Portmahomack

Colum Cille, Colum who was, Colum who will be
(Tiugraind Beccáin, in Clancy and Márkus 1995: 149)

Portmahomack

Monastery of the Picts

Martin Carver

EDINBURGH UNIVERSITY PRESS

© Martin Carver, 2008

Edinburgh University Press Ltd
22 George Square, Edinburgh

Typeset in 10/13pt Adobe Sabon
by Servis Filmsetting Ltd, Stockport, Cheshire, and
printed and bound in Great Britain by
MPG Books Ltd, Bodmin, Cornwall

A CIP record for this book is available from the British Library

ISBN 978 0 7486 2441 6 (hardback)
ISBN 978 0 7486 2442 3 (paperback)

The right of Martin Carver
to be identified as author of this work
has been asserted in accordance with
the Copyright, Designs and Patents Act 1988.

All illustrations are copyright Martin Carver and
University of York, unless otherwise stated.

Contents

List of figures	vi
List of plates	ix
Preface	xi
Acknowledgements	xii
Abbreviations	xv

PART 1 Exploring

1	Welcome to Portmahomack	3
2	Designing the expedition	16
3	What we found	37

PART 2 Age of Fame

4	The monks arrive	73
5	Carvers and thinkers	94
6	Architects and artisans	118
7	Serving new masters	136

PART 3 Legacy

8	Aftermath: St Colman's church	151
9	Ritual landscape, with portage	173
10	A holy place in history	191

Digest of evidence	203
Bibliography	227
Index	235

Figures

1.1	Early Historic Scotland, showing the location of Whithorn, Iona and Portmahomack	4
1.2	The lower portion of a cross-slab, found east of the church (TR1)	6
1.3	A large carved stone boss retrieved by grave-diggers (TR6)	7
1.4	Portrait of the inscribed stone (TR10)	9
1.5	Aerial photograph of Iona	12
1.6	Cropmark recorded at Portmahomack in 1984	13
1.7	Caroline Shepherd-Barron and Gillian Mackenzie raising money for the Tarbat Historic Trust	14
2.1	Early kingdoms of the North Sea	18
2.2	Prehistoric cultures: distribution of henges and carved stone balls	20
2.3	Early historic cultures: map of place names and Pictish symbol stones	21
2.4	Areas of evaluation, with contours	27
2.5	Duncan Johnson	28
2.6	'Strip and map': inspecting the surface of the archaeology without harming it	29
2.7	The excavation design	35
3.1	The excavation of the Smiths' Hall (S1)	38
3.2	Church under scaffolding in 1996	40
3.3	Annette Roe, supervisor, and Fred Geddes, architect, consider the options	40
3.4	Areas excavated in the church	42
3.5	The 'Boar Stone' (TR22) *in situ* in the foundation of Church 2	43
3.6	Katie Anderson and Donna Urquhart look into the crypt	44
3.7	Cist grave under excavation	46
3.8	Medieval burial under excavation	47
3.9	Overview of Sector 1	50
3.10	Enclosure ditch under excavation	52
3.11	The sequence in Sector 1	55
3.12	Overview of Sector 2, seen from the south	56
3.13	Nicky Toop sampling the main east section in Int. 14	57
3.14	The sequence in Sector 2	63
3.15	Last-minute preparations before opening day at the Centre in 1999	65

Figures

3.16	Prince Charles opening the Centre, 1999	66
3.17	Overall plan of the excavated area	68
3.18	Timeline	69
4.1	Carved stone ball from St Colman's church	74
4.2	Filtration pit, for purifying water with charcoal	75
4.3	Monastic period burials	77
4.4	Sarah King's identifications of age and sex	78
4.5	Cist burials from Portmahomack	79
4.6	Head support or pillow burials from Portmahomack	79
4.7	Elevation east wall of the crypt (F3)	83
4.8	The churchyard, showing its development from an oval original	84
5.1	The Craw Stane at Rhynie, Aberdeenshire	95
5.2	The simple scratched cross on TR24	98
5.3	The grave marker TR33, found inside the church	99
5.4	Examples of grave markers at Portmahomack and on the west coast of Scotland	100
5.5	The Calf Stone (TR28/35, detail)	101
5.6	Pictish symbols on the Tarbat peninsula	108
5.7	Model of the form of Cross C	109
5.8	Fragments of Cross D *in situ*, scattered over the demolished workshops	111
5.9	Fragment of Cross D, showing double strand interlace	112
5.10	Corner of the shaft of Cross D	113
5.11	The Dupplin Cross	114
5.12	Fragments from the Portmahomack corpus being studied at York	115
6.1	The culvert (F431) leading from the pool	119
6.2	The road leading to the terrace wall, culvert and cistern	120
6.3	The tawing tank (S4)	121
6.4	S9 and yard, finds distribution	122
6.5	Cattle bones set in rows at right angles	123
6.6	Model of the vellum-making process	123
6.7	S1, in its first phase, and S8	127
6.8	S1 – a post-pit being dissected	127
6.9	Objects from the neighbourhood of S1 associated with metal- and glass-working	128
6.10	X-ray of glass stud inlaid with metal	129
7.1	Excavators defining the pebble Road 2	136
7.2	Metal-working hearth (F148)	137
7.3	Small hearths for workers with precious metals	137
7.4	Plan of Period 3 metal-working area beside the pool	138

7.5	S1, after its refurbishment, and S8	141
7.6	Hoard of silver coins and ring-silver found in the Portmahomack churchyard	143
8.1	St Colman's church from the south-west	153
8.2	The evolution of St Colman's church, twelfth–twentieth centuries	154
8.3	Foundations of the west wall of Church 2	155
8.4	Chamfered plinth of Church 4, seen in the architect's test pit	157
8.5	Medieval burials under excavation in the nave	160
8.6	Fragment of leather shoe from Burial 43	161
8.7	Grave cover seen at the east end	162
8.8	The tomb and memorial of William Mackenzie	165
8.9	Recording the memorials of the seventeenth–nineteenth-century churchyard	167
8.10	Monumentality at Portmahomack	169
8.11	Graffiti in the twentieth-century church	170
9.1	Map of the Tarbat peninsula	174
9.2	The site of the Shandwick monument in its shelter	179
9.3	The Hilton of Cadboll replica	181
9.4	The Tarbat peninsula as represented on John Speed's map, early seventeenth century	185
10.1	Sunset over Portmahomack	191

Plates

Between pages 144 and 145

1a) Portmahomack: members of the digging team relax on the beach
1b) St Colman's church, with the Dornoch Firth beyond

2a) The Dragon Stone (TR20)
2b) The Apostle Stone, reverse side of the Dragon Stone (TR20)

3a) Excavating the nave of St Colman's church in 1997
3b) Ard marks in Sector 1, cut by the inner enclosure ditch

4a) Sector 2 under excavation in 2005
4b) What became of the mill: the road foundations, culvert and cistern of the eighth century being dissected

5a) Features under excavation in 2007 (Sector 2)
5b) Excavation of cattle bones *in situ* in the vellum-working yard

6a) Fragment, possibly from the Apostle Stone, found in the workshop area (TR201)
6b) The Calf Stone (TR28) under excavation by Katie Anderson

7a) Evidence for vellum-working from Sector 2
7b) Evidence for the working of precious metals from Sector 2

8a) The sequence captured in the south-facing section on the east side of Sector 2
8b) The sequence captured in the west section of Sector 2

Preface

This book is a preliminary account of the discoveries at Portmahomack intended for students, historians and those with a general interest in how the countries of Europe began. The full report of the research, intended for long-term scholarship, will appear when all the supporting analyses are complete, which will take, as these things do, another decade or so. This is to be published by the Society of Antiquaries of Scotland and the National Museums of Scotland and will be supported online by seven volumes of Field Reports. This book is an ambassador for the publications to follow, which will be enriched by contributors better qualified than I am. The current offering will contain some of the erroneous impressions of a first encounter, but such blemishes will hopefully be outweighed by the benefits of immediate report. Excavating at Portmahomack was an experience that was uniquely challenging and inspiring, even in a rich lifetime of experiences of the kind that only archaeology offers.

Readers whose interests have been aroused are urged to visit Portmahomack itself at the earliest opportunity. There they will find not only a village of considerable charm in a Firthland setting, but also, within St Colman's church, the captivating museum of the Tarbat Discovery Centre. Here are displayed a selection of the finest objects and artworks unearthed by the expedition. The exhibition also presents to visitors, in a graphic and entertaining manner, the story related here.

Martin Carver
York
1 January 2008

Acknowledgements

I was invited to come to Portmahomack by Caroline Shepherd-Barron, chairman and founder of the Tarbat Historic Trust. The Trust's aim was to restore the old church of St Colman, redundant and nearly derelict in 1994, and archaeology proved to be a vital partner in this venture. We archaeologists were helped in turn by Highland Council, which supported the initial project evaluation through the good offices of Graham Watson. The future of the church depended not only on its long-term curation by the Trust, but on its long-term viability as a Visitor Centre. Kick-started by funding from the Heritage Lottery Fund, the Tarbat Discovery Centre's integrity and survival has owed much to the initial design of Higgins Gardner, to its managers George MacQuarrie, Kate Collard and Michelle Cadger, to members of its Trust – particularly Anna Ritchie and Isabel Henderson – and especially to its inspiring first chairman Caroline Shepherd-Barron and its stalwart current chairman Tony Watson. We had hoped, as many do, to complete our researches and maintain our Centre through private sponsorship and visitor revenue. But there was always a shortfall, and it gives me special pleasure to salute the crucial roles in completing the project and keeping the Centre viable by the National Museums of Scotland and by Historic Scotland. Their officers will know how much we relied on their support, judgement and faith to get the job done.

The archaeological project itself was the product of teamwork, dependent on the commitment, imagination and hard work of many talented people on site and off. A very particular debt is owed to Field Archaeology Specialists Ltd (FAS), the professional field research company managed by Justin Garner-Lahire, which ran the excavation, survey and analytical programmes. From the beginning of the project, this collaboration between a professional fieldwork company and a university has set a model for modern archaeology that others will succeed in emulating but are unlikely to better. Our administrators, Roy and Faith Jerromes, made life in a highland field cosy and well appointed.

On site, Annette Roe supervised the study of the church and wrote the Field Report for Sector 4, Madeleine Hummler supervised the Field School and wrote the Field Report for Sector 1 and Cecily Spall supervised the excavation of the workshops and wrote the Field and Data Structure Reports for Sector 2. Since 2003, Cecily has been my co-researcher responsible for directing the excavations. Her impeccable standards and thoughtful investigations have produced many of the best ideas to come out of the project, especially on the making of vellum and other monastic crafts.

As well as seeking comments from my digging colleagues, I have received valuable advice and helpful opinions about what is published here from Isabel Henderson (Chapter 5), Dauvit Broun (Chapter 7) and particularly Anna Ritchie, who reviewed the whole text. I am also grateful to Kellie Meyer, for her observations while a doctoral student at York, particularly on Hilton, Shandwick and Nigg. The proposed narrative and interpretation of the site was also tested in its final season against four panels of academic visitors, who kindly gave me a whole day of their time in exchange for a dinner. I am particularly grateful to Cecily Spall, Nicky Toop and Becca Pullen of FAS for checking, creating and managing the illustrations. The final result owes a great deal to meticulous editing by Hilary Walford and thoughtful production by EUP.

Sponsorship

The archaeological evaluation (1994–6) was sponsored by Highland Council (£30,000). From 1996 to 2001 the excavations were funded by the Heritage Lottery Fund (£233,361) and from 2003 to 2007 by Historic Scotland and the National Museums of Scotland, with important contributions from Highland Council, Ross and Cromarty Enterprise, the Society of Antiquaries of Scotland and the Russell Trust (£170,000).

The Department of Archaeology, University of York contributed the services of the Director for fourteen years (equivalent to £140,000).

The total equivalent cost of the archaeological research project from its initiation in 1994 to the completion of fieldwork in 2007 is calculated to be £573,361.

Landowners

Our thanks to James and Douglas Gordon, and to the Church of Scotland and their tenant, Billy Vass for permissions to undertake the research.

We have relied on the generosity of the Tarbat Historic Trust, led by its chairmen, Caroline Shepherd-Barron and Tony Watson, and members past and present: Eric Barnes, David Clarke, Monica Clough, Hamilton Cormack, Janet Gill, Isabel Henderson, Michael Lang, Gillian Mackenzie, Ellen Macnamara, Heather and Willie McRae, Finlay Munro, Anna Ritchie, Dave and Gill Scott and Lachie Stewart.

And we want to record our gratitude to our other friends in The Port for their innumerable kindnesses, in particular Jan and Martin Dane, Kate Collard, Jane and Richard Durham, Donald and Catherine Urquhart and Stewart and Sandra Smart.

Officers responsible for managing our partnerships with the National Museums of Scotland were David Clarke, Andy Heald and Fraser Hunter; and with Historic Scotland were Patrick Ashmore, Sally Foster, Rod McCullagh, Sabina Strachan and Laura Hindmarch.

The removal of the sculpture to the National Museums was initially put in hand through the good offices of June Ross and Mark Eliot, stone conservators of Highland Council.

ACADEMIC ADVISERS

I am grateful to the following for their advice and comments and for the pleasure of their company, mainly as visitors on the four Study Days held on site during the final season:

> Leslie Abrams (Cambridge), James Barrett (Cambridge), Niall Brady (Irish Discovery Programme), John Bradley (Maynooth), Stefan Brink (Aberdeen), Ewan Campbell (Glasgow), David Clarke (NMS), Claire Cooper (Edinburgh), Malcolm Cooper (Historic Scotland), Tom Clancy (Glasgow), Rosemary Cramp (Durham), Eric Fernie (London), Sally Foster (Historic Scotland), Mark Hall (Perth), Jill Harden (National Trust for Scotland), Isabel Henderson (Nigg), Catherine Hills (Cambridge), Laura Hindmarch (Historic Scotland), Madeleine Hummler (York), Heather King (Dublin), Raymond Lamb (UHI), Chris Lowe (Headland Archaeology), Rod McCullagh (Historic Scotland), Aidan MacDonald (Cork), Bernard Meehan (Dublin), Roger Mercer (Edinburgh), Chris Morris (UHI), Betty O'Brien (Dublin), Julian Richards (York), Linda Richards (Leeds), Michael Ryan (Dublin), Julia Smith (Glasgow), Graham Watson (Highland Council), Alex Woolf (St Andrews), Susan Youngs (London).

We also relied on Stephen Carter, Allan Hall, Patrick Ashmore, Janet Montgomery and Sarah King for important scientific advice.

THE TEAM

> Supervisors: Justin Garner-Lahire, Cecily Spall, Annette Roe, Madeleine Hummler, Roy and Faith Jerromes.
> Recorders: Katie Anderson, Tony Austin, James Brennan, John English, Dave Fell, Hamish Fulford, Jules Giecco, Lars Gustavsen, Candy Hatherley, Lizzie Hooper, Richard Jackson, Alastair Jupp, Doug Kippen, Leo O'Brien, Becca Pullen, Ralph Shuttleworth, Gigi Signorelli, Dominic Salsarola, Toby Simpson, Steve Timms, Nicola Toop and Dave Watts.
> Architect: Fred Geddes.
> Buildings Recorder: Martin Jones.
> Mechanical excavator operator: Kim Mackenzie.

In addition we benefited from the contributions of some 100 trainees and 200 volunteers. While I cannot list them here, I hope they will have happy memories to match our gratitude to them.

ILLUSTRATIONS

I am grateful to the Royal Commission for permission to reproduce Fig. 1.5 (Crown Copyright), to Historic Scotland for Fig. 5.11 (Crown Copyright), to the Trustees of the National Museums of Scotland for Fig. 1.2; 1.3; 1.4; 6.9; 7.6, to Tom Gray for Fig. 5.1; 5.2; 5.3; 5.5 (Copyright Tom and Sybil Gray Collection), to Sarah King for Fig. 4.4, and to the Tarbat Historic Trust for Fig. 1.7; 3.16.

All line drawings and photographs were generated by staff at FAS, with the exception of Fig. 5.7 by Elizabeth Hooper and Fig. 8.7 by Trevor Pearson.

Abbreviations

NOTE ON ARCHAEOLOGICAL ABBREVIATIONS

In archaeological investigations, every operation and all records of discoveries are systematically labelled so that other scholars can find them and examine them in later years. In this book, intended as a summary for every kind of reader, technical argument and notation are kept to a minimum. However, since later scholars may want to track some of my more dubious assertions to their sources, references to archive data are given. Here is the key to the taxonomy used:

The areas to be investigated are designated as **sectors** (1–4 in this case). Every archaeological operation undertaken is numbered as an **intervention**, Int. for short (Int. 1–29) which may be further divided into **modules**. Recorded **structures** are numbered and carry the prefix S; structures are sets of **features** (prefix F), and features are sets of **contexts** (soils and stones defined by excavators on site as deposited together). Features are numbers of 1–3 digits prefixed by F; contexts are numbers of 4 digits. Thus F132/1404 means context 1404 in Feature 132. Over 200 pieces of Pictish **sculpture** have been found at Portmahomack. These, numbered TR (for Tarbat), appear throughout the book. The archive is held by the University of York but once the full research report is published it will be placed on line within the Archaeological Data Service.

List of abbreviations

AOD	Above Ordance Datum
AU	*The Annals of Ulster (to AD 1131)*, ed. and trans. S. Mac Airt and G. Mac Niocaill (Dublin: Dublin Institute for Advanced Studies, 1983)
Bulletin	*Bulletin of the Tarbat Discovery Programme* (1995); see http://york.ac.uk/dept/arch/staff/sites/Tarbat
ECMS	*The Early Christian Monuments of Scotland*, ed. J. Romilly Allen and J. Anderson (Balgavies: Pinkfoot Press [1903], 1993)
F	feature
FSA	*First Statistical Account*, otherwise *Old Statistical Account* (Edinburgh 1791–9); published as Sir John Sinclair, *Analysis of the Statistical Account of Scotland* (Edinburgh: W. Tait, 1831)
HE	The Venerable Bede, *A History of the English Church and People*, trans. and intro. Leo Sherley-Price (Harmondsworth: Penguin, 1968)

Int.	intervention
LC	Adomnán of Iona, *Life of St Columba*, trans. and intro. Richard Sharpe (Harmondsworth: Penguin, 1995)
NGR	National Grid Reference
NMR	National Monuments Record
NMS	National Museums of Scotland
NSA/SSA	*New Statistical Account*, otherwise *Second Statistical Account*, by the ministers of the respective parishes under the superintendence of a committee of the Society for the Benefit of the Sons and Daughters of the Clergy (Edinburgh: W. Blackwood and Sons, 1845)
ONB	*Ordnance Survey Object Name Books*
OPS	Cosmo Innes, , W. Anderson, J. Robertson, J. Brichan, and J. McNab, *Origines Parochiales Scotiae: The Antiquities Ecclesiastical and Territorial of the Parishes of Scotland*, 2 vols (Edinburgh, 1851–5)
OS	*Orkneyinga Saga. The History of the Earls of Orkney*, trans. H. Pálsson and P. Edwards (Harmondsworth: Penguin, 1981)
PSAS	*Proceedings of the Society of Antiquaries of Scotland*
RCAHMS	Royal Commission on the Ancient and Historical Monuments of Scotland
S	structure
TR	Tarbat sculpture
TSA	*The Third Statistical Account of Scotland*, by the Scottish Council of Social Service (Edinburgh and London: Oliver and Boyd, 1951 [1952])

Part 1

Exploring

CHAPTER 1

Welcome to Portmahomack

The further north you go in the island of Britain, the more beautiful the scenery becomes, the hills wilder, the skies wider, the air clearer, the seas closer. Even for those not born in Scotland, you feel as if you are driving towards your beginnings. Many holiday-makers take the western road to the isles, or, if lucky enough to have a boat, the sea road, which allows them to visit a hundred pleasant islands. But the east coast too has its special maritime character: long broad estuarine firths providing access to rich farmland. This region of firths was the homeland of the Picts, a now lost people of the Dark Ages (the fourth to the ninth centuries AD) famous for their brilliant and highly individual carving on stone. Nicknamed *Picti* (the painted people) by the Romans, the Picts were simply Celtic Britons living in the eastern part of Scotland. Their sculpture and the meagre references to them in texts show that they were great players in their day, but they have proved surprisingly elusive to archaeologists and historians alike. When our campaign began in 1994 there were more than 150 sites known to have had Pictish monuments, but no excavated Pictish cemeteries, settlements or churches. This may help to explain how it was that a small fishing village at the far end of the longest headland in the Scottish north-east came to serve as a stepping stone in the story of Europe.

A long twisty road, not quite wide enough for its traffic, takes today's traveller from the A9 up the Tarbat peninsula to Portmahomack (Fig. 1.1; Plate 1). The peninsula pushes out towards Norway, and from the top of the Hill of Nigg you can see three seas: to the south, the Cromarty Firth, a former harbour to the British navy, now a park for superannuated oil rigs; to the east, the Moray Firth and beyond it the coastline of the redoubtable men of Moray, and beyond that the misty form of Bennachie in the Grampians, where the Caledonii confronted the armies of Rome; and, to the west, the Dornoch Firth, with tier after tier of highlands in shades of blue and purple. At the tip of the peninsula stands a lighthouse with red and white bands, built by Robert Louis Stevenson's uncle; and a few miles south of this lies Portmahomack, a cluster of white houses on two streets curving around the best beach in the region. The jetty built in the eighteenth century to take grain and salmon south now has only a few fishing boats left. Neither wholly a working port nor wholly a spa, it is a perfect destination for families with small children tough enough to play sandcastles in a strong wind, people who like things a little bit wild, people who like sea spray by day and do not mind rain lashing the shutters at night, who want to see the mist dissolve suddenly and reveal the hills – and who cannot wait for their long journey from the city to end so that they can throw open the car door and admit all the adventurous freshness of the Scottish highlands.

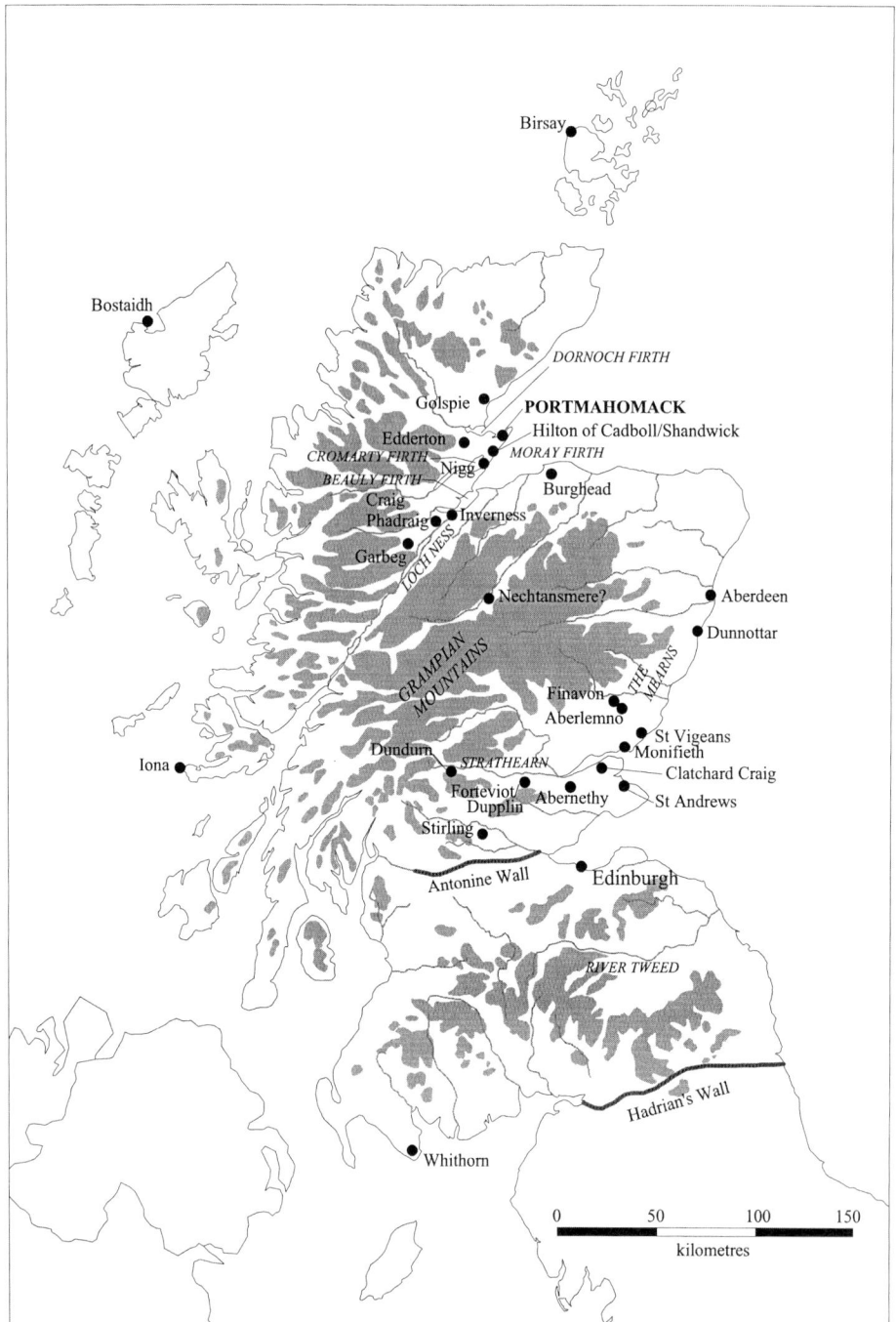

Fig. 1.1 Early Historic Scotland, showing the location of Whithorn, Iona and Portmahomack.

It would not have been easy to guess in 1994 that this village was once one of the most famous places in Britain. But there were clues. Two large erect Pictish stone slabs stood elsewhere on the peninsula – at Nigg and Shandwick, and a third had famously once stood at Hilton of Cadboll and now graced the National Museums in Edinburgh (these monuments are discussed in Chapter 9). At Portmahomack itself, St Colman's church, standing above the beach at the south end of the village, was said to have had a certain history. Known locally as Tarbat Old Church or 'The White Church', it had flourished as the parish church until the Disruption of 1843, when the minister and most of the congregation had walked out and founded the Free Church, now a great grey pile rising between St Colman's and its beach. For the next hundred years, the old church, with its relict knot of parishioners and Church of Scotland minister, enjoyed a genteel old age, occasionally offering titbits of its still obscure past to visiting antiquaries. In 1946 the regular worship of the two Church of Scotland congregations was transferred to the United Tarbat East Church of Scotland, and Tarbat Old Church began to slide into oblivion.[1]

In retrospect, thanks to the revelations that have been made since (and the little that was written down at the time), we can reconstruct something of these twilit years, Tarbat's long century of rediscovery. The great monuments at Nigg, Shandwick and Hilton of Cadboll were all blown down in hurricanes in recent centuries – and hurricanes they must have been to unseat and break stone slabs 6–8in (15–20cm) thick. Nigg and Shandwick were re-erected, and Hilton, after a period of indifference face down on the seashore, was transported to Invergordon Castle, where the owner was accumulating a lapidarium in his ornamental garden. Five famous enthusiasts, Charles Cordiner and Charles Petley in the late eighteenth century, John Stuart in the mid-nineteenth and J. Romilly Allen and Joseph Anderson at the turn of the twentieth, toured Scotland in order and kept the flame of interest flickering for the carved stones of the Picts. All came to the Tarbat peninsula and to Portmahomack, and the antiquarian assets of our area were further enhanced by the investigations of several church ministers, the celebrated naturalist Hugh Miller, resident at Cromarty, and his son Hugh Miller junior.

In 1776 Charles Cordiner, our earliest antiquarian visitor, observed splendid monuments at Shandwick and Hilton, and was then escorted by Mr M'Leod of Geanies to the Tarbat churchyard, where he saw several fragments of other 'obelisks', no less inferior but 'shattered to pieces'.[2] The pieces (which we know as 'TR2') were still there in 1845 when George Dunoon, the Tarbat schoolmaster, reported that 'fragments of what is said to have been a Danish cross' were still to be seen scattered among the grass in the churchyard. 'A low, green mound adjoining the east gable of the church', he says 'was still pointed out as the site on which it [the *Danish Cross*] stood.'[3] That green mound had an evil reputation: 'There was a tradition that [victims of] the plague had been buried there,' says Hugh Miller visiting in the 1880s,

> and so rooted was the aversion to disturbing it, that it was not until the late parish minister took a spade in hand and actually threw off his coat to dig *in propria persona* that the grave digger could be induced to break into ground accursed by the presence of the plague. There are still no grave stones. The place is allotted to a community of poor

Fig. 1.2 The lower portion of a cross-slab, found east of the church (TR1). (Source: NMS)

fishers on the outskirts of the parish. It was found to be thickly covered with pieces of sandstone.[4]

Although not necessarily seen by Cordiner, and not mentioned by the Revd D. Campbell (the minister who wrote the *New Statistical Account* for Tarbat), a quite separate piece of sculpture was already in the churchyard in the early nineteenth century, since it had been removed from there to Invergordon Castle by the time Stuart drew it (TR1; Fig. 1.2).[5] It had been situated further to the east of the green mound and consisted of the wreckage of another great cross-slab, fallen and broken into two. The larger piece had been reused as a grave cover, and it was the shorter lower piece, with a snapped-off tenon, that was still lying about in the churchyard. Its face was ornamented with a vine-scroll border, and along one edge were carved four symbols belonging to the Picts. Other smaller pieces were also in the grass: one was a stone boss in the form of a circle nearly a foot (30cm) across, shaped like a wreath and containing six bosses around which adders wound (TR5). Another was a triangle of sandstone ornamented with a geometric fretwork (TR8).

Mr Macleod, the occupant of Invergordon Castle, displayed the Hilton slab and Portmahomack's cross-slab (TR1) side by side in his garden. Smaller pieces were arranged in a room in the tower where they could be viewed by the curious. Others were stacked near the door with geological specimens of various kinds. This was an age of antiquarian enterprise. Over the water at Dunrobin Castle, the Dukes of Sutherland had scooped up the sculptures and other ancient objects that had come to light in the Golspie strip and were exhibiting them in polished wooden cases in their summer house. There they shared exhibition space with the stuffed heads of

Fig. 1.3 A large carved stone boss retrieved by grave-diggers (TR6). (Source: Tom Gray)

hundreds of exotic animals mounted on the walls, the trophies culled by a hunting family from three continents.⁶

Meanwhile, back in St Colman's churchyard, grave-diggers were making new discoveries. Sometime in the 1880s a Mr William Mackay retrieved a carved boss from 6–7ft (about 2m) down in the burial place of Ross of North Balkeith (TR6; Fig. 1.3). The same sensitive grave-digger dug up and retained an even more exquisite fragment of sculpture about 4yd (about 3.5m) from the east gable of the church in the burial place of Roderick Bain of North Tarrel (TR7). When Hugh Miller junior visited in the 1880s, these two pieces were on the window sill at the west end of the church, and he arranged for them to be donated to the National Museum of Antiquities of Scotland in Edinburgh.⁷ He was also present in 1889 to witness a startling discovery of another kind. On 28 March, during the digging of a grave some few yards from the east gate of the churchyard a 'line of hewn stones' appeared at a depth of 5–6ft (1.5–1.8m). From this wall, on the side nearest the church, and apparently from some crevice in the masonry, came 'several pieces of old silver'. A month later, the minister, the Revd Donald Macleod, caused an opening to be made in an adjacent space among the gravestones, in order to continue the investigation so far as the crowded condition of the churchyard would permit.⁸ The line of masonry was rediscovered at about 5ft (1.5m) from the surface as thin flag stones. It ran east–west and was coincident with the old churchyard wall, which had been moved some thirty-five years before (that is, in 1854). After digging down to a depth of nearly 7ft (2.10m), the excavator threw out a spadeful of earth and pieces of stone, together with three more silver coins, including a penny of the English king Edgar (AD 959–75). More silver was found when adjacent graves were dug in 1892. The eventual find consisted of thirteen coins, including ten of the Frankish king Louis le Bègue (846–79), and four silver penannular armlets. The latter were also coinage, since they were the Viking money of the day – the day being around AD 1000, when the objects had been buried, probably to hide them from marauders.[9]

At this time Miller astutely noted the character of the soil:

> In this excavation, and in other graves of the churchyard, the earthy mould in which the interments are made is found to extend to a depth of from 7 to 8 feet below the present uneven surface, resting on white sand. The bottom of this considerable growth of mould [earth] probably represents . . . the original surface of the ground, the native soil of which, in so bleak a spot, was doubtless very thin . . . Over considerable spaces of the churchyard, some thirty paces from the east and west gables [of the church], the spade of the grave-digger passes through a layer of shells of edible species . . . The date of this early occupation it is impossible exactly to fix.[10]

He also noted that 500yd (about 450m) east-north-east from the church in 1889 was a 'heap of heavy slag' from bog iron, together with some remains of an old forge round which older people said they remembered finding some silver coins. Near the manse (500yd east-south-east from the church) a 'layer of charcoal' was reported, 4ft (1.2m) down.[11] Early human burials had also come to light here and there on the peninsula, some accompanied by large slabs of sandstone. But it was only in the twenty-first century, towards the end of our campaign, that their significance has become clear. (These burials are discussed in Chapters 4 and 9.)

By the later nineteenth century, then, St Colman's church had permitted a glimpse of its antiquity to the discerning. But a most significant discovery was about to be made – arguably the most significant ever made at Tarbat, since it carried in itself the evidence for an early literate community. A carved stone, reused in the coursing of the garden wall of the Portmahomack manse a quarter of a mile (400m) from St Colman's church, was spotted by a visitor: the Revd J. M. Joass of Golspie, curator of the Duke of Sutherland's museum at Dunrobin (TR10; Fig. 1.4). This piece of stone was not very large,[12] but, unusually for Scotland and uniquely for Pictland, it carried a Latin inscription in bold upright letters belonging unmistakably to the earliest centuries of Christianity in Britain. The letters were insular majuscules, resembling those used in the gospel books of Northumbria (the Lindisfarne Gospels) or Iona (the Book of Kells), but it would be another eighty years before this connection was put in context by John Higgitt, the Edinburgh art historian.[13] Meanwhile, the find of Joass made its way to Invergordon Castle to join the other curiosities cherished by the Macleod family.

This discovery had already been made when, at the turn of the twentieth century, the great compilers of *The Early Christian Monuments of Scotland*, J. Romilly Allen and

Fig. 1.4 *Portrait of the inscribed stone (TR10). (Source: ECMS III, pl. XII, facing p. 83)*

Joseph Anderson, visited the Tarbat peninsula. The re-erected Nigg stone stood outside the vestry of its church overlooking a steep slope and dripped on by the rain, Shandwick stood in a field overlooking the firth and Hilton was at Invergordon Castle. In their survey (published in 1903), Allen and Anderson numbered ten fragments or sets of fragments as originating from 'Tarbat' – meaning Tarbat Old Church at Portmahomack.[14] Seven of these were at Invergordon Castle, two already in the National Museums and one still in St Colman's church. A visit of the Inverness Scientific Society in 1903 confirmed a similar tally and recorded the opinion that the churchyard at Portmahomack 'contained at one time three sculptured stones of the Columban period'.[15] Portmahomack had acquired its first acknowledgement of a deep seniority.

The Columba in question was, of course, St Columba, or Columcille, who lived in the sixth century, founded a famous monastery on Iona in about 563 and died there in 597. In 565 or thereabouts he made a famous journey into northern Pictland via the Great Glen, and this journey, and Columba's role as a possible apostle of the Picts, have long acted as lodestones for historians of a murky age.[16] The great mid-nineteenth-century tome on the *Origin of Scottish Parishes* credited St Columba with the foundation of the church at Portmahomack, pointing to its underground crypt, which still survived as a vault 30ft (10m) long.[17] In 1906 William Macfarlane elaborated:

> There is a large regular vault about 30 feet long near as broad as the church and so high that persons of a prettie good stature may stand in it. This vault is said to have been built by S. Columbus [sic] as a place of worship, and this tradition is supported by the name which a port about ¼ of mile to the N of the church does bear in sume old charters viz. portus Columbi, but now it is called Portmahobuagg, where there is a convenient harbour for barks and small ships and ane inn for intertaining of strangers.[18]

The author of the *Third Statistical Account* in 1957 noted: 'Though marked on old charts Portus Columbi, Portmahomack is the Gaelic Puirtma Cholmaig, St Colman's Port.' Its author identifies this Colman with the Bishop of Lindisfarne (660–4), and comments: 'It is known that he laboured much in Easter Ross.'[19]

So who was Portmahomack's famous ancestor, the pioneer holy man who gave the village its name and caused its crosses to be carved? Was it Columba, the founder of Iona, Christian missionary to the northern Picts in the later sixth century? Or was it Colman, and, if so, which one? The pioneer expert on Celtic place names, W. J. Watson, noted that *Colman*, a diminutive of *colum*, itself a diminutive of *columba*, Latin for a dove, was a name borne by 218 saints – which offers us rather too many choices to be useful.[20] In the mid-sixteenth century, Saint Colman, bishop and confessor, was said to be buried at 'Terbert' in the diocese of Ross, where the memory of his holy life attracted the continuing veneration of the faithful.[21] Since the saint's day cited is 15 February, this should refer to Colman of Lindisfarne (saint's day 18 February) rather than Columba (saint's day 9 June). In the opinion of the learned compilers of the Aberdeen Martyrology, the servants of Tarbat Old Church housed the relics of St Colman, Bishop of Lindisfarne, or thought they did. It is most likely that it was for the veneration of these relics that the medieval crypt was maintained (see Chapter 8).

Colman of Lindisfarne began his career as a monk on Iona, among his Irish compatriots, and in about 661 was selected as bishop (and abbot) of the Northumbrian monastery on the island of Lindisfarne, the place of origin of the Lindisfarne Gospels. Within a few years he was to find himself at arguably the most significant meeting ever held for the development of the church in Britain and its political future. The Synod of Whitby (in North Yorkshire), held in 664, was convened to agree the correct method of calculating the date of Easter, and of cutting a monk's hair (the tonsure), both ritual matters that stood for deeper traditions and allegiances. The saintly Colman, whose austere regime had been much admired by Bede, was no match for his opponent, the artful European internationalist bishop Wilfred. The issue was in any event decided by the Northumbrian king Oswy, thus demonstrating its political basis: Northumbria and its Christian Church were to align with Rome, and there would be no regional roads to Christianity. Colman, the loser in the debate, honourably resigned his post, and retired to Iona, and then to Innisboffin off the coast of Connacht and then to Mayo. Colman, loved by Irish and Angles alike, with a respect for older Celtic tradition, was an admirable saint to be revered by the medieval people of Easter Ross.

During the twentieth century the Invergordon collection of sculptural trophies was gradually transferred through the good offices of the Macleod family to the National Museums in Edinburgh: the Hilton slab and TR1 in 1921 and nine further fragments in 1956. In retrospect it might be thought that much of the nascent historical interest in the Tarbat peninsula was surrendered at the same time. Only a few carved stone fragments came to light during the ninety years following 1903, and the recording of their provenance was poor. One was reported from St Colman's by D. J. Ross, Merchant, of Portmahomack and given to the National Museums in 1927 (TR12). Another was found while a grave was being dug at a depth of 6ft (about 1.8m): the greater part of the slab it belongs to remains in the grave, under the coffin, but no lover of art or archaeology was on hand to record where the grave was situated (TR13). Another was seen in the churchyard briefly by James Ritchie in 1914 before it was destroyed (TR15).

The Royal Commission on Ancient and Historical Monuments was active in the area in 1956, its investigator noticing an early carved stone in the relieving arch of the west tower (TR14). A 1966 investigator pronounced the church as essentially eighteenth century, but noted that it incorporated early remains. The addition of a north aisle to accommodate a heritors' loft and burial vault was 'a typical adaptation of a medieval church in reformation Scotland'. Geoffrey Stell again recorded St Colman's church for the Commission in 1982, and warmed to the theme of its earlier history: 'At the east end is what appears to be a genuine late medieval vaulted crypt which takes up one third of the length of the church.'

For most of the twentieth century a pall of historical silence lay over the peninsula. But from time to time prescient art historians drew intermittent attention to its possibilities. In 1972 Julian T. Brown launched his case for the Book of Kells having been made in Pictland, with Tarbat as a possible centre for its production: 'One or more court monasteries or churches must have existed among the Picts; and if we cannot say where they were, the groups of stones from St Andrews, Meigle, Aberlemno, and the Tarbat–Nigg area . . . show what sort of work they were able to do.' Isabel Henderson was also a powerful early advocate for a Pictish monastery at Tarbat: 'The slabs in Easter Ross certainly suggest that this district supported at least one ecclesiastical foundation – perhaps at Tarbat, where there are fragments of a number of particularly fine cross-slabs.'[22] In 1982 John Higgitt published his ideas on the inscribed slab found by the Revd J. M. Joass, noting: 'At Tarbat, or somewhere very close by, was an ecclesiastical centre with contacts that went beyond Pictland . . . This centre was capable of producing books.'[23]

At a speed best described as cautious, scholarly opinion was converging on the idea of a monastery at Portmahomack. But very soon the excitement mounted,

Fig. 1.5 Aerial photograph of Iona, showing the monastic ditch or vallum. (Source: RCAHMS)

thanks to a new discovery, made this time from the air. Ian Keillar and Barri Jones, well-known aerial archaeologists in pursuit of the traces of Rome in the north, were reaping a rich harvest of sites of all periods in the Moray heartland in the hot summer of 1984. Turning for home across the firth, they spotted, and captured on camera, a cropmark around the old church at Tarbat. Incomplete though it was, this cropmark suggested a ditch marking out an enclosure, D-shaped in plan, that reminded all who saw it of the D-shaped enclosure bank and ditch that survives around the monastery on Iona (Figs 1.5, 1.6).

By a happy chance, these new glimpses of Portmahomack's historical *persona* coincided with an initiative that was to set the whole enquiry buzzing with energy. Impatient of watching the old church of St Colman descend into destitution, a company of local movers and shakers formed themselves into the Tarbat Historic Trust[24] and in 1980 bought the building from the Church of Scotland for £1. As a result of its ownership of this property, the Trust shouldered the responsibility of restoring it and keeping it standing, something that became more difficult to do every day that it was not done. Money was the principal desirable – to mend the roof, waterproof the walls and refurbish the interior where trapped birds were dying. The first steps were heroic: car boot sales and donations (Fig. 1.7), and tireless work by volunteers, patching the holes and clearing up the mess. The north aisle had been

Fig. 1.6   Cropmark recorded at Portmahomack in 1984 by Barri Jones and Ian Keillar.

boarded up, and behind the boards lay a pile of timber work belonging to redundant coffins and coffin-carriers. The crypt, too, had been sealed, hiding another pile of debris. Applications for large grants, from local and national government, met with the predictable response of overburdened agencies. In 1980 there were countless redundant churches in Scotland, few of which had found their own champions. The repair of a church after decades of neglect costs hundreds of thousands of pounds. Where was the money to come from?

It seemed that the agencies did have one rule of thumb to determine the degree of merit in a candidate for a grant: it needed to demonstrate historic value – the value that comes with being a stage for historic events, or having surviving ancient fabric or objects. Even though all the pieces of sculpture found in that and in the previous century were now in the National Museums in Edinburgh, the body of the church itself, its idiosyncratic belfry and its crypt, were recognised as having a certain potential. That potential had been raised by John Higgitt's paper and Geoffrey Stell's visit of 1982, and still further by the cropmark discovered in 1984. By 1991 the Tarbat Historic Trust recognised that one likely way of raising the historic value of a place was to employ an archaeologist, and accordingly it commissioned Jill Harden, a freelance professional from Glen Urquhart. Inside the church the crypt was cleared, producing, among other finds, another four pieces of carved stone, found and cherished at some earlier date. Three of these, the volunteers were delighted to discover, fitted together (TR17–18). Outside it, with the help of the Trust's assembled volunteers, Jill Harden cut a section through the cropmark ditch. She found it to be 8m wide and at least 2m deep. Within it, a peaty fill was sampled, and the samples radiocarbon dated

Fig. 1.7 Caroline Shepherd-Barron and Gillian Mackenzie raising money for the Tarbat Historic Trust at a bring-and-buy sale. (Source: THT)

by Glasgow University: they ranged from the second to the sixth centuries AD (for all radiocarbon dates from Portmahomack, see Digest, A3). There was a little disappointment with this result, which seemed too early: 'The ditch, which surrounds the church and encloses about 3.5 hectares,' commented Jill Harden, 'had certainly been dug before a monastic settlement could have been established at Portmahomack.'[25]

Would the Portmahomack settlement once again subside into anonymity? It might have happened, but we cannot know that, and I now have to take up the story myself. In 1993 I had completed my fieldwork at Sutton Hoo and had done two seasons at the early Islamic site of Achir in the Atlas mountains of Algeria. This had ended badly: I was declared to be a spy by an Arab newspaper and, although I was bravely supported by friends who knew better, the future of the project was looking a little awkward. My investigations into religious and political change in the Maghreb would have to wait, and meanwhile I turned my attention back to the discovery of early kingdoms in the North Sea area. And when, at the invitation of the Tarbat Historic Trust, I looked at the site at Portmahomack for the first time, it seemed to me a site of irresistible promise.

Notes

1. *TSA* (Tarbat parish).
2. Cordiner (1780: 66, 75); *ECMS* III. 88–95. All the pieces of sculpture found at Portmahomack are numbered with the prefix TR; this observation probably refers to TR2.

3. *NSA* 461.
4. Miller (1889: 442).
5. Stuart (1856: plate xxx). The list of these dispersed fragments that led early antiquaries to Portmahomack is included in the Abbreviated Catalogue of sculpture from Portmahomack, which will be found in the Digest, A5.
6. This museum is still in existence, and is remarkable as much for its evocation of the nineteenth-century antiquary as for its prehistoric collections.
7. Miller (1889: 435).
8. Miller and Macleod (1889: 314)
9. Graham-Campbell (1995: 143–4); four armlets and six coins survive in the National Museums.
10. Miller (1889).
11. Miller and Macleod (1889: 317).
12. It was measured as $19 \times 12 \times 6½$in (c. $48 \times 30 \times 16.5$cm).
13. Higgitt (1982).
14. *ECMS* III. 88–95.
15. An opinion repeated in *TSA*: 'The churchyard has also yielded fragments of three Celtic crosses of the finest type, made of the warm yellow sandstone from the tall coast cliffs near Rockfield, and from other places and caves round the coast.'
16. See *LC*.
17. *OPS*, vol. 2.2, p. 434.
18. Macfarlane (1906–8: vol. 1, p. 215).
19. These 'old charts' have yet to be rediscovered; but see Chapter 9 for some of the sixteenth century and later.
20. Watson (1926: 278).
21. 'In Scocia Sancti Colmanni episcopi et confessoris sepultus dyocesi Rossensi apud Terbert. Cuius vite sanctitas morum honestas et virtutum merita ad eius gesta veneranda fideli populo prebent incrementa', Aberdeen Martyrology (Edinburgh University Library MS 50), under 15 Feb. See also A. Boyle, 'Notes on Scottish saints', *Innes Review*, 33 (1981), 59–82, at 65–6. Many thanks to John Higgitt for this reference.
22. Henderson (1975).
23. Higgitt (1982).
24. Originally the Tarbat Old Church Preservation Trust.
25. Harden (1995: 226).

CHAPTER 2

Designing the expedition

It all began, as many an enterprise does, with a telephone call. The caller was Caroline Shepherd-Barron, chairman of the Tarbat Historic Trust, and she had the best of motives for calling: she knew my cousin's mother-in-law. She had heard from her friend that I was an archaeologist: was this true? My partner, Madeleine Hummler, who took the call at our home in York, assured her that it was so, and undertook to resume contact the moment I returned from the USA, where I then was. This duly occurred. Having telephoned Caroline, I got on the next train north, and so got my first sight of the Tarbat peninsula, Nigg, Shandwick, Portmahomack and the church of St Colman. My hostess was warm in her hospitality and tireless in her conviction, not only that her church required a roof, but that this was a site of the greatest historic importance imaginable.

In many years of freelance research in eight countries, I have encountered enthusiasm and pessimism often enough, and one is always grateful for the former. But there is also on these occasions a sixth sense, a third voice, not easy to reduce to words. People who buy houses know this voice very well: it encourages them to buy or not to buy, without much visible supporting evidence. And yet it is the only reliable voice to heed. At Portmahomack, my third voice pronounced the site a winner, and so it has proved. I cannot claim any scientific probity here. I asked questions from a shifting raft of ignorance; such observations as I made were later to seem improbable, and my guesses often proved to be wrong. But there was a clarity in the landscape: the church on its hill above the beach, and inland the fields of the Glebe Field crossed by the enclosure ditch; these could not, so it seemed to me, fail to produce an early Pictish settlement. Accordingly I set about creating the conditions in which a very large part of it could be brought to the light of day.

At this point it would be fair to confirm the reader's suspicion that there is to be a certain amount of autobiography in this chapter – but it is only in this one. Soon we shall be following the course of what was actually found, and then trying to make history out of it. But for the moment the personal is inevitable, and for a number of reasons. First, the chapter concerns the design of projects, a matter to which I have dedicated a large part of my professional life. I do try to control the urge to give lectures (rants) on the subject, but often I fail. I have given my views on project design to startled passengers on trains, to ministers in their churches, to publicans in their pubs, to lovers wrapped in their sheets and to children careless enough to ask a question. Here the reader is reasonably safe, since I am going to let the project speak for itself: in this chapter how it was put together, and in the next how it actually turned out in practice. The sceptic will have the great satisfaction of noting that not everything worked.

The second reason for offering a personal account is that this project has had no official historian, and many of the protagonists have very different impressions of what actually happened, and to whose credit or blame. Not that I intend to apportion either – the credits agreed in general terms will be found in the Acknowledgements and in the museum that St Colman's church has now become. If my account has any value, it is in showing how archaeology actually happens, what people think of it at the time, the good fights we must fight and the compromises we should accept. No archaeologist would necessarily do what I did, but most, I fancy would like to know what was done and why.

My third reason is the strangest. Of all the people who were working on the early history of Scotland in 1994, I must be accounted one of the most ignorant. My path of learning may help explain both the delusions I came with, and the conclusions I came to. This can be interesting, because, contrary to public opinion, every archaeological researcher is a traveller along a narrow path, and just because the researcher is called a professor does not make the path any broader. New learning is required for every student supervised and every lecture taken, but even more so for every new site dug. The world of archaeology is so immense that a few feet from our chosen fairway we all stray into the rough grass of ignorance. By exposing the path taken, I hope not only to explain my objectives, and what they led to, but to share with the reader the challenge, the puzzle and the thrill of what this whole adventure was like.

My own serious infatuation with the Picts began in 1969 when I found F. T. Wainwright's book *The Problem of the Picts* in the military library in Celle, the north German town adjacent to Bergen-Belsen, where I was stationed.[1] It is probably difficult now to see this as a romantic book, yet it seemed so to me. The Picts were a people who commanded attention and allegiance. Whatever their inadequacies in recording their own history or their thoughts about anything at all, their carved stones, souterrains and hill forts spoke volumes: they were epics, eulogies and threnodies of a people with great heart. This was my first real understanding of why archaeology works: like all the best poetry, drama, music and films, it relates little but makes you write the script and fill out the characters in your own head. When I left the army in 1972 to become an archaeologist, I headed for Durham to take a course in Northern Britain 1000 BC–AD 1000. Unfortunately I was the only subscriber, so, well used to the vicissitudes of disappointed choice ('choice' has a special meaning in the army), I joined the other three students of my year in the study of the Anglo-Saxons, which, thanks to an inspiring professor,[2] I was to pursue professionally for the next twenty years.

When I made my way north in 1993, I had just closed down the ten-year excavation campaign at Sutton Hoo. The study of this seventh-century burial ground and its context had affirmed that the northern Europe of this time was composed of numerous small kingdoms, into which the Roman provinces had fragmented, and out of which had come the European countries we still have (Fig 2.1).[3] That much was probably uncontroversial; harder to prove, but a more exciting prospect, was the idea

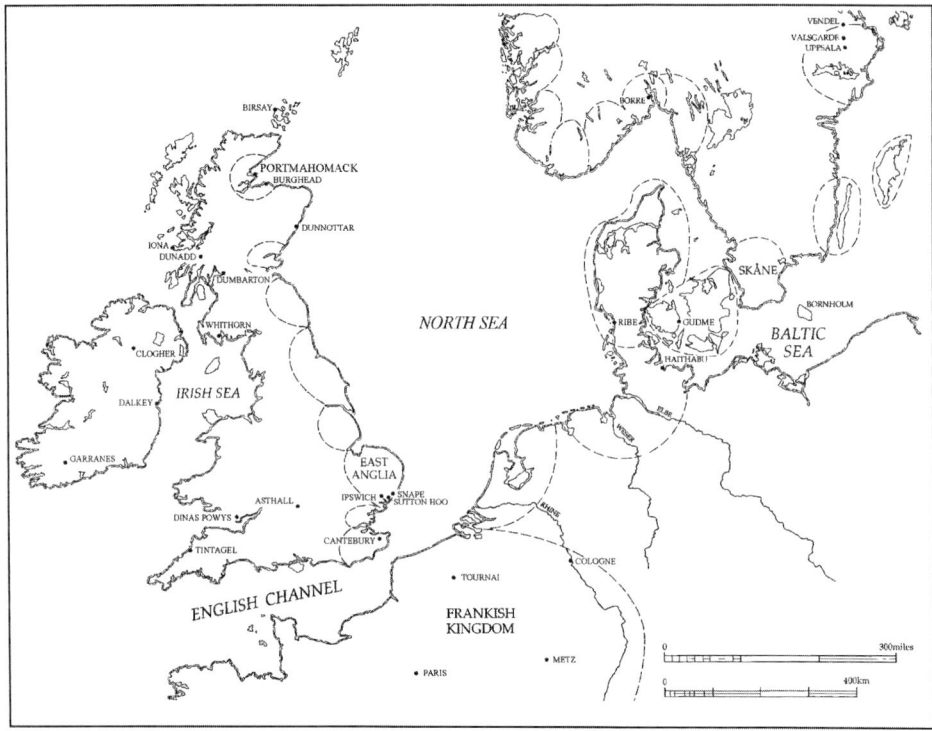

Fig. 2.1 Early kingdoms of the North Sea.

that each of these kingdoms had forged its own world view, its own religion and its own political agenda. This was suggested by the very different types of monument in which they each invested. Some communities, such as those active in East Anglia and in eastern Sweden, expressed themselves in the form of ship-burials and horse-burials. Others, in Scotland, Ireland, Wales and Gotland, made standing stone slabs, although with very different motifs on them. Some incised their memorials in Latin, others in runes and others again in ogam. It was not so much the strangeness of all this, appealing as it is, as the care taken to be different, to offer something special. It was this that led to the deduction that the monument-builders were following the dictates of their own souls, and, more crucially, that this almost uniquely was an age in which such individuality was permitted or tolerated – or at least could not successfully be suppressed. In Europe, religious thinkers, though not utterly inflexible, have always prized orthodoxy, and orthodoxies, in support of large-scale political hierarchies, have continued to dominate to the present day. The implication of the archaeology, that between the Roman Empire and the Christian Middle Ages was sandwiched a brief period of intellectual freedom, was seriously attractive.

The new project, then, was driven by a determination to find the origins of a Pictish kingdom and discover its political agenda through the study of sites and monuments. But the design of such a project would need more than a vague aspiration: it would require well-defined objectives, identification of material evidence that could

Research Agenda

In Scotland, as in other North Sea countries, we can model the picture of the sixth–ninth centuries in two ways: as archaeological evidence, particularly monuments, or as verbal evidence, particularly place names and personal names. The monumental map (Fig. 2.3) shows that the territory of eastern Scotland is a cultural zone marked out by symbol stones – boulders or carved slabs carrying the special insignia of the Picts. The symbols are found on two kinds of memorial, hitherto termed Class I, incised on boulders or unshaped stones, and Class II, incised or done in low relief on shaped rectangular slabs, carrying a cross on one side. Class I and Class II stones occasionally carry inscriptions in ogam – an Irish method of writing, probably derived from a sign language (like deaf and dumb), in which the letters were formed of horizontal or sloping strokes against a line. The term 'Class III' referred to cross-slabs without Pictish symbols, and Class IV to mainly small slabs that carried only a cross, incised or in relief. The problem with the designation was that an evolution was implied, Class I to Class III, an evolution of time and an evolution of thinking, neither of which is easy to demonstrate.[4] The geographical distribution is more helpful: the Class I stones are thickly distributed in Aberdeenshire, Angus and around the Moray Firth, and generally situated between the uplands and agricultural land. Apart from a few outliers in Skye and Orkney, the distribution reports eastern Scotland from Angus to Sutherland as the heartland of the Picts. The Class II stones, by contrast, cluster around supposed political centres on Tayside and the inner Moray Firth. The Classes III and IV, it can be assumed, mark out other Christian centres of some kind.

Various other kinds of site and object share a coincidental distribution with the symbols, although their customary dating takes them further and further back in time: square ditched barrows (second–sixth centuries), souterrains (first–sixth centuries), vitrified forts (early Iron Age, sixth–ninth centuries BC) and henges and carved stone balls (Bronze Age or Neolithic) (Fig. 2.2). For the builders of square ditched barrows, the association with the symbols is intimate, since in several cases stones incised with symbols have been found at or near the barrow summits.[5] Symbols are also found carved on Bronze Age standing stones, as at Edderton, or the stones of Bronze Age stone circles (see Chapter 5). Thus, whatever was to be the influence of Christianity – the big new sixth-century idea from the Mediterranean – the homeland of the Picts already had its own monumental character, as prominent to them as it still is to us. Whether or not we succeed in proving that the later monuments made active reference to the earlier, it can be accepted that the people of what is now eastern Scotland lived in the eighth century in a land long marked out as a discrete cultural zone.

It is an ecological zone too: it has a dry climate, the best farmland, but a difficult coast for sailing, with very few islands or natural harbours. The contrast with the

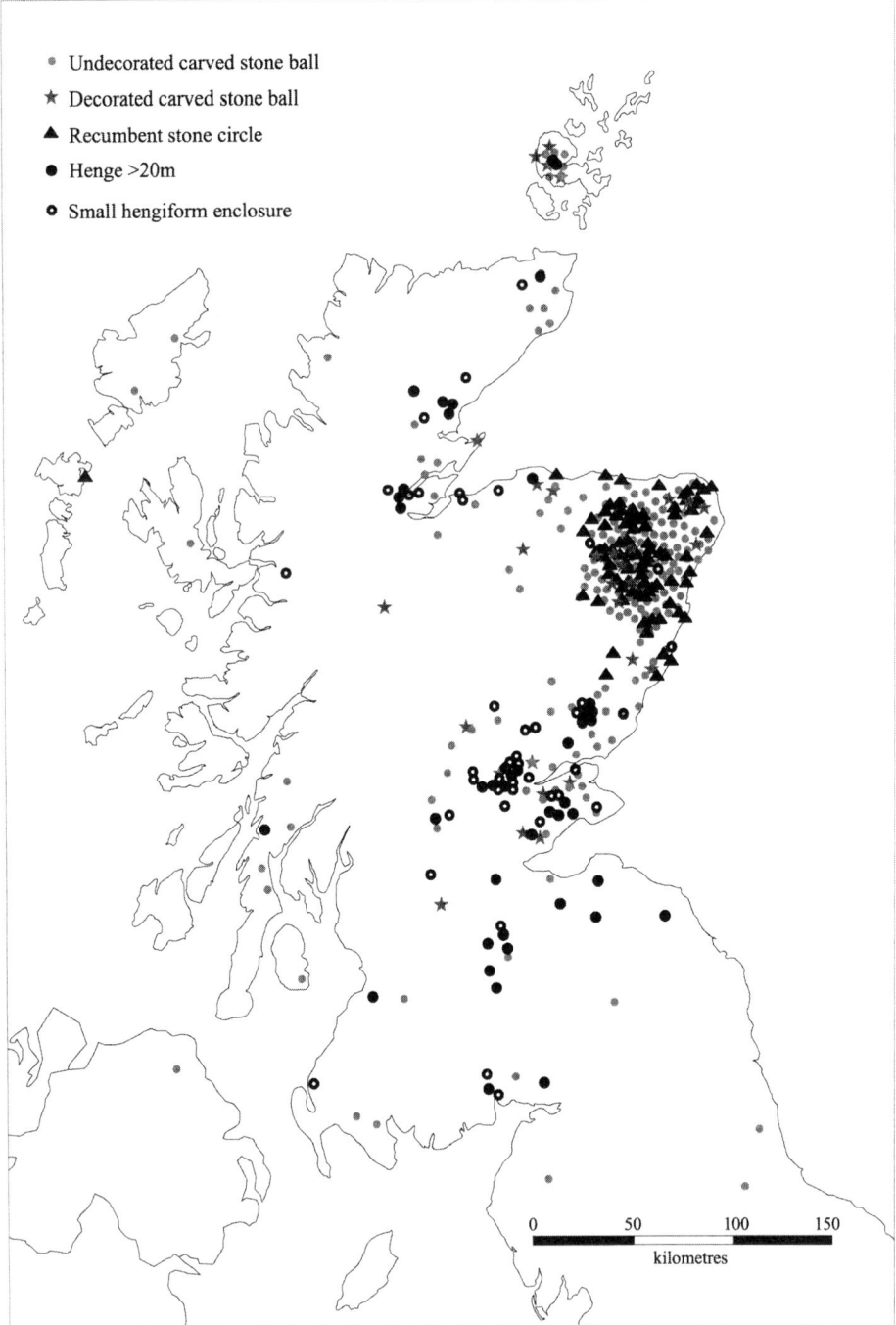

Fig. 2.2 Prehistoric cultures: distribution of henges (after Bonsall) and carved stone balls. (After Edmonds 1992)

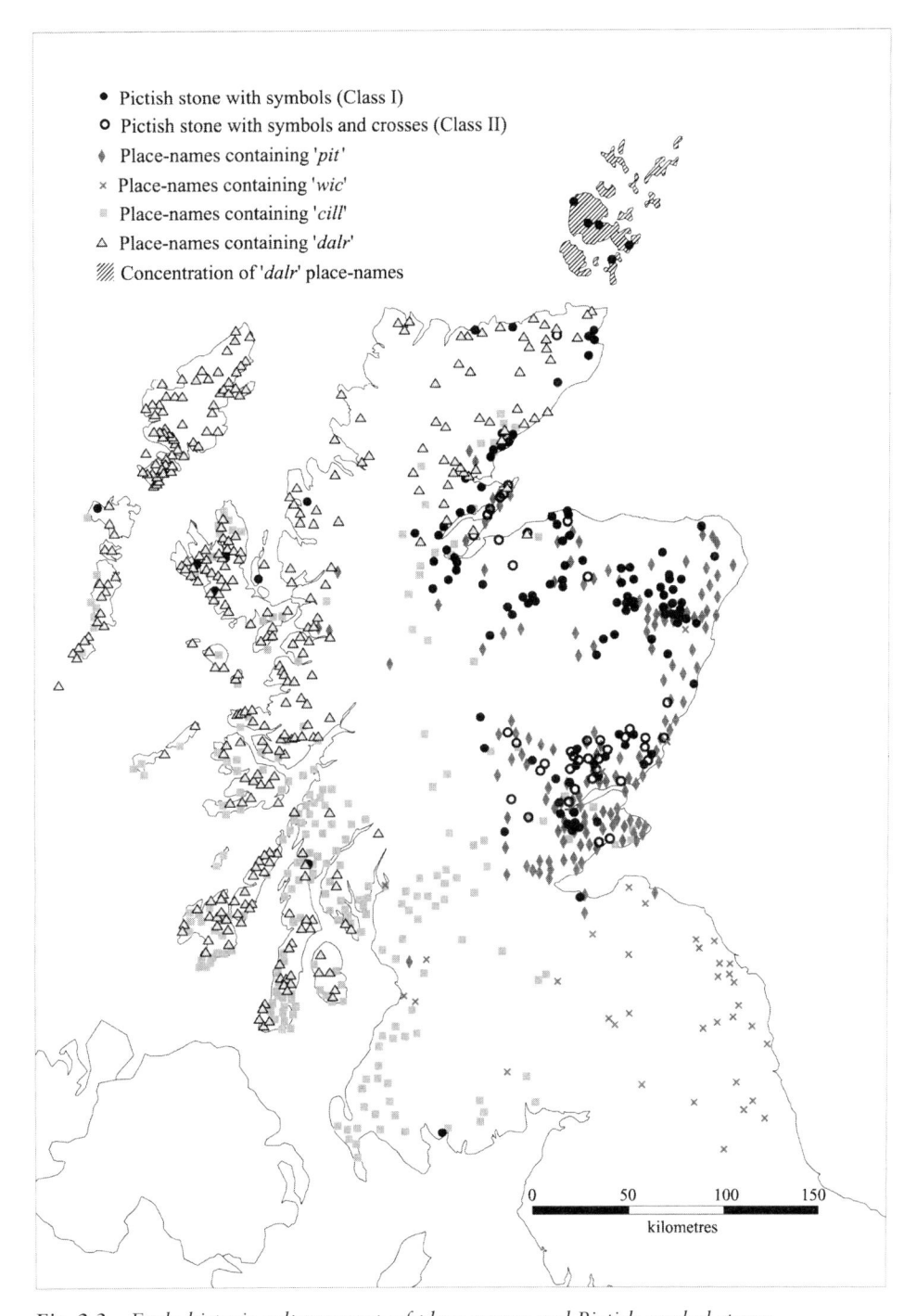

Fig. 2.3 Early historic cultures: map of place names and Pictish symbol stones.

west of Scotland could hardly be greater: a steep land of many hundreds of island and sea lochs, with extensive upland grazing, a lot of rain and many bogs. Those of a determinist disposition can also note that most of Scotland's ferocious midges live on the west rather than the east side. There is a long mountain range, Druim Alban, the spine of Britain, between the east and west archaeological zones. If we knew nothing more, a prehistorian would not be surprised if the east and west of Scotland entered history as two separate countries.

And it is reported as such by the Venerable Bede in the early eighth century:

> At the present time there are in Britain, in harmony with the five books of the divine law, five languages and four nations – English, British, Scots and Picts. Each of these has their own language; but all are united in their study of God's truth by the fifth – Latin – which has become a common medium through the study of the scriptures.[6]

This diversity of language has been preserved for us in the form of place names, the distribution of which leaves little doubt of the localities in which they predominated: east (Pictish), west (Scottish), south-east (English) and south-west (British). Since Scottish is closely related to Irish, a language zone can be proposed that encompassed the northern part of the Irish Sea, and included Ulster, Argyll and the western isles (Fig. 2.3).

So far so good. But Bede goes on to tell us that the Picts were immigrants from Scythia, that they made their way to Ireland to get wives, and that, having obtained them, they agreed that, in the event of a disputed succession, they should choose a king from the female royal line rather than the male: 'This custom continues among the Picts to this day.'[7] How long ago all this is supposed to have happened is not said. The Romans knew the people of eastern Scotland as Caledonii, and defeated them at the battle of Mons Graupius (maybe intended for Grampians), at which the locals famously fought naked. By the end of the third century, they had acquired the Latin nickname *Picti* ('painted') and were rampaging southwards, often in cahoots with the *Scotti*.

These ancestral scraps have been contrived into a freakish history that is still cherished by modern lovers of the Picts. The Picts were led by their women, who had several husbands and made them compete for their favours. In the folk tales, three brothers set out for the Pictish castle, tall and blank like a broch, with no way in, and were set various tasks. The youngest brother won the princess and thus the kingdom, since the two went together. The men generally went about naked (they were hardy) but covered in tattoos – like the Scythians, whose tattooed remains had been found in well-preserved tombs in modern Georgia. And the tattoos were the source of the symbols that, by historical times, were rendered on stone. The incomprehensible Pictish ogam must be Scythian, or else the Picts were pre-Celtic people who spoke a non-European language. Yes, it all seemed to make sense – but of course it didn't. This enticing vision of seductive strangeness still lingers on, but has now to be relegated to the nursery of history. The general opinion now is that Picts were simply Britons living in eastern Scotland. They had a Celtic language that resembled Welsh. They had male leaders and kings and wore clothes most of the time.[8] But they may

Table 2.1 Historical summary

Dates AD	Event
297	Picti mentioned by Eumenius
367	Picts and Scots overrun Hadrian's Wall
sixth century	Ninian in Whithorn; missions to the southern Picts?
563–97	Columba in Iona
565	Columba's mission to the northern Picts
565–85	Bridei, son of Mailchon, king of northern Picts
672–93	Bridei, son of Bili, king of Picts
685	Picts defeat and massacre English army led by Ecgfrith of Northumbria at Nechtansmere (in Badenoch?)
697	Curadán, missionary and bishop, active in Easter Ross
679–704	Adomnán abbot of Iona
c. 706–24	Nechtan, son of Derile, king of Picts
710	Nechtan corresponding with Ceolfrith of Jarrow about the practice of Christianity
729–61	Angus son of Fergus, king of Picts
731	Bede's *History of the English Church and People* completed
789	Constantine, son of Fergus, king of Picts
c. 811–20	Constantine, son of Fergus, king of Picts and Scots
839	Picts of Fortriu defeated by Norse
866	Fortriu plundered by the Norsemen
1035	Macbeth loses the battle of Tarbat Ness

Sources: derived from *HE*, *LC*, the *Annals of Ulster* and other written sources. See also Woolf (2006).

well have employed tattoos, and it is certainly possible that Pictish women, like those in eastern Sweden, had rights of property and inheritance, particularly in the pre-Christian period.[9] The real problem is that we have seen so little of the Picts on the ground.

In his *History*, Bede saw Christian conversion as closely associated with the emergence of the English nation. What about the Picts and Scots? Principally from Bede and from Adomnán's *Life of St Columba*, we have three conversion stories for Scotland. The earliest, placed in the fifth or sixth century, was due to St Ninian (or Finian) based at Whithorn in Galloway. His missionary activities took him north and east, into lands of the Britons and perhaps the southern Picts. The second is owed to St Columba or Columcille, who arrived from Ireland to found a monastery on Iona off the coast of Mull in AD 563. He presumably found himself in an already Christian milieu, since he set out two years later on a famous mission to the northern Picts. He and his companions travelled by boat along the Great Glen, a journey marked by the first appearance in history of the Loch Ness monster, which tried to eat one of the holy company.[10] Somewhere near Inverness, he met the Pictish ruler Bridei son of Mailchon[11] in his stronghold, and had a discussion with him about the nature of the world. Columba calmed storms, and used white pebbles for healing purposes, which also floated on water,[12] chanted the forty-fourth psalm in an unbearably loud voice,[13] beat Broichan, the king's chief wizard, in a competition to control the weather[14] and caused the gates of Bridei's fortress to open.[15] All this caused Bridei to treat the holy man with respect, but he stopped short of accepting Christianity on behalf of his people.[16]

However, some families were seemingly converted, and, more significantly, Adomnán reports that Columba founded monasteries in Pictland at that time. Relating that a great plague had struck Britain and Ireland, but had spared the people of northern Scotland, living either side of the Druim Alban, he adds: 'Surely this grace from God can only be attributed to St Columba? For he founded among both peoples the monasteries where today he is still honoured on both sides.'[17] In a footnote to this passage, the editor Richard Sharpe remarks dryly: 'One could wish that Adomnán had named the monasteries that St Columba had founded in Pictland and Scottish Dalriada.'[18] 'Still honoured today' means the early eighth century, the time at which Adomnán was writing, and one can take it that the places concerned would have been well known then, and that none of the Christian community could easily foresee a time when they would be abandoned and even their location totally forgotten.

The third part of the conversion narrative intimately concerns Bede himself, and this is largely where we get it from. In AD 710 Nechtan, king of the Picts in the south, sent a letter to Ceolfrid, abbot of Jarrow in Northumbria, asking him to elucidate their practice on the date of Easter and the form of the tonsure for monks. Bede himself seems to have composed the official reply, which argued (at length) for the primacy, and Roman conformity, of Northumbrian practice. According to Bede, his advice was well received:

> When this letter had been read in the presence of King Nechtan and many of his more learned men, and carefully translated into their own tongue by those who could understand it, he is said to have been so grateful for its guidance that he rose among the assembled chieftains and fell on his knees, thanking God that he had been accounted worthy to receive such a gift from England.[19]

Bede, like many Englishmen since, was given to indulge comforting visions of Scottish gratitude. Subsequently, around 716, monks of the Columban persuasion were expelled from Pictland, although shortly afterwards Iona itself adopted the 'Roman' Easter. What differences of thinking were masked by these apparently marginal matters of keeping the date of Easter and the tonsure? 'Whenever adherents of the Celtic practice came into contact with followers of the Roman practice, there could be argument,' remarks Richard Sharpe, and the argument was 'about diversity or unity'.[20] For all the scholiastic discussion involved, at Whitby the Gordian knot was cut by the king, Oswy, and it was another king, Nechtan, who took the plunge in Pictland. This shows that, whatever the roots of the argument, these were political decisions, questions of alignment.

The archaeological reading of ideological change also implies something rather more complex than 'Conversion' or 'Christianisation', something more subtle than the simple acceptance or non-acceptance of the Christian package. The investigations at Sutton Hoo suggested, to me at least, that, by seeking explanations of influence and power, the influence of the core on the periphery, we had often failed to place the initiative where it properly belonged, in the mind of the monument-builder. I saw a burial mound or a carved stone slab, not as an emulation of other people's culture, but as a creative and individual expression that draws on the very wide variety of learning that was potentially available. The local community made its choice, and in general it was not trying for authenticity and failing; it was defining its own authenticity. I felt that, whatever we might find at Portmahomack, we would be reading what the people who had lived there, then, had wanted to say. Just as much, or even more than in the case of the texts, we would have to read between the lines. The main questions we were required to answer about the material culture we encountered were not: 'Is this Christian? Whose influence is seen? What ethnic groups are these?' But – more simply – we needed to discover the factors that caused our site and its monuments to be created: why that, why there and why then?

In brief, the principal documentary sources provide us with a sparse framework, thanks to Bede and Adomnán, referring to the period immediately before they wrote – that is, the mid-sixth to early eighth centuries. At that time, the Scots in the west, the Britons in the south-west and the Angles in the south all have an interest in the Picts and the lands they occupy. The Angles attempt conquest by military means; but the Scots and the Britons use ideological conquest through Christian missions. Belatedly, the English join the game and use their newly converted politicians to bid for Pictish alignment. By the early eighth century, there is a strong impression that communities all round Scotland are sharing hymn sheets, if not always singing in harmony.

The rest of the eighth century is obscure, our principal witnesses having fallen silent, but there are kings of Pictland, apparently Christian, and an assumption that there are bishops at their courts and monasteries in their endowment. Curadán or Boniface is an important figure in the north-east, promoting the Christian infrastructure. The majority of the Pictish cross-slabs would appear to belong to this century. From the early ninth century there are new players in the form of the Norsemen, who make a strong pitch for Shetland, Orkney and Caithness, and eventually settle there. They are no friends to the monastic movement, but may soon have adopted the trappings and alliances of Christian kingship.

The period from the ninth to the eleventh centuries is perhaps even more of a Dark Age than the one that preceded it. Shadowy figures, mostly derived from later documentation, circle each other in the Firthlands: Sigurd and Thorfinn from Orkney, Mael Brighte and MacBeth from Moray, Constantine and Angus II from Tayside. For the north-east, the picture has been brightened recently by Alex Woolf, who demonstrated that the region of *Fortriu*, long thought to have been in the south of Pictland, can sit better north of the Mounth. If Fortriu comes north, so does the Battle of Nechtansmere (685) and a number of kings and bishops and Viking raids – all referable to the land called Fortriu. (These matters are discussed in Chapter 7.)

These considerations and thoughts, clearly much abridged here (see Table 2.1), provide the underpinning for the first part of the construction of a Project Design – the Research Agenda. It was an extensive shopping list, beginning with the social organisation of the Picts, which alliances they had fostered and when, how or whether they had accepted or adopted or adapted Christianity. On these matters, the assertions of Christian writers were not to be trusted, since they had motives of their own for supposing that all peoples are ruled by kings, and that Christian teaching is ultimately irresistible. There was also the question of the disappearance of the Picts from history, and whether they had been subsumed by the Scots or the Norse or neither or both. And there was everything to learn about the material culture that had provided a context for those magnificent stone-carved monuments.

To this end we wanted first of all to have a decent sight of *any* Pictish settlement, since none had been excavated on a sufficient scale to understand how it functioned. This was also true of an early medieval monastery – should this prove to be one. None had been found in Pictland, or exposed on a comprehensible scale elsewhere in Britain and Ireland; the enquiry had been largely directed at named sites where the relevant heritage authority had been reluctant to give permission for more than a small intervention. This was a well-meaning stricture, designed to conserve the greater part of a precious historic site for the future. But it does not work in the long term; Iona, for example, is lacerated by small trenches, many making no sense and remaining (perhaps for that reason) unpublished, and we are no nearer to knowing how the monastery there was laid out.[21] Similarly, we had only a vague idea of what constituted a Pictish building, and little knowledge of Pictish craft, agriculture or burial. In brief there was rather more on the agenda than off it.

Deposit Model

The second requirement for successful design was to know how far any of our questions could actually be answered at Portmahomack. This required the construction of a 'deposit model' – the mapping of the archaeological deposit as extensively as possible with a view to discovering its depth, date and state of conservation. Supposing there was nothing there? Supposing there had been, but it had been minced into oblivion by years of ploughing? Supposing, on the other hand, the site was well preserved and there was wood to find, lift and conserve. Needless to say, there were implications here, not only for the chances of answering our questions, but for what it would cost to do so.

Archaeological excavation is destructive, since it involves the dismantling of the strata, so the trick in predicting strata quality is to use non-intrusive or non-invasive methods as far as possible. The church of St Colman was expected to have at least a medieval, if not an earlier stage, so that whatever there was would be interesting. However, it could also be anticipated, without calling on any special ingenuity, that the interior would be full of graves, and that these graves would have cut into each other, disturbing and scattering the skeletons that had been buried earlier. The churchyard too was clearly cut about by graves, but this was, in any case, a no-go

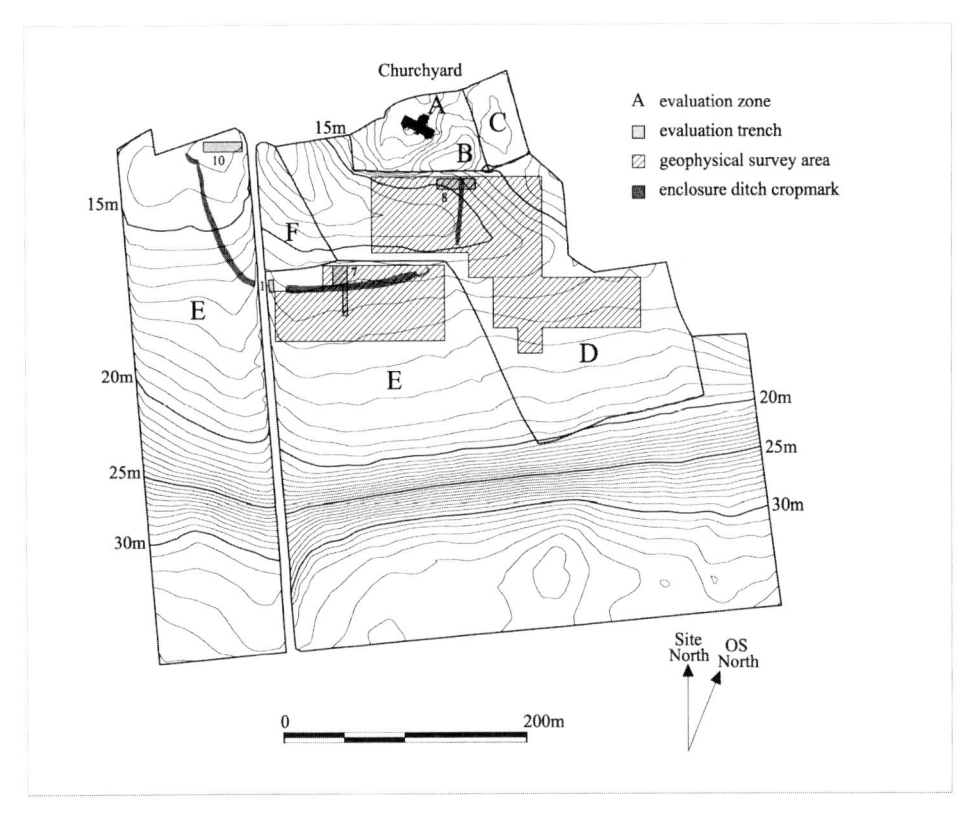

Fig. 2.4 Areas of evaluation, with contours.

area, determined as such by the local community, as I will shortly relate. Our energies during the evaluation phase were therefore concentrated inside the church (A on Fig. 2.4) and on the land outside the churchyard: to the north, between the church and the beach, to the south, the Glebe Field owned by the Church of Scotland (F and D), and, south of that, the field owned by James and Douglas Gordon (E).

Among the fancy modern methods of seeing through the ground without disturbing it are resistivity, magnetometry and radar, all of which report 'anomalies' that refer to buried ditches and buildings. At Portmahomack, magnetometry quickly confirmed the line of the enclosure ditch and pointed to a hearth in the southern field; but that took us only so far towards a Pictish settlement. Luckily we had some other methods at our disposal, each of which would report promisingly on what lay beneath.

The most powerful of our secret weapons was a gentleman by the name of Duncan Johnson who lived adjacent to the site, which he had in fact ploughed for some forty years (Fig. 2.5). Now retired, he was in the habit of having a morning cigarette watching us at work, a welcome change after the forty years in which others had watched him. One morning we got chatting, as the resistivity meters and magnetometers beeped and shouted their way across the fields. He had a delivery that was wry,

Fig. 2.5 Duncan Johnson, farmer and friend.

humorous and understated, not unlike Dave Allen, the late lamented comedian, which it is worth imagining as I relate the following conversation.

> *Duncan* (casually): Now what would you be doing, I wonder?
> *Myself* (with some condescension): We are looking for a Pictish settlement
> *Duncan* (incuriously): What are those devices?
> *Myself* (with added condescension): They are electronic devices. We are using them to find buried houses.
> *Duncan* (with faint irony): Have you found any?
> *Myself* (robustly): Not yet.
> *Duncan* (after a lengthy pause and a drag on the cigarette): Would you like to know where they are?
> *Myself* (reality slowly dawning): I certainly would!
> *Duncan* (companionably): We'll go together then.

We walked into the northern part of the centre of the Gordons' field, where he stopped and said: 'I should dig here if I were you.' Needless to say I did, and up came the circular end of the remarkable building that we were later to refer to as 'Structure 1'. Duncan guided us also to the north end of the Glebe Field, where he anticipated more buildings; and they were there too (Structure 4). In retrospect, this was of course no mystery. The subsoil here is pure sand. Not only must stones of any kind be imported from elsewhere (such as off the beach), but the assiduous ploughman must stop and remove any that are pulled out by his plough. It needed a local ploughman, as opposed to an archaeologist, to recognise the ancient settlement of his

Fig. 2.6 'Strip and map': inspecting the surface of the archaeology without harming it.

region. Such people are worth many thousands of pounds' worth of electronic machinery.

The area opened in the vicinity of Structure 1 was the first of four trial trenches designed to test the depth and integrity of strata inside the enclosure (Fig. 2.4). Reassessed now, they can be seen to have been inadequate. In particular, they failed to anticipate what now seems so crashingly obvious: the presence of a buried stream running through the Glebe Field, and its accompanying deep strata with waterlogging and preserved wood. But early monasteries do not respond well to narrow trenches – or narrow questions. More productive was a method first advocated by O. G. S. Crawford, developed by Brian Hope-Taylor on the Anglo-Saxon palace at Yeavering (he called it a 'primary horizontal section'), and fine-tuned on the sands of Sutton Hoo, where we called it 'horizon mapping'.[22] It really applies only to a site covered by a shallow ploughsoil; the ploughsoil is removed with a mechanical shovel, by back-blading to ensure the tracks of the mechanical excavator do not damage the opened surface, and then cleaned with shovels and trowels. The main disadvantage is that a large volunteer workforce is required, with trowelling lines of ten to twenty persons (Fig. 2.6). This is not easy to achieve in professional archaeology, but for a university there is usually a ready supply of students, and the chance for local volunteers to lend a hand greatly increases a project's social acceptance. This process, also known as 'strip and map', did not involve any excavation: it was a map of what lay under the plough, did not cause damage to any of the archaeological deposit and for this reason it was classed as part of the evaluation stage. When a surface had been mapped and recorded, it was covered up again, using black polythene sheeting and sandbags ('strip, map and wrap'). Horizon mapping gave us a 'road map' of most of the excavation area, and it was from this map that decisions were taken about what to study by destructive excavation. If all or part of an area had to be examined again, it was dug to the level of the polythene by machine and quickly recovered to its near original condition. Several areas, such as that of the Hall (S1), were opened and wrapped in five or six seasons.

A small number of other trenches were dug, and occasionally they proved useful. On the beach side of the Tarbatness Road was a small building plot, where a Mr Petty was planning to build a holiday cottage, with attractive views out across the Dornoch Firth and the western hills beyond. It was the last plot on the ridge not yet built on, and an important opportunity for those who wanted to understand the archaeological strata better. An area 16 × 8m was opened in 1996 under the supervision of Dominic Salsarola, who tackled it lustily. The results were to prove disappointing: it was sand and more sand, with eighteenth–nineteenth-century rubbish pits. 'A sand site has no bottom' runs the old adage (mine at any rate) – in other words you should never be too sure that you have reached undisturbed strata in sand. It has a nasty habit of hiding early activity beneath its inscrutable blankets. It fools all archaeologists regularly – and would be doing so again. But here at least, as we went down through more than a metre of clean sand (the top of the subsoil near the road was 14.70m AOD), the conclusion had to be drawn: this was a sand dune, and, until recent times, no one had ever lived there. This suited the model of our site. The monastery lay on the ridge, behind the beach, overlooking the sea, and there had been nothing in front of the church, which could see and be seen far across the firth. Outside the churchyard, on the south side of the road, it was another matter. Here, in the Glebe Field, named by us Sector 2, was arguably the most complex continuous medieval deposit yet encountered in Scotland.

The outcome of the deposit modelling exercise was that the enclosure existed, and there were buildings with stone foundations within it. The finds showed that the place had been occupied at least from the eighth century (the date of the sculpture) to the tenth (the date of the hoard) and that the church at least had been active in the Middle Ages. Our test trenches and the strip and map showed that the subsoil was scored with ditches, slots and post-sockets, and that the occupants had left behind thousands of animal bones and seashells. At the outer limits of the enclosure the site was buried by 250mm of disturbed soil, while towards its centre the deposits lay much more deeply. Between the church and the beach, the trench had shown us only sand dunes, much disturbed by dumping of rubbish in the eighteenth and nineteenth centuries and by the building of holiday homes in the twentieth. All this offered a guide to the underground geography of the buried site at Portmahomack, even if we could not as yet know its precise date, duration or function. The importance of knowing as much as we did before committing ourselves, and the Tarbat Historic Trust, to the expense and duration of a major project can hardly be exaggerated. The aim was to match what we wanted to know to what had survived and so compute the cost of the investigation. Only then could we propose how much should be dug, and where, and with what expectation.

Social Context

There was, however, still one more factor contributory to the design and thus to be taken into account: the social context in which we were to work, and the local context in particular. Some local attitudes to the proposed project were already extremely clear, and we were fortunate to have the encouragement and support of the local group that had initiated and encouraged the research programme from the outset. Led by its chairman, Caroline Shepherd-Barron, the members of Tarbat Historic Trust treated us like honoured guests, and we were feted and feasted, and liberally supplied with whisky and roast lamb. After the honeymoon was over there were occasional ups and downs; those unfamiliar with the ways of archaeologists sometimes regard them more as labourers than scientists – perhaps it is all that sweat and mud; but in truth we are both and should be content. More problematically, the Trust did not represent everybody in the village or the locality, and owned only the church, so there were other parties to woo before the larger project could be accepted by the broader community. By a strange piece of luck, James and Douglas Gordon, who owned the south and west fields through which our enclosure ran, declared themselves almost immediately as the friends of archaeological research. They had won a competition as the 'Fittest Family in Easter Ross', and their prize was a holiday in Egypt. This gave them a great deal of satisfaction, and their return to Easter Ross after this holiday coincided with our arrival. We could not offer them a pyramid, but the deep past of their own country was clearly as attractive. The owners of the Glebe Field were the Church of Scotland, with whom a deal was swiftly struck, and their tenant farmer, Billy Vass, was to remain an enthusiast over the next decade.

Serious opposition came from two quarters, both associated with St Colman's church and its churchyard. Although the church was nearly derelict in 1994, there were those who did not relish its being given some sort of artificial facelift. Others made it clear that there should be no digging in the churchyard, not even to lay electric and water services for an eventual museum. Cultural resource managers will observe that there was a notable gap here between the Trust's perceived and its effective authority. The Trust had permission to cut a trench through the churchyard from the elders of the Church of Scotland and from Highland Council (which owned it), so its attitudes to subsequent objectors were liable to be dismissive. But, of course, a Scottish burial ground is actually owned by the descendants of those buried in it, the owners of the 'lairs', and their opinion on whether or not the ground should be disturbed is subservient to no one. Although there is a map of the lairs, held by the Council, there is no guarantee that families or their grave-diggers will have followed it with any great accuracy. To dig in a Scottish burial ground (other than to bury someone) therefore requires permission from a very large number of people, few of whom would recognise the Council or the church elders, let alone a self-appointed trust, as speaking for them. This was made abundantly clear when we dug a first trench in order to lay power lines to the church; it followed the recommended line on the north side of the church, apparently with all permissions in place. But infuriated lair-owners arrived and announced that we were on the point of striking the very recent burial of a relative, and they proposed to protest in the most vociferous terms, and duly did, from Inverness to Glasgow.

There was a real problem here, as real as those encountered by archaeologists working in territory curated by descendant communities in Australia or North America. Respect for local views is not a matter of ticking boxes or recruiting the eminent and the official. It requires legwork on the ground. John Macleod, the Free Church Minister, helpfully mapped the local susceptibilities and advised me to visit Finlay Munro, a local expert who was most certainly a lover of history, and no enemy to those that he believed loved the old church as he did.[23] I sat with him in his prodigiously heated parlour, supplied with tea, whisky and potted meat sandwiches, being instructed in what he would regard as acceptable conditions. He agreed that St Colman's would fall down if not repaired, but felt that there was no necessity to tear the heart out of it. Its new life as a museum was not one that appealed to him, but all he required was one area in it reserved to prayer, where the sacred character of the building was to be respected and preserved (we chose the crypt). We might dig a trench through the churchyard, but only if we followed the line of the path. Sadly he did not live to see his advice followed (which it was), and it is possible that he did not want to. The new work, including the trench along the churchyard footpath, was preceded by a public meeting and advertising on local radio and in the post office: not just in official circles, but in the much broader, less formal, and more important 'circle of the descendants'.

The evaluation of the project had now assessed the research agenda, the deposit model and the social context, and it was time to start composing and costing a programme. However, there were still some major negotiations to do, because this was not to be solely an archaeological project. There were, in essence, three main organisations involved, each of which wanted something slightly different from the venture. The Tarbat Historic Trust wanted to restore St Colman's church, to see it once more as a landmark and a seamark for Portmahomack. The University of York wanted to research the site and tell its story, as a contribution to the early historic archaeology of Europe. Highland Council also wanted to see the research done, and its case officer, Graham Watson, was himself a Pictish scholar.[24] The Council was less convinced that the restoration of the church was a high priority, but if it was to be achieved it was vital that the building had some long-term use, preferably of educational benefit to the community. These differences in objective led initially to some fairly spectacular misunderstandings, which melted away once they had been integrated into a single project.

The argument for the integrated project ran like this. The restoration of the church would be expensive, and would get grants at the right level only if a long-term use for it could be found – a long-term use of high community value. The church of St Colman was sitting in a settlement of the northern Picts, about whom we knew very little. In order to understand their economy, their social organisation and their ideology, we would need to investigate the layout of the settlement on a large scale: trenches would not do. If it had been, at some stage of its life, a monastery, the need for a large-scale investigation was still more essential, since so little was known about the function of these places in the sixth–eighth centuries, and so little had so far been seen through the medium of small trenches. On the other hand, the large-scale excavation that was demanded promised to yield something special: a rounded image of a Dark Age settlement and a great number of finds that could serve as exhibits.

These were, so to speak, the moving parts of the machine: the dig would supply the artefacts and the story to create a long-term museum and visitor centre, which would in turn justify the capital required to restore the building. Each bit was essential to the others. The archaeological research programme in particular required to be integrated into such a development; no national research council could have funded an excavation on that scale. A certain amount of money had already been promised by agencies like Historic Scotland, hoping that we would get this far. Others like Highland Council and Ross and Cromarty Enterprise were with us every step of the way. Now for the necessary larger sums. The European Regional Development Fund accepted that we were in a priority area for the stimulation of tourism. And the Heritage Lottery Fund indicated that we were in the running for the greater part of the £2m required, provided we could demonstrate that our project was of value to the community. However, the first major blow then fell: research could not be included under that heading.

It was interesting (if bizarre) to be told that the Heritage Lottery Fund – or the governments that drew up its rules – did not regard research as having any community value. This long-suspected but depressing verdict raised the question of why the government could use taxpayers' money to pay for research or research facilities in universities at all. Perhaps the government saw research as part of the competitive weaponry of UK plc, rather than as the enhancement of the lives of its citizens. Possibly no income, and no ethos, can be transferred between government departments. At any event, it became necessary to deploy new arguments, and the concept of evaluation and project design here made a useful contribution. Archaeological research, I explained, was no longer what it had once been, a summer expedition sanctioned while it remained productive. Archaeological research was not self-indulgent; it was socially embedded. It no longer resembled either treasure hunting or gardening, but rather the building of a house. The archaeologist was its architect, proposing a well-designed, detailed and finite programme as a result of careful evaluation. The programme had a set of objectives, a set time scale and would involve only a specific piece of ground. In short, the principles of evaluation and project design meant that everything was fixed in advance, including the price. The archaeological research programme was, in fact, a capital expenditure, necessary to supply the material to exhibit in the museum to give the restored building its rationale. The project was, in fact, all of a piece. On 4 July 1996 the committees of the Heritage Lottery Fund agreed, and authorised the release of the grant that thereby gave the project its official go ahead. We were on our way.

The rest of this book is concerned with the archaeological discoveries that were made over the next ten years (the next chapter) and what they might mean (the following seven chapters). But I will refer from time to time to the building of the Tarbat Discovery Centre and the ingenuity and bravery of its Trust in the face of innumerable setbacks, just as I will not stint from relating how those on site struggled to understand the strata they were defining. This is because archaeology does not exist in a vacuum; every visitor, every supporter, as well as every volunteer and professional excavator, leaves a mark on the record for better or worse. Although an archaeological excavation is often thought of as a scientific expedition, it is a lot more like making a film. A discovery, a breakthrough, a smiling face, an affectionate liaison or a site seen once in brilliant evening light all stimulate the progress of the work and the understanding of the results, just as poor weather, excessive alcohol, fatigue and the miseries of love and jealousy impede it. No one is immune from these exigencies.

The right way to end this chapter is to offer a résumé of the archaeological research programme as it was proposed in 1996, and as it was followed, with a few minor variations since then. Although the expectations of excavations inside the church were not great, such excavations would in any case be necessary in advance of our own conversion of the building into a museum and visitor centre. Furthermore, as urged by Anna Ritchie, leading Pictish scholar and member of our Trust, the excavation of a Scottish church was not such a common occurrence, and, if not for the Pictish era, would pay dividends for the Middle Ages and later. And so it proved. Our excavations inside the church were to include every part of the ground plan commensurate with safety. The fabric of the church was to be stripped, preparatory to its repair and repointing. Here the archaeologist would work in close collaboration with the architect, Fred Geddes, whose knowledge of historic buildings was superior to ours and who in fact shouldered much of the recording of the fabric. The objective was to provide the complete history of the church and the structures and features on the same site, from its beginning to its last days as a ruin in 1994. The churchyard was obviously also a key area for early occupation, but it was not on offer, apart from the observations possible in the service trench cut along the footpath. Outside the modern churchyard wall, the nearest we could get to the church was in the corner of the Glebe Field adjacent to the Tarbatness Road and west gate of the churchyard. A recent excavation in advance of a housing estate at the monastic site of Hoddom, in Dumfries, had been focused (by the development) on the territory just inside the enclosure ditch. There the excavator Chris Lowe had found a number of agricultural and possibly manufacturing features.[25] It was clear that an exploration of the total geography of the Portmahomack site should include the enclosure, inside and out, as well as the church and as much space as possible in between the two. This led to the excavation area shown in Fig. 2.7. The investigations were conducted in four sectors: Sector 1 was the south field, Sector 2 the Glebe Field, Sector 3 the area beyond Tarbatness Road, and Sector 4 the church and churchyard. Within each sector, the archaeological operations or interventions were applied, Ints 11 and 25 in Sector 1, Ints 14 and 24 in Sector 2, and so forth. (The full list of interventions will be found in the Digest, A1). All the interventions marked on Fig. 2.7 were archaeological excavations.

It was also necessary to explore the context of the Portmahomack site, so this formed an integral part of the project as a whole. As noted from the sculpture (see Chapter 1), Portmahomack was intimately connected in date and ideology with sister sites on the Tarbat peninsula at Nigg, Shandwick and Hilton of Cadboll. What were

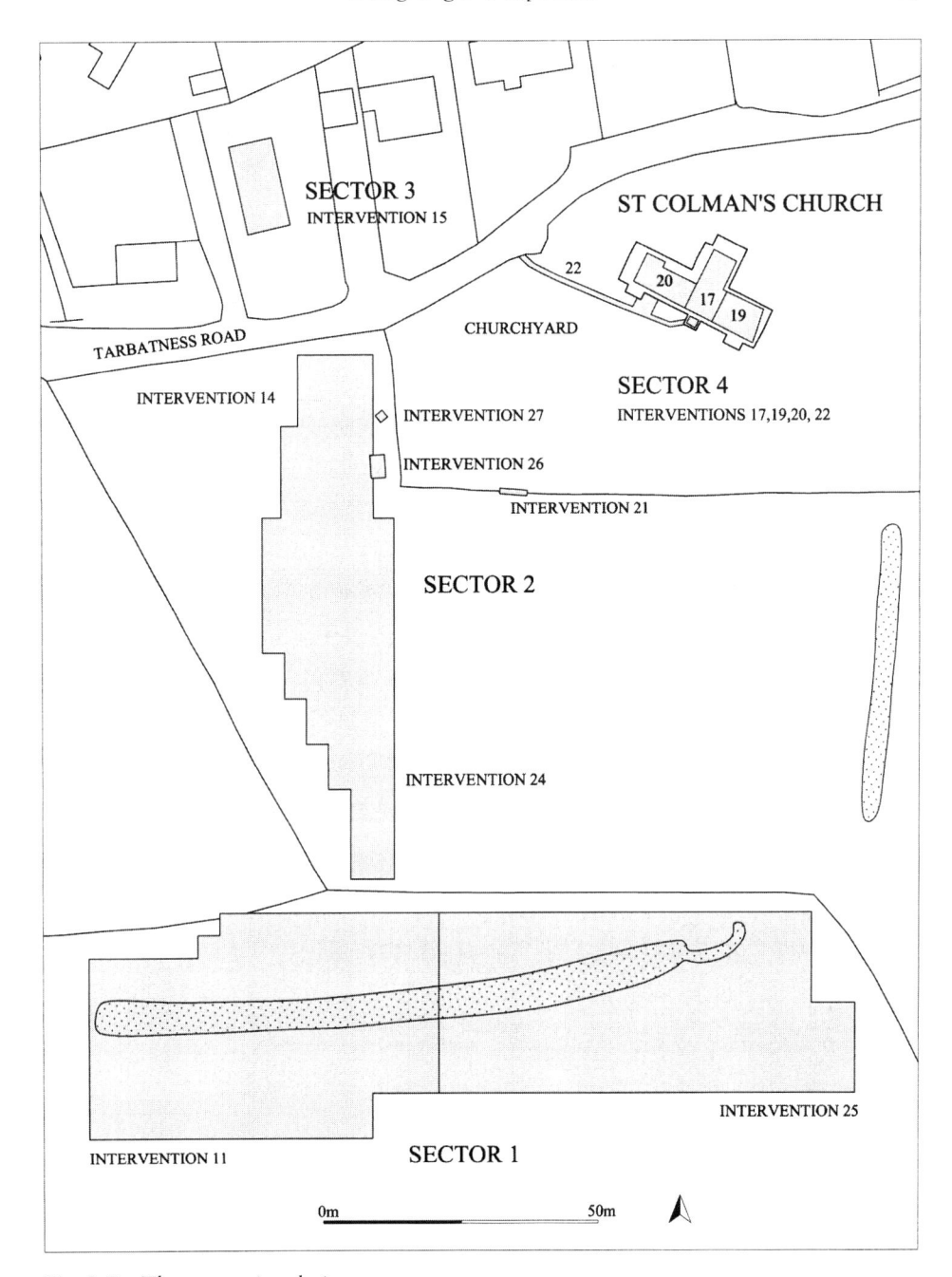

Fig. 2.7 The excavation design.

these places, and how did they relate to each other? The Tarbat name implied that there had been a portage, where boats were dragged across the neck of the peninsula.[26] Where was it? When was it active? What became of it? Lastly, since the investigation concerned the political objectives and destinies of putative communities adjacent to, but not necessarily in agreement with, each other, it was desirable to explore the neighbours in the Firthlands: the fortress at Craig Phadraig with its single piece of sixth-century imported pottery; that at Burghead with its 'bull' plaques; the Golspie strip with its numerous symbol stones; the square ditch barrow cemetery at Garbeg; the candidates for early monastic sites at Kinneddar and Rosemarkie. Little of this could be done immediately. Our agenda was truly huge, but it needed to be: without a large canvas the sketches of our first encounters underground risked having no perspective or landscape. These are essential aspects of the human world, as opposed to the world of the worm.

Notes

1. Wainwright (1955).
2. Rosemary Cramp
3. Carver (1998c; 2005a).
4. A major review of Pictish art has just been published by the leading insular art historians of our day, Isabel and George Henderson. They present us with a broader classification (not favouring Classes I–IV) and emphasise the leading role that Pictish artists played in the dissemination of Christian ideas (Henderson and Henderson 2004).
5. Ashmore (1980).
6. *HE* I. 1.
7. *HE* I. 1.
8. See, e.g., Smyth (1984); Alcock (2003).
9. For Swedish women, see Gräslund 2003.
10. *LC* II. 27.
11. Dauvit Broun would prefer us to write this as Bridei son of Meilochon.
12. *LC* I. 1; II. 33.
13. *LC* I. 37.
14. *LC* I. 1; II. 34.
15. *LC* II. 35.
16. For a general assessment of Columba's experiences among the Picts, see Sharpe (1995: 3–34).
17. *LC* II. 46.
18. Sharpe (1995: 350).
19. *HE* V. 21.
20. Sharpe (1995: 37).
21. McCormick (1997); O'Sullivan (1999).
22. For references, see Carver (2005a: 43).
23. Mr Munro was co-author of a history of St Colman's church (Fraser and Munro 1988).
24. Friell and Watson (1984).
25. Lowe (2006).
26. The 'Tarbat' name is from Gaelic *tairm-bert*, 'over-bringing'. Tarbat place names, most common on the west side of Scotland, were the sites of portages for Viking ships, and likely to have been earlier. Watson (1926: 505–6); see also Chapter 9.

CHAPTER 3

What we found

The signal to begin our formal exploration was given in July 1996. The funding package was in place, permissions had been obtained and the contractors selected. We would excavate the Pictish settlement, restore a historic church and build a museum inside it. The logic of this sequence of action was not entirely accepted by all the players, and there was an initial tension in the programme. The Trust wanted the church restored and the museum built as soon as possible, and the Heritage Lottery Fund shared this view. The restored church, rather than the research outcome, was considered 'the product' for both parties, and they wanted it 'delivered' before the committees were much older and before all the prices needed revising. The archaeological excavations were expected to take six years, but the restored church, its museum and car park were to be opened in less than three. Evidently, the exhibition would reflect the state of knowledge when the excavation was only halfway through. The church would need to be investigated first, since it was to be the subject of restoration and redevelopment. Fortunately, the church excavations were to give us the entire sequence of occupation, from its beginnings in the sixth century to its ending in 1996 – more than enough to furnish a museum.

Work began at once in the church and on the site of the car park. But in the fields beyond, the strip-and-map operation, initiated in 1994 and 1995, also continued with a squadron of students and volunteers. We were thus advancing on a very broad front, which was risky, but deliberate. The principal objectives of the excavation relied on opening the whole of the proposed large area, without any faint-hearted compromise. But the circumstances of large-scale research excavations are capricious: sponsors retained by the slender thread of new history can suddenly lose interest and cease funding. This favoured a strategy in which the big picture was to be seen as quickly as possible, to be followed by more detailed selected studies as confidence in support for the long-term project grew.

At any one time, about six professionals, ten volunteers and fifteen students attending the Field School, rising to a midsummer maximum of fifty, lived together on a camp site in tents and caravans, situated on the Gordons' field, its location shifting slightly each year as new areas were examined. The chief dangers to the excavation team at Portmahomack were the damp and the drink, neither of which was ever wholly tamed. The weather was not disagreeable; the sun often shone, and when it set over the Dornoch Firth it provided a spectacular show. At night the sky was huge and starry, and often showed revellers the glimmer of dawn in the east while the red light had scarcely vanished in the west. But rain or shine the damp came every evening

Fig. 3.1 The excavation of the Smiths' Hall (S1), with the camp-site and offices in the background.

and every morning and crept uninvited into the tent and sleeping bag, which was often still damp from a previous downpour. The palliative was to go to the pub and drink whisky, made locally down the centuries since human bones first chilled, and for all we know since the first people set foot on the Tarbat peninsula. Rabbie Burns, who knew all about the pleasures of *usquabae*, also knew how hard it was to leave a warm pub: 'While we sit bousing at the nappy, An' gettin' fou and unco happy, We think na on the lang Scots miles, The mosses, waters, slaps and stiles, That lie between us and our hame, Where sits our sulky, sullen dame.' It was only a mile down the tarmac road to the Castle Inn at Portmahomack, but it was hard to make the journey back, not so much to a sulky dame, as to a night in the skeletal grip of a soggy, clammy sleeping bag.

These perils were offset by investment in a well-appointed camp-site run by two caretakers of genius: Faith and Roy Jerromes. Courtesy of Shepherds of York, we had acquired four large portakabins and a washhouse, which included offices for the recorders and the care of finds, a kitchen, an all-weather crew room with television, and a shower, and were connected to mains water and electricity. One of these portable buildings was converted into a kitchen, from which Faith Jerromes dispensed hot meals, health, comfort and medicine. Roy Jerromes had a workshop by means of which everything that was broken got mended. Lucky are the digs that can boast such a dedicated infrastructure. Let nobody suppose that archaeology is just a matter of travelling, looking, digging and thinking. Big historical problems need big-scale archaeology, requiring large teams working well together. This, in turn, means peerless administration, careful management, efficient tools and good food, as well as ceaseless investment in the happiness of the workforce and the high opinion of the community. On site, contriving this is what excavation directors mainly do.

Putting these pious thoughts back in the script, what actually happened in practice? Excavations took place in four areas ('Sectors', see Fig. 2.7), each excavation being on very different terrain. In the southern part, in the Gordons' field, the land was flat, with the central ridge of the peninsula rising behind. From the top of this ridge, you could see across the Moray Firth to the south and across the Dornoch Firth to the north. We laid out Sector 1, an area 140 × 40m, along the flat land at the foot of the ridge, embracing over 100m of the enclosure ditch that had led us to the site. Here 30cm of ploughsoil gave out directly onto flat sand subsoil, cut by features of all periods. Sector 1 was excavated mainly by large groups of students supervised by Madeleine Hummler; strip and map took place from 1994 to 2000, and excavation continued until 2003, including that of the great Smiths' Hall (S1) by Cecily Spall (Fig. 3.1).

At right angles to Sector 1 was another large strip, Sector 2, 100 × 30m, running northwards across the valley towards the churchyard. Here the deposits were deep, and sometimes wet, and urban in their complexity: they contained multiple layers and disturbed stone structures and many thousands of finds. It required excavators working individually and often thinking and recording for longer than they were digging. This was largely a job for professionals, and, after the initial clearance in 1996, the team tended to be small and expert, led initially by Justin Garner-Lahire and latterly by Cecily Spall with important contributions from a number of company staff.[1]

Sector 3 was the land across Tarbatness Road, which was evaluated with a 4 × 8m trench under Dominic Salsarola. It appeared to be largely sand dunes, sterile until the eighteenth century, and was not taken further (and not described further here). Sector 4 was the church, the scene of a comprehensive study of the whole upstanding fabric together with the excavation of as much of the interior as we could reach (Fig. 3.2). It involved the excavation of 200 skeletons, the three-dimensional survey of many wall fragments and the extraction of eleven pieces of Pictish sculpture. This operation was led by Annette Roe in collaboration with architect Fred Geddes (Fig. 3.3). The study of the church had to begin immediately in 1996 and finish by 1997, so that its conversion to a museum and visitor centre could begin. In a small way, this was a rescue project, a recording in advance of development. We set out to rescue the church from ourselves.

We dug in seasons, since the many days that would be lost through darkness, cold and wind between October and May meant that excavation at that period was uneconomical and inefficient. As already mentioned, the sectors were not addressed one after another, but all began together, after two years' evaluation, in 1996. So, since I cannot present them in the order in which they started, I shall risk offending the reader's sense of logic by presenting them in the order in which they finished: Sector 4, Sector 1 and Sector 2. Because the sites were so different from each other, they

Fig. 3.2 The church under scaffolding in 1996.

Fig. 3.3 Annette Roe, supervisor, and Fred Geddes, architect, consider the options.

demanded a difference of approach, with their own special and attractive challenges, and consequent risks of inconsistency in records, or uneven emphasis. The reader must judge how far the account of the monastery has been skewed by the variable survival of its parts. But my hope is that the contrast in the discoveries made in each sector will reflect, rather, the diversity of the lives that these early occupants of the Tarbat peninsula were obliged to live.

THE CHURCH: SECTOR 4

The church building consisted of a nave 25m long, with a two-storey square addition projecting off its north side, referred to as the north aisle (Fig. 3.4). Two vestries were appended to the south wall. At its east end a flight of steps gave access to a door halfway up the wall – the entrance to the sacristy. At the west end, another flight of steps gave access to a loft. Here the roof was topped by an idiosyncratic yellow sandstone belfry, frequented by seagulls, some of which had died extravagantly inside the roof. All the outside of the church was covered with a once white harling. Inside, a timberwork vestry and a dais fronted by a lectern rose at the east end. On the wooden floor in front of the lectern could be seen the entrance to a crypt, sealed with a wooden trapdoor. The west end and the entrance to the north aisle were blocked off by vertical dowelled planking, which continued around most of the interior of the nave, creating the effect for the parishioners in their pews of being inside a huge wooden box.

By July 1996 the pews had been dismantled and carted away for storage in the barn of one of the Trustees, farmer Dave Scott, and the crypt had been cleared of debris by the Trust under the supervision of Jill Harden. New clearing-up operations, for the restoration and for the excavation, began together. On 23 August the vertical wooden planking was removed, revealing the openings to the north aisle and the west end, as well as the plastered inner faces of the nave walls. Set into the east and west walls of the north aisle were two commemorative plaques showing that it had been constructed before 1623. On the floor of this hidey-hole were the tumbled debris of decades, including coffins and coffin-carriers, all duly carted away by the Trustees.

The first target of the archaeological excavation was the floor area of the north aisle and the central part of the nave, making a rectangle measuring 5×12m (Int. 17, Fig. 2.7). The main purpose of digging here was to see whether this small-scale intervention could answer some basic questions about the relationship of the visible features: the north aisle and the nave, the nave and the crypt. It was intended just to put a toe in the water and see if any strata had survived, the expectation being that ground under the north aisle would offer a legible sequence, while that under the nave would be scrambled by numerous burials and thus remain incomprehensible.

It proved to be the other way round. The wooden floor of the nave was swept and its planks were lifted. Underneath the floor was a dry sandy layer containing bottles and broken teacups, resembling the debris of some ghostly underfloor party. Under this layer was an earlier floor of stone slabs, now broken and dispersed from each other on a layer of sand bedding. No sooner had the layer of bedding been removed than the

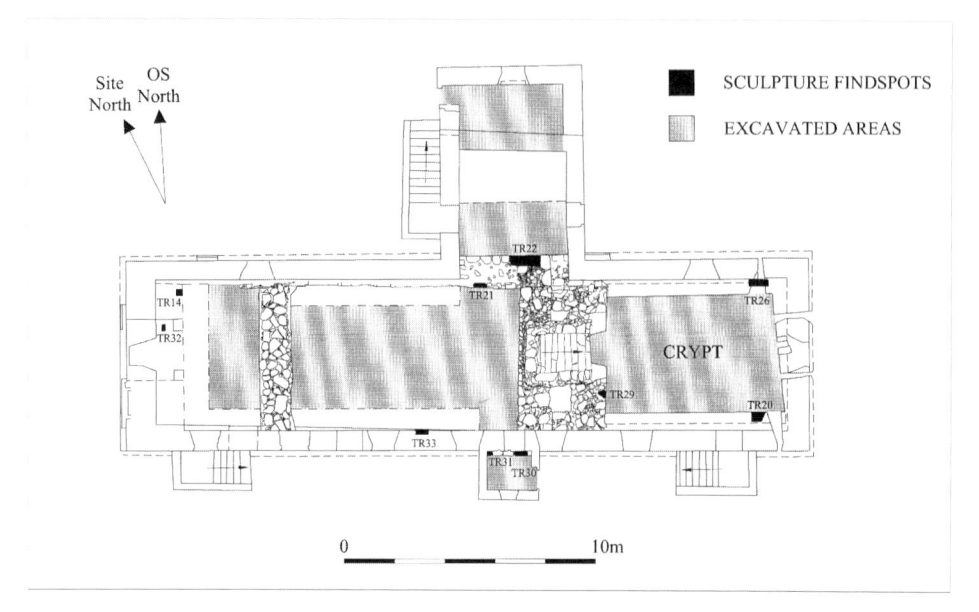

Fig. 3.4 Areas excavated in the church, showing the outline of the principal church buildings and the find spots of sculpture.

remains of a buried wall 1.20m wide appeared, crossing west to east under the opening to the north aisle. It was constructed of two rows of stone blocks infilled with rubble and a soft white mortar. The wall had been reduced to ground level when the north aisle was built, showing that it had belonged to an earlier church, and potentially a much earlier one. Lying flat in the surviving wall top, where it had been reused as building stone, was an early stone grave marker with a simple, but deeply incised cross (TR21). It was lying immediately under the sand and just needed dusting off, so the builders of the aisle and the stone floor (in the seventeenth century) must have seen it, but evidently without any great distraction to themselves.

The lowering of the ground on the north side of the wall of the older church revealed its courses and showed that it included the north-east corner of its nave. As the dry mortary soil was brushed way from the wall face, a large block made its appearance at the quoin, and, on its face, figures in relief that gradually took the form of animals, upside down. One of these was clearly a boar, which provided the block with an immediate nick-name (the 'Boar Stone', TR22). It now lay upside down, reused in the wall of an early church, which had thus been constructed after the eighth century (the date of the sculpture) and demolished before 1623 (Fig. 3.5). In one of its later manifestations, this same wall had incorporated a chamfered plinth, a typical thirteenth-century refinement. This plinth was eventually tracked all around the exterior of the nave, with the aid of a number of architect's test pits (Int. 18), giving us the preliminary deduction that the nave at least was thirteenth century, but was not itself the earliest church. Once of these pits, dug at the east end, also exposed a fine medieval grave cover (see Fig. 8.7).

Fig. 3.5 The 'Boar Stone' (TR22) in situ in the foundation of Church 2 (twelfth century).

The relationship of the main crypt with the nave was explored in the central part of the excavation. Annette Roe removed the rubble backfill from a series of cuts relating to different versions of the steps. She showed that the steps leading to the present crypt, which took the form of a barrel vault, were of a single build with the north aisle, so that the two developments had occurred together – something radical and all embracing that would soon find its chronological home in the Reformation period.

Within the crypt itself, the excavation begun by Jill Harden and the Trust was swiftly completed (Ints 13, 19). Lighting was installed, the walls were brushed and the protective sheet removed. White mortar splashes on a brown soil matched the pointing or repointing seen in the barrel vault. Beneath was a dark spongy layer thought to be the remains of a rotted wooden floor. Beneath this was a clay surface flecked with mortar and marked with Roman numerals X, IV. The east and west walls were not parallel to each other, and the barrel vault had been inserted between them. The west wall, where the steps entered, was scorched by fire and carried a mason's mark on its door jamb. The east wall, punctuated by later lights to the exterior, contained a small aumbry, and its foundations descended some 1.5m into the subsoil.

From these slender clues Annette Roe conjured a sequence that has stood the test of time: the barrel vault, seventeenth century in date (like the north aisle), had been added to a pre-existing rectangular crypt. This crypt should be medieval. The

Fig. 3.6 Recorder Katie Anderson (on the right) and publican's daughter Donna Urquhart look into the crypt.

scorching was confined to an episode that affected only these walls. The east wall, on its eccentric alignment, should be that of a still earlier building, inviting its attribution to a very early Christian period.

The seventeenth-century vault in the crypt was to produce our most important piece of Pictish art – thanks to the sensitive nose of Niall Robertson, a celebrated stone-finder of the Pictish Arts Society, who was then working with the excavation team. In the south-east corner of the vault, his fingers, gauging out the soft clay between the stone courses, had felt the rounded forms of the underside of a relief carving. Fred Geddes and Justin Garner-Lahire inserted props to take the weight of the curve of the vault above the sculpture and then dismantled the courses that held it captive. The stone, carefully freed with wooden spatulas from its clay bonding, was lifted by four persons and laid on the floor of the crypt. The effect was sensational: although still covered with patches of clay, the form of a rampant fanged beast could be seen advancing in a framework of spirals. The other side of the stone was also carved, showing, beneath a smudged surface, a row of clerics with books. No one was in any doubt that this object, speedily nicknamed the 'Dragon Stone', had raised the potential of our site to entirely new levels (Plate 2). Joanna Close-Brooks, doyenne Pictish prehistorian, noticed on her first visit after the discovery that the spiral frame of the 'dragon' closely matched that on the inscribed stone found by the Revd J. M. Joass a century before and many metres away in the garden wall of the manse. What amazing monuments had been dismantled here – and what chances we were being offered to return to the days of their glory! Altogether, excavations connected with the church brought to light eleven pieces of early historic sculpture, not counting three others that remain *in situ*.

By the end of the 1996 season, this stage of the church excavations had met its objectives, but had suggested others. Consultation with Anna Ritchie, who emphasised the historical importance of a complete Scottish sequence, and with company director Justin Garner-Lahire and architect Fred Geddes, who supported the feasibility of its investigation, led to a decision in the early summer of 1997: we would excavate every part of the nave commensurate with safety (Int. 20 Plate 3a).

The excavation of the nave was accomplished with the aid of large numbers of sandbags needed to support the dry sand of the balks, which in turn were providing support for the walls of the church. On 31 May Annette excavated the cobble foundations of a west wall that had pre-dated the west end of the church, and so nearly completed the jigsaw puzzle of the sequence (see Fig. 8.3). She had now identified an early stone church in the eccentric wall of the crypt, a later small rectangular chapel (erected after the eighth century, the artistic date for the sculpture included in its foundations), a thirteenth-century church with a chamfered plinth coincident with the present church, but including a partially subterranean crypt, and the addition of a north aisle and refurbished vaults in the seventeenth century. This framework would be greatly enriched by the study of the walls and fixtures that was to follow.

The principal reward of the second stage of excavation lay in the definition of 185 articulated and stratified skeletons. Not only was the prediction of an unreadable mass of burials confounded, but the sequence was contained by a series of reasonably visible stratigraphic horizons, which would allow a tight sequence to be proposed. Underneath the flagstone floor already defined (Horizon F) was a family of mortar floors (Horizon E). Beneath these was a yellowish sand found over most of the nave area, and attributed to the construction of the thirteenth-century church (Horizon D). Beneath it was an extensive layer of brown sand (Horizon C) into which the walls of the first medieval chapel were cut. We know now that this horizon separated the burials of the parish church from those of its monastic predecessor. Beneath it was a pink sand (Horizon B), which masked the earliest graves of all, which were cut into the earliest surviving buried soil (Horizon A). Also cutting into the earliest buried soil was a narrow gulley, with a curved black lining, resembling wooden bark – a ditch, in which some kind of timber pipe had been laid (F129; see Fig. 4.3). Later in the sequence came two bell-founding pits: one that would be dated to the eleventh century, and the other to the sixteenth (F107, F4). These, providing bells for the first medieval and the first Reformation churches respectively, helped to anchor the sequence of burial with the sequence of churches.

Even before analysis and radiocarbon dating, it could seen that the graves belonged to two separate periods. The earlier, which pre-dated the medieval chapel, were cist burials – that is, skeletons contained by large stone slabs, so that they lay in a stone chest (*cist*) (Fig. 3.7). In a lesser variant, the skeleton had just two stones placed either side of the head, and occasionally another above it. There were no finds with these bodies, which were all adults, and a suspicion that they were mainly men would be confirmed. The second group of burials was of men, women and children,

Fig. 3.7 Cist grave under excavation by Dave Watts.

Fig. 3.8 Medieval burial under excavation by Roy Jerromes.

laid in the ground in increasing numbers until finally terminated by the flagstone floor (Fig. 3.8). Some of these had been placed in wooden coffins, others had shroud pins. With them were medieval coins, a fragment of a stone gaming board and sparse fragments of pottery, including an aquamanile and a chafing dish. One skeleton still wore a leather shoe in which a piece of toe had miraculously survived. In other cases, the alkaline conditions had allowed the survival of hair on the head and pubic hair, strange dark whisps of life on the bleached bones.

It seemed that this second group was a medieval population, buried in the enlarged nave of a parish church up to the point that the flagstone floor and the north aisle were built. This moment could be broadly correlated with the Reformation, when burial was permitted only for the great, or the good, in the vaults or tombs specially constructed for them. Since grave had naturally disturbed grave, there was, in addition to the invaluable sequence of articulated skeletons, an immense quantity of disarticulated human bone. This was examined by Don Brothwell and Donna McCally, and then, in respect for the sensitivities of local people that had already been expressed, the bones were reburied on 8 August 1997 with a ceremony conducted by the Church of Scotland minister the Revd Stewart Low. The ceremony was brief, but those attending were distracted by the unusual character of the occasion. The minister, accompanied by numerous boxes of human bones, stood on the wooden dais at the east end with Annette and myself. Others stood at the low level reached by then in the nave, looking up at the dais, and before it, at the tower of rubble jacketing the later steps to the crypt. Nestling in this rubble was an example of that rarest and most enigmatic of prehistoric objects, a carved stone ball. It was spotted during the ceremony simultaneously by Donna and by the Trust's chairman, who, understandably, could hardly contain her excitement until the ceremony had ended to claim and announce the find (see Chapter 4). This was only the second serious prehistoric artefact to emerge from any of the excavations, but its findspot, in the packing of a seventeenth-century stairwell, gave rise to thoughts of early antiquaries and collectors.

The recording of the fabric of the church took place at the same time as the excavation, but at a faster pace. The whole outside and inside of the church were stripped of plaster, cement and harling, and the wall fabric laid bare. But it could not stay that way for long; the weather demanded it should be repointed and roofed before winter, and, in addition, the chariot of the Heritage Lottery Inspectors, goaded by the Trust, was hurrying ever nearer. In short, we had an unparalleled opportunity, but no time to relax and enjoy it.

The restoration of the church was in the hands of Fred Geddes, architect of Inverness, who could profess and apply both historical knowledge and archaeological awareness. This made an important difference to the viability of the project, since in the nature of the work the restoration and the recording had to go hand in hand. It required, in effect, a full-time recorder, permanently on call and at a state of orange alert – like a carp fisher who may doze in the expectation of being instantly awakened by the electric bell. We had not budgeted for such a person, so were doubly fortunate in our architectural partner. He prepared all the elevations and plans and alerted us to areas of archaeological interest or historical puzzle. The task was made more viable by the well-documented fact that the greater part of the church had been taken down and rebuilt in 1756. The walling of the eighteenth century, while not lacking in interest, posed far fewer questions than that of the eighth.

Nevertheless, we were determined that the architectural sequence would be one of the most detailed yet for a Scottish church, and accordingly buildings archaeologist Martin Jones was also commissioned to examine it, including all wall fabric, roof spaces and furnishings (Int. 23). He divided the church into one exterior (A1) and fourteen interior zones (A2–A15) and studied them minutely using a mixture of context and feature description and thinking aloud in plain language. Ideas were passed to Annette, who would check their compatibility with the recording below ground. This generated a continually evolving story for the building. Its gaps and contradictions were passed to Fred, in the form of plans and elevations pencilled with questions. Is there a blocked doorway here? Was there an earlier stair? Is this window integral or inserted? These questions could be answered as restoration proceeded.

The architect also needed to dig some pits adjacent to the foundations, all of which proved informative in some measure (Int. 18). By the spring of 1998 the restoration was well advanced and the team was stretched: Annette was in York and Martin in New Zealand. But the story of the church had now acquired scenery and actors: the first parish churches with their crypt; the major rearrangement at the Reformation; the church of the Heritors with their snugly furnished quarters flanked by poor lofts; the near desertion at the Disruption. This long-running drama

Table 3.1 Nine churches at Portmahomack

Church 1	Eighth century	Lower half of east wall of crypt, which may have formed a wall for an early stone church.
Church 2	Twelfth century	Rectangular building with south door
Church 3	Twelfth century	East end chancel added
Church 4	Thirteenth century	New version of Church 3 with extensions west and east; east end crypt fashioned from the ruin of Church 1
Church 5	Seventeenth century	With flagstone floor; doorway; north aisle; burial vault; MacKenzie Tomb; new vault and lights in east crypt; relieving arch at west end
Church 6	1756	North wall of nave rebuilt; blocked doorway in south wall; west gallery; north gallery; doors in south wall, windows; door to gallery
Church 7	Late eighteenth century	New north aisle with upper storey; east wall rebuilt; flue for stove, fireplace; blocked doorway reused as window in west wall; new first floor; remodelled trapdoor to vault; window, vestry; door; pulpit door; raised wall plate; memorial to William Forbes and children (1841); blocking under arch
Church 8	Early nineteenth century	Roof raised by 1.07m; external masonry staircases to north aisle; east and west galleries
Church 9	After 1843	Church renovated after 1843; wooden floor; graffiti on west wall of north aisle, first storey; new vestry window; Macleod enclosure; memorials to Donald Macleod and sons (1874)

took us from Columba's early monastery to the modern world in nine phases (see Table 3.1 and Chapter 8).[2]

THE ENCLOSURE AND THE SOUTHERN WORKSHOPS: SECTOR 1

The monastic enclosure ditch, identified from the cropmark, ran through the flat field south of the church owned by the Gordon family, who generously gave us access to it. A search of the surface was rewarded by a few pieces of medieval pottery, but it

Fig. 3.9 Overview of Sector 1.

was not until Duncan Johnson showed us where to dig that confidence rose in the presence of early settlement. At the point indicated, the trial trench (Int. 7) contacted the rounded east end of what would become our S1, a unique and uniquely complete eighth-century building of some grandeur. There was no trace of it in the ploughsoil now (the loose stones being lifted when the plough had disturbed them), but we felt it wise to investigate whether the topsoil held any evidence for finds or strata. Accordingly a small section of the ploughsoil was taken down by hand and sieved, and very tedious it was. The result, a handful of medieval pottery and no layers, removed any remaining inhibitions about taking the ploughsoil off by machine. We used a toothless back-actor, excavating to 30cm and then back-blading to within 2–3cm of subsoil. With a few exceptions the subsoil was stone free, and the blade of the mechanical excavator was able to produce a fine smooth surface. This was then shovel-scraped to remove any remaining ploughsoil, and then trowelled, once, twice and up to five times, until the surviving archaeology showed clearly against the subsoil, the art of 'horizon mapping' (Fig. 3.9).[3]

Their visibility usually assisted by spraying, before and after trowelling, the anomalies on and in the surface of the subsoil would appear in contrasting shades of buff: the broad buff-grey band of a ditch, the buff-brown circles of post-holes and pits, and the more equivocal ragged edges of hollows. Some of these would later turn out to be natural: the scoop occupied by the roots of a former tree or rabbit holes, while many of the straighter lines belonged to drainage channels laid in recent times. As with previous practice at Sutton Hoo, the assumption was made that everything not excavated by us would be preserved for the future; so excavation need not be total, but targeted. The results from Sector 1 therefore reflect decisions made in response to the deep reconnaissance proved by the mapping process; and the map was, in general, available before these decisions had to be made.

The first underground system encountered was that of the land drains, which came in two main types. The more familiar were the drains containing pottery pipes, and the older were the more ingenious rubble drains, where beach cobbles were laid in a narrow trench. Taking a walk on 16 August 1996, I met George Munro, an octogenarian then building himself a house on the top of the ridge overlooking the Firths. He had farmed the land we were working on, even before Duncan Johnson. His school had had an allotment at the west side of Sector 1, beside the road, and as a schoolboy he had won prizes for growing vegetables on it. I asked him about the rubble drains, and he said that such drains could be found in a herringbone pattern under the whole field, which sloped down from where we were to the church. I wondered why such a slope should need draining. Ah, but it didn't. The drains were there to collect water, not to remove it. What we were finding was the Portmahomack water supply, which had operated before the mains were installed after the war. Water was collected by feeder drains all over the hillside and fed into a main collector, which in turn fed the wells. There were two wells, one near the church and the village well, which was the other side of the road, near the War Memorial. Thus enlightened, I fell to wondering by what strange mixture of practicality and myth the water supply had been finally reinvented as a heritage item known as The Baptistery (see p. 183).

These beneficent drains had cut through two systems of early ploughing. The first was easily recognisable from its broad shallow waves roughly 1 rod, pole or perch (5¼yd or *c*. 4.8m) crest to crest, oriented approximately south-east–north-west, and typical of the 'rig and furrow' of the Middle Ages. The truncated furrows obligingly contained pottery and coins of the twelfth–fourteenth centuries. They ran over the backfilled enclosure ditches, showing that the monastic enclosure had been finally ploughed away by medieval farmers. The other system of ploughmarks was earlier still, indeed earlier than everything, being cut by both the inner and the outer enclosure ditches of the monastery. It consisted of numerous thin, broadly parallel wandering lines showing against the subsoil, with a north–south orientation (Plate 3b). These traces of cultivation should have been made by an ard, and, if early medieval, should have been betrayed (as at Whithorn) by 'plough pebbles' – the small pebbles with one flattened edge that gave a longer life to a wooden ard. And, sure enough, plough pebbles were soon recognised (see Chapter 4).

It became clear that there had been two enclosure ditches: the inner one lay to the north, and had been soon filled in (see below). The outer one, enclosing the larger precinct, was that seen on the aerial photograph (Figs 1.6, 3.10). An attempt had been made to improve water retention by erecting little wattle fences on either side, and it was this wattle that produced a date between 660 and 860 (see Digest, A3). Inspired by George Munro, I soon decided that this ditch too was there to collect and canalise water that flowed off the hill. A number of features followed the inner flank of the ditch: a thick mat of redeposited boulder clay, and a number of intermittent fence lines, while the outer edge of the ditch showed that tracks of animals and/or

Fig. 3.10 Enclosure ditch under excavation by John English.

people had become established along the edge (F101). At a point towards the west end, the outer edge of the ditch broke down into a drinking place marked with the innumerable hooves of cattle. There was no hint of defence here, only of farmers managing water to serve their estate. Even if the inner band of dumped clay was sometimes referred to as a 'rampart', it was likely to have been nothing more than a band of up-cast. At a third section, the ditch was 5.50m wide and more than 1.5m deep, and was here backfilled with branches and tree stumps that had been cut down and thrown in (F132/1404). These trees had probably been growing along the ditch; this, then, was how the life of the ditch ended, with a robust operation, in which the overgrown banks were cleared, the bank was pushed back in and levelled off and the ploughing of rig and furrow began.

The investigation also included an area outside the enclosure ditch, notably at the east end, where there was a sequence of three intriguing if elusive buildings (Fig. 3.11). The earliest was a gully that formed a perfect circle 13.5m in diameter, and had been cut by all subsequent features (F31). Its fill was a pale grey podsol, like the fill of the ard marks. Cutting it on the east side was a strange structure (S5), which took the form of a ditch, shaped like a horseshoe in plan, with six post-pits and a dark anomaly in the middle. It had been seen on the aerial photograph and could be traced on the ground as a parchmark, 19 × 13m in extent, in the hot summer of 1995. It had then been hailed as everything from a chambered tomb to a Viking ship-burial, but in the event became a more humble building, concerned with crop-processing. It proved to contain six post-pits in two rows with, in the centre between the posts, a rectangular pit 3 × 1.5m with pitched stones at the edges and filled with much charcoal. Rather vaguely associated in plan were five other post-pits, one still containing an oak post (F172). In a mind hungry to find early settlement evidence, these tantalising fragments could have represented farming activities beginning in the Iron Age. But radiocarbon dating later showed that S5 was contemporary with the monastery in the seventh–ninth centuries and remained concerned with crop-processing until the tenth or early eleventh century (see Digest, A3).

The main focus of excavation in Sector 1 was to become the area occupied by a most splendid early historic building, our so called bag-shaped building or more prosaically, S1 (Fig. 3.1; see Chapter 6 for interpretation and Digest, A7, for its components). Its study was to continue with annual exposures for nearly ten years. In 1994 we knew it as a semi-circular trench with a stone feature forming a 'spoke' and imagined it to be the beginnings of an Iron Age wheelhouse. In 1995 it was shaped like a horseshoe, but by 1996 had acquired its west end. It was now shaped in plan like a bag – or, perhaps more appropriately, a sporran. When it was finally dismantled in 2002, the main components of the building were confirmed as a perimeter wall, round at the east end and square at the west, containing a symmetrical array of post-pits. Excavation of the post-pits revealed that some posts were square in section, many were supported on stone pads and a number had been replaced. In the centre of the round east end was a hearth, which contained animal bones, nuts and slag and gave a radiocarbon date range of 760–900. At the extreme east end was a stone-lined channel that had been added late to the building (F67/F79; Fig. 7.5). Signs of burning on the sandstone pieces used to line it suggested a heating duct of some kind, presumably introducing hot air into the building from the south. There was a cluster of post-holes outside the building at that point.

The design of this remarkable building, its method of construction and its functions before and after a major refurbishment were to provide key insights into the history of the monastery and the minds of its occupants. The analysis of its features by Madeleine Hummler distinguished two separate phases, with, it is suggested, two separate functions. The first consisted of twelve upright posts on padstones, together with the porch and perimeter wall and the hearth in the centre. This building, associated with animal bones and a scatter of metal- and glass-working debris, was assigned to the eighth century and has become the Smiths' Hall of Chapter 6. The second was a less tidy but still symmetrical redevelopment, in which all the posts were replaced by double posts, an external buttress supporting an internal upright. The hearth was superseded by a stone-lined flue, bringing in hot air from the south. These arrangements imply that upper floors were built at the east and west end, and that something on them needed heating or drying. As the National Museums' David Clarke pointed out, the form of the building is analogous to early modern structures in western Scotland used for drying grain. So it was that the second phase of the building, placed by radiocarbon in the ninth or tenth century, emerged as the Kiln Barn of Chapter 7.

At ploughsoil level, the S1 neighbourhood was unusually rich in animal bones (especially cattle), and the seasons brought increasing hints of artisan activity – fragments of moulds and crucibles and slag of bronze and glass. But the centres of activity were elusive, consisting of structures without finds and finds without structures. A foundation trench (S2) formed a rectangle 13.80 × 7m, which had cut through S1, and another (S6), 14 × 5m, was outside its west end. These are likely to have been later sheep pens. Another structure (S3) poked out of the north section, and was more promising as it shared the shape of the Hall. To the north-east of S1 was a highly visible curving band of black earth, which on first exposure was hailed as a souterrain – the underground store typical of the Picts. It proved on excavation to be a well (S8), which had begun as a small pit with a timber lining and ended as an untidy waterhole disfigured by flooding and the scramble for access.

Important evidence for the activity practised in the region of S1 was captured in the layers dished into the top of the backfilled inner enclosure ditch (F179). The layers were investigated in two contiguous stretches and searched carefully for signs of structure. The finds included fragments of moulds, crucibles, trays, slag, a whetstone and iron objects – and, of course, quantities of animal bones, which seemed to gather wherever humans had been busy. At first there was some uncertainty about whether this material had been worked *in situ*, or was just waste tipped in from somewhere else. However, the character of the finds scatter did not resemble dumping, and a number of linear features and pits, and at least one hearth, could be construed as indicating a workshop. As S3 occupied a similar position over the backfilled inner enclosure ditch, it was suggested that here was a working area at least 24m long dedicated to making metal and glass objects.

There was some evidence that this artisan quarter had spread further to the south. A leat taking water from the outer enclosure ditch had overgrown with turf before capturing mould and crucible fragments, slag, hammerscale, a whetstone and animal bone. All this material had presumably been dumped from workshops nearby. A cluster of scoops and root pits suggested that the old artisan area enjoyed a period of bucolic decay before being given back in the twelfth century to the serious business of agriculture.

The story of Sector 1, therefore, can be resolved into four periods (Fig. 3.11). A round house at the south-east corner may represent Iron Age people displaced by the enclosure (or remaining supplicant outside it). These were the people, perhaps, who were responsible for the ard marks belonging to the earliest cultivation we have, which we place in the sixth century or before (Period 0). These ploughmarks were cut by an inner enclosure ditch that should belong to the earliest phases of the monastery (sixth–seventh centuries: Period 1). By the early eighth century (Period 2) this inner ditch had been filled in, and a new, bigger enclosure ditch was dug further south. Two, maybe three or more, large bow-ended buildings were constructed next to or over the site of the inner ditch. The best preserved, S1, was constructed with a timber frame carried on post-pits with a stone foundation and perimeter cladding wall. The neighbourhood of S1 formed an artisan quarter, with materials relating to glass- and metal-working being preserved in the dished surface of the inner enclosure ditch and in other dips and hollows.

In Period 3, the ninth–eleventh centuries, S1 was radically reconstructed, and became a Kiln Barn, with a well sunk beside it. Crop-processing was also active at

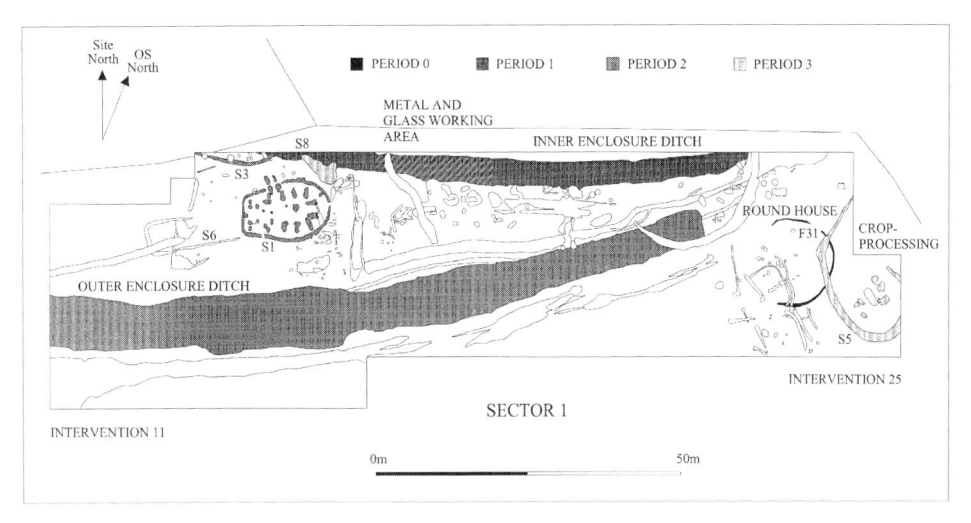

Fig. 3.11 The sequence in Sector 1.

the east end, outside the enclosure (S5). It is hard to see when the barn was disused, but its posts were removed, so it was decommissioned rather than abandoned. Trouble with water led to the ditch being 'bled', with ditches taking overflow into the valley. While they could still see the enclosure ditch, farmers had gone over to sheep, leaving traces of a number of pens. The outer enclosure ditch was eventually abandoned and filled in with the trees that grew beside it, and ploughed over with rig and furrow. This was the true beginning of Period 4, which we might put at the beginning of the twelfth century.

THE NORTHERN WORKSHOPS AND POOL: SECTOR 2

The excavation area in the Glebe Field was a long broad strip 100m long and 30m wide (with variations), laid across a valley (Fig. 3.12). It ran north–south, down into the valley bottom and up again, so that the deposit was nearly 2m deep in the middle, but at either end thinned out to 30cm. It had been cultivated for several recent centuries as part of the Glebe Field that supported the minister of Tarbat church. Inevitably, the plough had dragged soil from the north and south ends and filled up the middle. As we were to discover, the middle area had actually started life as a marsh with a stream running through it, which had been dammed by the monks to form a pool.

Excavation began on 13 July 1997, with the stripping-off of 30cm of the modern ploughsoil. At the north end, nearest the modern road, we immediately touched a stone building. Justin maintained from the first (correctly) that this building, an approximate rectangle with a slab-lined tank at its centre and pebble surfaces around it, belonged to the earliest, not the latest, part of the sequence. Several years later, when the central part of the site had caught up, it was identified as a tank for washing and processing leather to go with the vellum workshops (S4). So for many

Fig. 3.12 Overview of Sector 2, seen from the south.

seasons it was repeatedly exhumed and revived and cherished and wrapped, like the precious prow of a sunken ship, the rest of which still lay under several feet of black mud.

Definition under the deepening ploughsoil was achieved with clearance by shovel, followed by cleaning by trowel, until out of the dark fog it was possible to discern a horizon from which the bulk of the archaeological sequence could be said to begin (or rather end). The latest feature was a stone dyke (a dry stone wall), which ran north–south across the black morass of the valley to make a field boundary, and the whole of the valley bottom was laced with drains – some open ditches, some containing cobbles and some pottery pipes, others now clogged with mud – all signs of the struggle of later farmers to evacuate water from this part of the field. They were not to know that the offending area concealed a now buried, but still functioning, early medieval dam, expressly designed to keep the water there. We next encountered spreads of seashells, which might have been mixed into the humus to lime it, but appeared to be much less random than that – more like heaps of shells that had subsequently been flattened by later ploughing. The hypothesis that has survived best is that these heaps were the result of fishermen preparing bait, and the latest pottery, East Coast Red ware and Scarborough ware, suggested that this activity belonged to the fourteenth–sixteenth centuries. Under the shell midden in the centre was a ribbon of rubble laid across the valley (context 1326), with a square area at the centre, which we thought might be a well head (it was the dam). At its north end, the ribbon of rubble became a pebble road (F18), petering out as it climbed up the hill.

Fig. 3.13 Nicky Toop sampling the main east section in Int. 14.

Stratigraphic excavation is sometimes claimed as simple by those who have encountered only simple deposits with visible strata. At Portmahomack any complacencies of this nature had to be rapidly confronted. The strata had survived in many different forms – in some areas rich, highly coloured and unmistakable, in others sparse but suggestive, like disturbed pebbles and rubble, in others barely visible – but of course just as crucial for the sequence. We learnt to read activities and sequences from the bottom up, using the free sections of larger pits. The subsoil was sand or gravel or hard glacial till (in the valley bottom). On the north side there were many different layers of apparent subsoil, which turned out to be major levelling operations. Within these layers of 'natural' subsoil, strong grey turf lines had formed. Deposited on these bright sand or dark turf surfaces were numerous hard cobbles or softer sandstone slabs. These had been brought in from elsewhere (that is, from the beach) and so were always candidates for buildings. Only very rarely was the sandstone faced, so that every structure had to coaxed out of a river of amorphous blocks scattered by collapse or later ploughing. Working-areas were eventually discerned by finds on sandy floors, but they had covered themselves and their surroundings with sprawling stiff multi-hued heaps that we termed the 'clay-silts'. These were composed of millions of tiny patches of clay or laminae of sand a few millimetres thick, and to begin with we worked through them, attempting to define contexts, without the benefit of knowing what was underneath. It was plainly a task requiring several centuries to complete, and we were learning little from it. It was like trying to record the Bible a letter at a time, taking no account of the words, let alone the sentences. The clay-silts were eventually managed by digging in quadrants (modules 4 × 8m) and recording running sections between them. They proved to represent not only workshop waste, but waste reused as packing for construction.

There is a tendency on this sort of site to see buildings everywhere, because you cannot actually see them anywhere. Here we were lucky: the experience of S1 in Sector 1 showed that our Picts knew how to build, and we did not need to patronise them by inventing dozens of sub-square shacks supported by stakes or balanced on stones. We therefore, and to an unusual degree, applied continual analytical interpretation at every stage, like a picture restorer, standing back every few minutes to see what image was struggling for definition among the wealth of possible scenes embedded in the palimpsest.

Between 1996 and 1999 Justin and Steve Timms defined numerous post-holes, culverts and hearths over the northern part of the site. Some of these features seemed to have been cut into the pebble road and at least one hearth had medieval pottery (F35). Some hearths were round, or two circles together, and their slag contained hammerscale and implied iron forging. All this seemed to belong to a late medieval shanty town of iron workers. To have a medieval settlement of any kind in this part of Scotland was no small asset, but there were accumulating hints of the survival of phases earlier than that. From the ploughsoil we had retrieved a bronze fragment of the eighth century, resembling a book plaque, another fastener of some kind, perhaps also for a book, and a comb (broadly dateable between the sixth century and the twelfth). But these were well out of any early contexts. Now, however, a concentration of metal-working evidence began to accumulate, and there were features with it. Beside the pebble road in the south-east part of the site, moulds, crucibles and a stone-kerbed hearth appeared (F148). Here were metal-workers casting bronze and possibly silver objects. The find of an oval carnelian gem, its back face chipped by extraction from its setting, suggested the recycling of gold, perhaps from a ring or necklace of Roman or Byzantine origin.

Understanding of the deposit's broader structure was assisted by the chance to view it sideways. On the east side of our excavation area was to be the storage tank for the oil to supply the church heating, which needed to be housed in a deep pit. This was dug archaeologically in 1997, and it gave us an invaluable preview to the complex strata of the workshop excavation: it was multi-layered and up to 1.5m deep (Int. 26; see Fig. 2.7). The earliest features were large robust stone-lined channels or pits, unidentifiable at that stage, but clearly associated with the management of water or heat. Above these stone features was a strongly coloured layer of scorched sand, a horizon created by a fire that was to play a major role in our story. Early layers could also be seen in the sides of every major pit and gully. For example, near the north end, a large late rubbish pit containing thirteenth–fourteenth-century pottery showed in its sides that it had cut through nearly 50cm of earlier strata (F13). In general, the pre-medieval layers thickened as you went down the hill, being fathomless at the bottom of the valley.

Appearing from beneath the ploughsoil in the lower part of the valley was a curving drystone terrace wall (F149), which was later to be joined by other megalithic constructions (see Fig. 3.14). The curving wall connected to a packed mass of uncut stone – that ribbon of rubble crossing the valley – which in turn slowly resolved itself into a dam (F440; S7), made of giant blocks of stone interrupted by narrow leats (F431, F432). The black morass to the east was now explained: it was a filled-in pond, originally contained by a dam to the west and a curving revetment wall to the north. Digging out the pond itself was a daunting prospect, in spite of the romantic possibilities it held for organic preservation – monkish garments, suitably rent, a redundant manuscript perhaps, tossed into the dark pool by a Viking. It was tested with two large trenches, one running the length of the east side, the other embracing the south face of the revetment wall. The peat sequence was dated by radiocarbon: a marsh had formed in the valley bottom during the Iron Age, and the streams that ran through the marsh were dammed between 590 and 720 (see Digest, A3). There was plenty of pollen and a number of wooden posts but very few artefacts. The most significant cluster consisted of fragments of moulds and crucibles, up against the revetment wall at the bottom of the pond. The metal-workers had been throwing their debris into open water.

All this was promising enough, but in June 1997 a wholly unexpected element joined the Glebe Field sequence. Trowelling, and then, with increasing incredulity, brushing the surface of a stone pushing up through the ploughsoil, excavator Katie Anderson saw that she was cleaning a sculpture in low relief depicting a family of cattle (Plate 6b). The two adult cows, male and female, tended a calf, the bull licking its offspring with a curling tongue. In the slanting sunlight of a particularly fine evening, the appearance of this scene after a hard day moving earth seemed little short of miraculous. This slab, to become widely known as the 'Calf Stone', lay horizontally, and later excavation revealed it had been employed as the lid of a culvert in which other fragments of the same stone frieze had been recycled as lining (TR28/35). The builder of the drain had simply commandeered a decorated slab of the eighth century and broken it roughly to size in order to line his drain (F166). But this was only the beginning. In 1998 fragments of sculpture began to make their appearance by the road, in its ditch and beside the mill pond. Finding new pieces of Pictish carving became an almost daily delight for the excavators through 1999, and continued intermittently in later seasons until we had increased our total tally to 225.

Nearly all these fragments were sharply carved: double-strand interlace, a common theme, exquisitely rounded, animal snouts, beaks and hooves, hardly worn by exposure. And the breaks were sharper still. In contrast to the sculpture found in Church 2 (see Table 3.1), or to the Calf Stone, these fragments were deposited from a monument broken up soon after its carving (see Chapter 5). Several pieces were burnt, and all lay in, on or above a highly distinctive carpet of burning; at first just blackened earth, but then reddening and brightening to sands of glowing orange and blinding white, with writhing borders of black. This was the horizon that Justin had found in

Int. 26, and that was soon to appear in its distinctive raiment all over the site. It was to be designated the 'primary burning'. It took much longer to discover what had been burnt: in 2004 we were to see burnt heather, wattle work and turf – the materials of the monastic buildings – *in situ*.

Underneath the primary burning, and almost as ubiquitous, were layers of yellow and grey ashy clays, referred to as the 'clay-silts'. They appeared to consist of thousands of minute laminated scatters, small dumps of ash, spread and trodden in, every day, for years. They lay either side of the pebble road, which soon had its pebbles removed to reveal the sand and slag on which it had been based (F18; 2568, 2556). But underneath it, instead of shifting more sand, the trowel began to scrape on a series of sandstone slabs. Some were so decayed that they were now little more than sandy patches themselves, but the sub-square locus of the patch showed where they had once been. This was the earlier version of the road, Road 1, a fine metalled surface, showing itself bordered by a stone kerb of upright stones, nearly continuous, poking here and there through the pebbles of Road 2 (Plate 4a). This remarkable construction, which had a ditch on either side, resembled something Roman. But it was certainly not built by Romans. It was a Roman lookalike, a reference to Rome, and can only have been built, *iuxta morem Romanorum*, in the manner of the Romans, 2,000km north of Rome in the seventh or eighth century.[4]

What had happened beside this road? As the area on the west side of the road was relieved of its clay-silts, we came upon an area of soft white sand, creating a 'yard' in which a number of finds, at first ad hoc and inconsequential, was gradually resolved into one of our most important assemblages. An iron tool took the form of a crescent blade, typical of the tools used to cut and scrape leather. There was plenty of animal bone, but it was all of a similar kind: cattle metapodials – in other words, just their feet. Some of these were set in rows, making lines or V-shaped or rectangular patterns on the ground (Plate 5b). Some had been sharpened like tent pegs. Every visitor and every friend was quizzed about these strange arrangements. The common response – 'edges to hearths or flower beds' – signally failed to satisfy. By the end of the 2003 season it was possible to claim that the area to the west of the road was a workshop for leather and wood-workers. But much more was to come, thanks to the meticulous collection of every type of material that could possibly be anomalous, including every pebble, whether it bore signs of working or not. The result was a collection of small white pebbles, a curved knife, many sharpened cattle metapodials and heaps of seaweed ash. Cecily Spall's researches, particularly among the practices of modern parchment-makers, were to demonstrate that this curious assemblage had its origin in the manufacture of vellum. The Portmahomack community was producing manuscripts.

Between the yard, with its hearth and rows of metapodials, and the washing tank (S4), was an area of pits of various shapes and sizes limited by a ribbon of stones on the south side. In 2005 Cecily was able to weave these shreds and patches into a credible building (S9), with roof posts and stone foundations for a turf wall; in brief, something very like S1 (without which we should probably not have recognised it). In its centre was a particularly fine hearth, of several phases, with stake and post sockets around it for a cowl or some related construction. The vellum- or parchment-makers, like the metal-workers of Sector 1, now had a sheltered place to work.

By 2006 a number of crucial episodes had been defined for Sector 2 (see Fig. 3.14):

- the building of a paved kerbed road (Road 1);
- a workshop making vellum to the east of Parchment-Makers' Hall;
- a dam, and a terrace wall, containing a pool;
- a major fire, consuming timber and turf buildings;
- the breaking-up and dumping of carved stone monuments;
- the laying of a pebble road (Road 2);
- bronze-workers at the south end, near the open water of the pool;
- iron-workers at the north end, with timber structures and culverts, among them the culvert lined with the Calf Stone;
- fishermen, with shell middens;
- ploughland, divided by a stone dyke boundary.

This was a rich and highly significant sequence, but it took ten seasons to get into order, not only weeks of meticulous trowelling but hours pouring over the contrasting and sometimes contradictory records of context cards, plans, photographs and sections. Given the ephemeral traces of structures and the discontinuous layers, it may be doubted that we could have understood this sequence if it had not been for the robust structures of Road 1 and Road 2 and the key horizons of primary burning and sculpture dumping. The *only* pottery recovered was medieval in date (twelfth–fifteenth centuries), and all of it was later than the second road. Without the general horizons of road and fire, the deposit could have been destined to be lumped together in a single pre-ceramic phase. Our mistakes were by no means made only with the trowel or the recording of contexts; these errors were human enough given the difficulties of definition. We also made fundamental errors of analysis, of which the most spectacular lay in the attempt to date the episode of burning and the dumping of broken sculpture associated with it. There was a wealth of material to draw on, and we drew on the obvious: big lumps of charred timber likely to offer the radiocarbon laboratory the kind of meaty samples they like: recognisable stuff and no danger of contamination. The date duly came back as mid-fifth century, a date for the destruction of a monastery that would take some explaining (especially if the Vikings were to be held responsible).

We had, of course, dated, not the fire, but the cutting-down of the timber of the buildings that had burnt down. Probably not even that. The timbers were oak and would have had heartwood that died up to a 100 years before the tree was felled. And the heartwood would have survived a fire best in large chunks. The material we really needed was from organisms that died in or just before the fire: the insects living in the thatch – or, failing that, the thatch itself. Through the good offices of Historic Scotland, and Patrick Ashmore in particular, a validated radiocarbon dating programme was later to succeed in bracketing this event to between 780 and 830 (see Digest, A3).

This deepest and most complex part of the site, nearest to the church and nearest to the sea, continued to bring to light surprises, until, in 2006, we felt we had finally exhausted them. In 2005 the washing tank and its immediate surroundings were studied further to ensure we had learnt all we could and to make sure there were no earlier phases lurking beneath. But at the north-east end of Int. 14, the sand just would not clean up. There were some anomalies inside the old test pit, as Toby Simpson had commented in 1996. Doing the retesting in 2005, I muttered in my notes: 'There are perhaps features earlier than S4, possibly a grave. The distinction is, however, pretty fine.' After that I went off on a week's holiday to Provence with some of my family. A few days later, in a hot car on the way to a hot beach, the mobile rang. It was Cecily calling to announce the discovery of a grave north of S4. Not just a grave but a magnificent cist burial lined with large slabs. It was, she thought, one of three in parallel. The old adage (a sand site hides its bottom) had proved itself again. So the workshops had been added to part of the early cemetery seen under the west end of the church, a cemetery that now looked set to have graves all the way along the ridge (see Chapter 4).

The last season in 2007 was focused on two main objectives: testing for the earliest activities on the site, and finding a mill. Prehistoric material had been extremely sparse, but it was essential to discover if there had been a settlement before the monks came. The original shape of the land proved to be a gently sloping valley with a marsh at the bottom, itself formed in the Iron Age (530–370 BC; Digest A3). But the land on the north side had been levelled up to make an approximately horizontal surface by cartloads of turf, sand and gravel, layer after sterile layer that had to be laboriously and carefully removed. Beneath them, the first activities on the earliest horizon proved to be monastic and all about water: a wicker-lined well, a charcoal-filled pit, gullies and a stone-lined cistern (F527, F572, F534, F530). But we could say that there was nothing underneath. We had finally reached the bottom.

Finding the mill proved less successful – perhaps because it wasn't there. The dam and pool in the central part of the valley were clear enough, and there was a fine stone-lined culvert running through the dam, of the kind that might have held a penstock – the square timber pipe that focuses a jet of water onto a horizontal wheel. So far so good. Removing rubble west of the dam showed a complex of huge boulders functioning as capstones and flat stones set on edge, which suggested the beginnings of a wheelhouse. 'Most complete Medieval stone mill found', I allowed the local newspapers to say. And during the wet summer of 2007 we toiled among the megalithic conglomerate, trying to make this come true. The water level rose each night and had to be pumped out each day, and a large tonnage of stone rubble, clay, sand, wooden branches and twigs was painfully extracted. The excavation continued deep into natural deposits, well below the level of the stones and the mouth of the chute. But there was no trace of a wooden wheel, or its paddles, or a millstone or the timber beam needed to support one. The earliest configuration was that of a culvert and a stone cistern accessed from the paved road, Road 1 (Plate 4b). Later, the area had been filled in with rubble to create a causeway for the pebbled road, Road 2. If there had been a mill on this spot originally, it would appear to have been completely demolished, perhaps to make way for a new version further down the slope. The picture was by no means 100 per cent conclusive. But excavators are always obliged

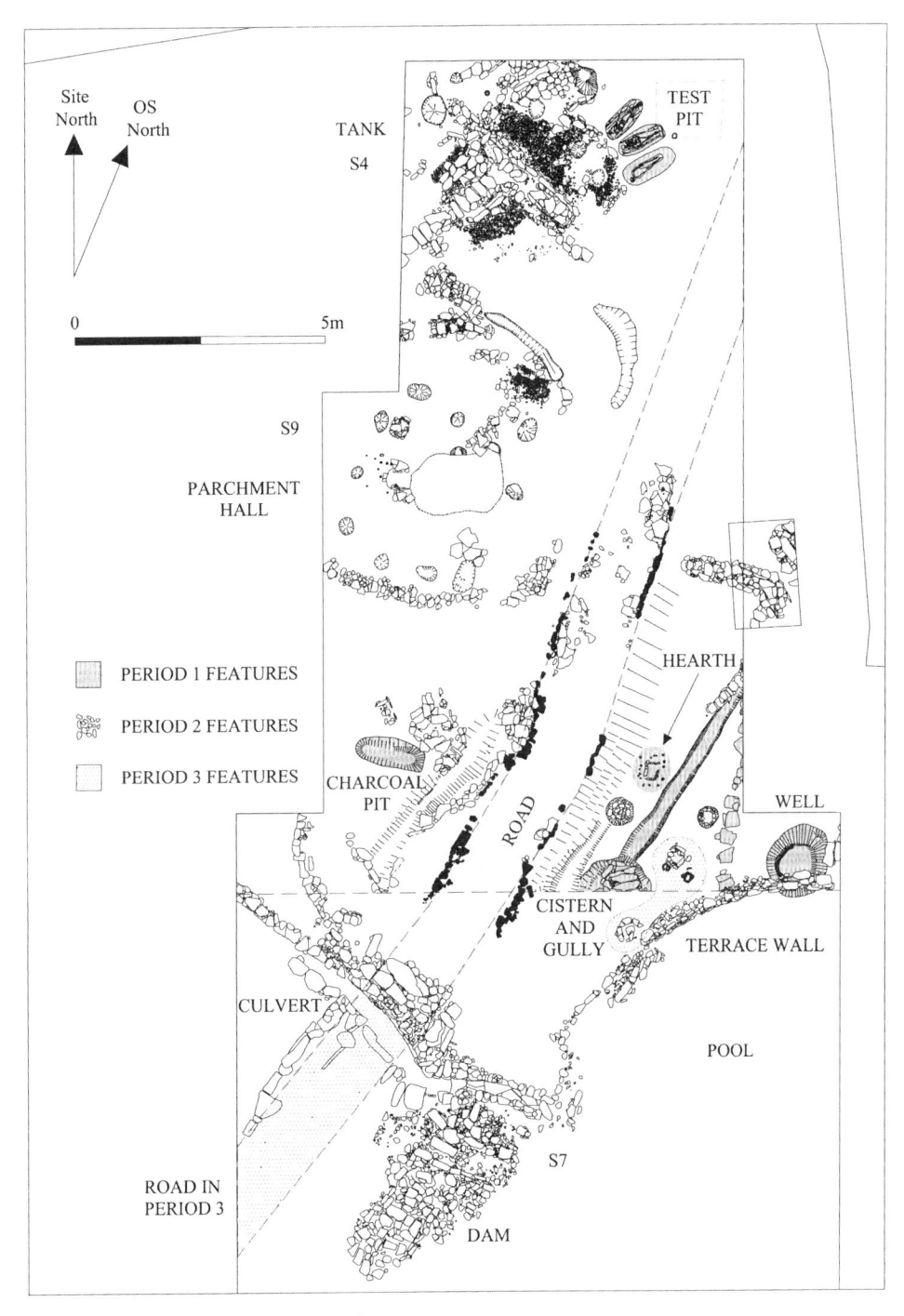

Fig. 3.14 The sequence in Sector 2.

to leave some matters in the realms of the might-have-been or the half-way-clear, at least until records have been thoroughly analysed.[5]

The sequence to be unveiled in the following chapters was thus forged and hammered by a decade of argument and testing, particularly on site. We were fortunate to have the attitude, the tradition and the time to dedicate to this kind of perpetual on-site seminar. On its own, the well-recorded sequence of individual contexts (which nevertheless commanded our dedication) is necessary, but not sufficient; essential, but often contradictory and equivocal. Yet again, it had proved important to apply two other principles and two other procedures: on-site feature recording with its built-in battery of questions, not just about present strata but about past activities; and the pressure to understand everything before we removed it, or at least to understand that we had investigated everything possible before it went in the wheelbarrow. These stresses of research excavation are the necessary price to pay for the privilege of disturbing precious historic sites. The purpose of excavation is not to record archaeological deposits, but to study them.

After further analysis, the Sector 2 story gradually unfolded. The sandy ridge above the sea had been a burial ground before it became a monastery. Once older finds had been taken into account, it seemed the burial ground extended southwards to Balnabruach, where the graves were of Bronze Age and Iron Age date. To this the monastery added burials of its own. In the sixth–seventh centuries (Period 1), the area consisted of a slope of rough ground or grazing, descending gently into a marsh fed by running water from the east. The marsh must have provided little drinking water, because culverts leading down the hill ended in stone-lined water collectors.

At a given moment, which radiocarbon dating puts not before 650, this area was subject to a massive development (Period 2). The valley was dammed and a terrace wall built to protect the land to the north. A paved road was laid on a causeway of sand and gravel leading up to the terrace wall, where it provided access to running water. Areas either side of the road were levelled up, and dedicated to hide-processing: the preparation of leather (west), with probably the slaughter of the cattle (east). The preparation of leather came to include the manufacture of vellum to make books; the hides came in with the feet on and were washed in a stone-lined tank, and then thinned and stretched and smoothed for delivery to the scriptorium (probably nearer the church). A large bow-ended building sheltered the vellum-makers.

These golden years of the monastery came to an end in a great fire, which took place no earlier than 780 and no later than about 820. It was accompanied or followed immediately by the breaking-up of at least four monumental crosses. It was succeeded by a mucky, murky period from around the ninth to the eleventh centuries (Period 3). The mill continued, the road was remade and the old vellum workshops turned to metal-working – making objects of silver and bronze. Metal-working continued – now mainly of iron – into the twelfth century (Period 4). After this, the land beside the church, and probably owned by it, was used by fishermen (or women) to extract shellfish and was periodically ploughed over. The ownership must have changed by the seventeenth century, when it became Glebe land to support the local minister.

Fig. 3.15 Last-minute preparations before opening day at the Centre in 1999.

Completing Sector 2 was the last act, the tail end of the excavation campaign, the hardest part and in some ways the most valuable. The camp site that had served us for a decade was struck in 2005; all the caravans and portakabins were sold or given away, and a small team toiled for the remaining few seasons operating from cottages or the neighbouring farm of our good friends the Dane family. But there was an important task still to complete: how to present the findings, and the remains of the site itself to the public.

THE TARBAT DISCOVERY CENTRE

The display of the results of the excavation formed an integral part of an integrated programme from the beginning. Without a display, there could be no continuing use, and therefore we earned no restoration grant. Without a restoration there could be no dig – at least not one of the scale and quality I thought necessary to address the research objectives.

Evidently, however, all the parties to the display wanted different things from it. For the archaeologists, the exhibition was simply part of their publication programme, and its aim was to tell the world about the new discoveries. For Highland Council, the principal aim was education: the Display Centre was to tell schools about early Scotland. For the Tarbat Trust, the aim was principally to give the local community something they could call their own; indeed this intention underpinned the conditions of the lottery grant. In practical terms this meant including the story

Fig. 3.16   Prince Charles opening the Centre, 1999.

not only of St Colman's church, but of its village, 'The Port'. In addition, all parties recognised that, to a greater or lesser extent, the church was itself a historic building, and needed to be presented as such, even if it now had an exhibition inside it. Others felt, contrariwise, that the historic building was still a church, and needed to be respected as such, even if services no longer took place within it.

These different objectives were resolved by hundreds of compromises in dozens of meetings, the form of the display pulling us to the more entertaining and then the more serious, to the more local and then the more international. No fewer than fifteen versions of the display panels were designed in response to these frequent changes of consensus. Our eventual design was that the nave and north aisle were to be dedicated to the archaeological discoveries, the east end to local history and the west end (the old poor loft) to activities for children. The basic design of the interior, thanks to the Higgins Gardner partnership, was a brilliant adaptation (Fig. 3.15). The north-aisle ground floor became the Treasury, housing the sculpture and most of the valuable objects, separated from the nave by a magnificent pair of sliding wrought-iron gates, with the vine scroll taken from TR1 – also adapted as the archaeological project logo – prominent in the centre of each one. As well as panels leading the visitor into historic Pictland, the nave had an 'archaeology pit', a lookalike excavation with overlapping shelves of strata, to indicate how time passes underground. The east end (St Colman's Gallery) had panels about the history of Portmahomack and guest cases for local exhibits. The west-end upper floor had a bank of computers with a preliminary archaeological archive of special studies on the texts, finds, graveyard and sites in the area, and it gradually filled up with other things to draw and play with.

The church itself could still be sensed. The restored crypt, with its early wall and aumbry, was a place of quiet, in which visitors could still imagine the spirituality that had once permeated the whole building. The walls of the twelfth-century church were marked out by brass rods or crazy paving, and at one or two places could still be glimpsed, lit up, below floor level under glass. The eighteenth century was represented in effect by the whole standing building, splendidly reharled in shining white. The Indian summer that followed the Disruption of 1843 was remembered in the pine panelling of the east end. The restored church, museum and visitor centre was opened on 24 September 1999 by Prince Charles (as Duke of Rothesay) and has been receiving visitors from all over the world ever since (Fig. 3.16).

The church was safe for the future, but this did not solve the problem of the rest of the site: what would become of *that* when excavations finished? There was little doubt that the fields within the monastic enclosure contained resources at least as precious and much more extensive than the well-cared-for church and churchyard. Historic Scotland recognised as much and has taken it all beneath its muscular wing. But a more difficult decision lay in the presentation of what had been excavated. We investigated the display of excavated buildings *in situ*, creating an open-air museum with reconstructed Pictish buildings, indicating the plans of structures with stones on the surface, planting a garden that reflected the monastic layout, or making a modern sculpture park, to continue, in an oblique way, the theme of great art on the peninsula. All these have come to nothing, not so much through lack of funds, as because, deep down, not enough people, including the stakeholders and often the begetter of the idea himself, believed that the locality would be the better for it.

The land of the Firthlands is in many ways its own best asset, and, sown with the stories of the past and the imagination, perhaps flowers best on uncluttered soil. So the visitor, with only a panel for company, looks out across the fields once cut by great open areas called Sector 1 and Sector 2 and builds a silent picture of artisans at work, their great halls, the smoke from the fires, the water pouring out of the pond through the leat away down to the beach, the cattle awaiting slaughter, the stench of tawed hides: a busy tiny town at the dawn of a European nation.

SYNTHESIS

The overall story is to be told in the chapters that follow. It is based on a preliminary study by the author of the stratigraphy in all sectors, underpinned by radiocarbon dates (Digest, A3). Fig. 3.17 shows the principal structures in Sectors 1 and 2. Fig. 3.18 offers a summary of the overall narrative employed in the rest of this book, in the form of a timeline. We can discern four periods of time in the early middle ages. In Period 1 (*c*. 550–*c*. 650) a monastery was established on a modest scale. In Period 2 (*c*. 650–*c*. 780) it greatly expanded its industrial base. Between *c*. 780 and *c*. 830 there was a catastrophic raid. In Period 3 that followed (ninth–eleventh centuries), metal-workers continued in action but there was apparently no monastic community. Period 4 (twelfth century) saw the beginning of the parish church and a new and different role for Portmahomack.

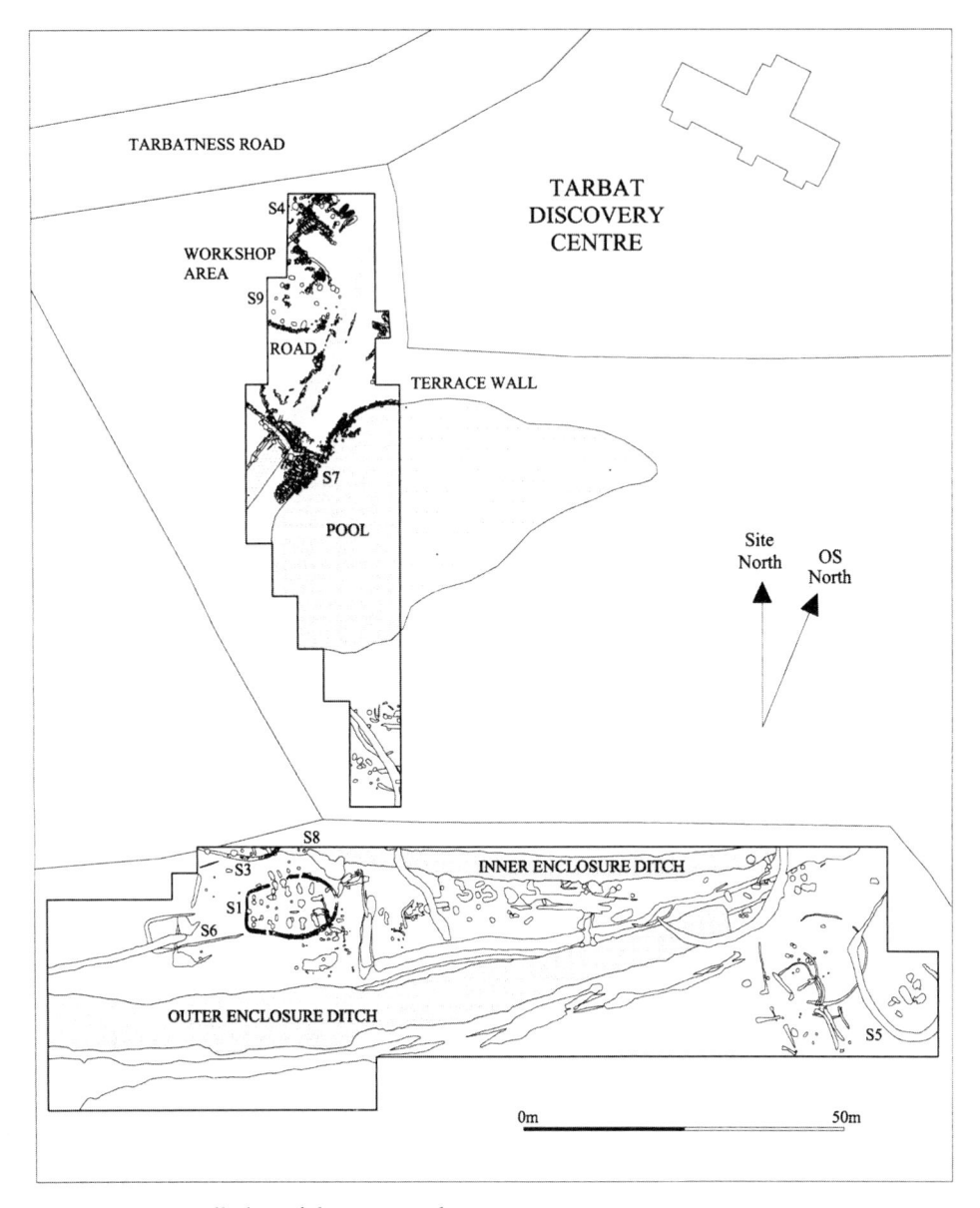

Fig. 3.17   Overall plan of the excavated area.

The early medieval monastery thus appears to have had its beginnings in the later sixth century, perhaps due to Columba himself, on the nearest thing he could find to an island at the far eastern end of the Great Glen that had led him from Iona. The monks first contrived a supply of water and began to work metal, but otherwise have left us mainly burials. We follow the sequence of burials, and discuss the possibility of a stone church in Chapter 4. Burials were marked by small stone slabs and large elaborately ornamented cross-slabs stood around the precinct of the church by 800

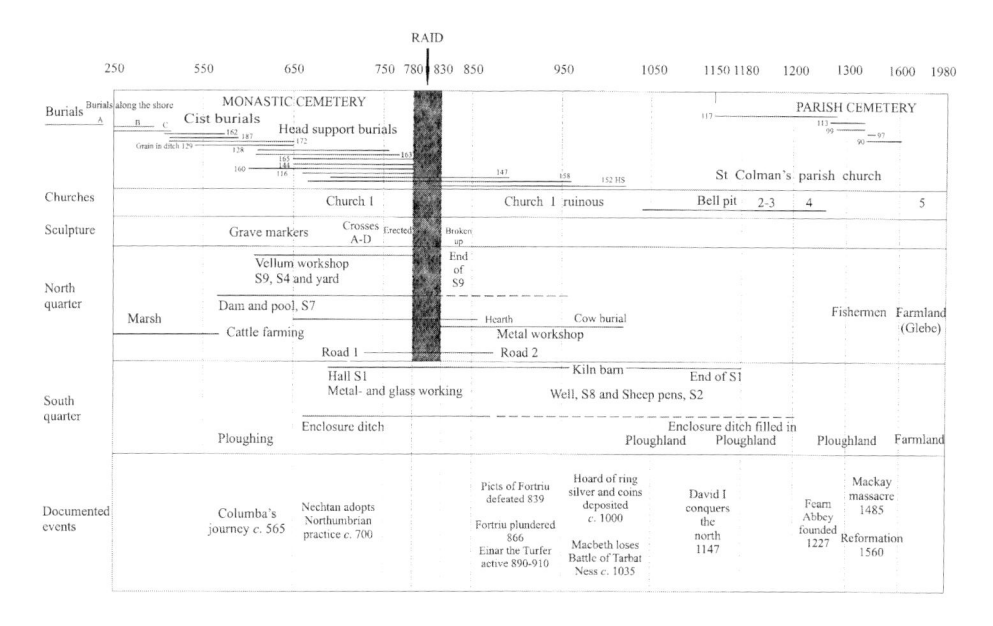

Fig. 3.18 Timeline: the radiocarbon dates are given in Digest, A3.

(see Chapter 5). During the eighth-century boom (Period 2) artisans made vellum in a northern quarter and church vessels in the south, operating from magnificent bow-ended buildings (see Chapter 6).

The northern quarter of the monastery at Portmahomack was destroyed by fire in the late eighth or early ninth century. But, although the attributes of Christian ceremony – church, sculpture, vellum and burial – were apparently stopped in their tracks, the industrial and agricultural parts of the old monastic motor continued to turn under new management in Period 3. The Smiths' Hall became a Kiln Barn, and the northern quarter was dedicated to metal-working. These events appear to belong to a vivid period in Scottish history, the ninth–eleventh centuries, when Norse and Gaels competed for supremacy in the old northern Pictish realm (see Chapter 7). Opaque as it was, making eye-to-eye contact with the era of Thorfinn and Macbeth was just as much of an adventure as travelling back to the time of St Columba. We were also exceptionally fortunate to be able to track the story of St Colman's church from its foundation in the twelfth century to the very end of the twentieth century, when it became the Tarbat Discovery Centre (see Chapter 8).

A context for these events has been sought on the peninsula and beyond. We searched for a portage connecting the Dornoch and the Cromarty Firths, and studied the role of Portmahomack's sister sites at Nigg, Shandwick and Hilton of Cadboll (see Chapter 9). In its heyday, the eighth century, the Tarbat monastery must have been a place famous in Britain, Ireland and beyond. Its experience can be said to reflect a great deal of the thinking of early Europe (see Chapter 10).

It is right to end this chapter with a caveat. The archaeological discoveries presented in this book have been trailed in many publications, and this book is itself only a forerunner of the full report, which will be prepared over the next ten years. The reader will oblige the author by treating the chapters that follow as watercolour sketches made in the countryside, while the weather held and the images were fresh. It is not intended as the last word on this remarkable site, but the start of a debate, one that will hopefully deserve the attention of all who wonder how nations form and fail.

Notes

1. Notably Katie Anderson, Dave Fell, Hamish Fulford, Lars Gustavsen, Candy Hatherley, Becca Pullen, Juliet Reeves, Gigi Signorelli, Toby Simpson, Steve Timms and Nicola Toop.
2. This phasing, due to Annette Roe, was first published in *Bulletin*, 3 (1997), 3–13. For the story, see Chapter 8; for the walls and features that go to make up each of the nine churches, see Digest, A4.
3. See Carver (2005a: ch. 3) for a discussion of the use of Horizon mapping and Recovery Levels in excavation. Recovery Levels refer to the precision of excavation and recording applied, e.g A. (with a machine), B (with a shovel), C (with a trowel). All features at Portmahomack were excavated at Recovery D, except graves (E) and features that were lifted for study in the laboratory (F).
4. Bede (*HE* V. 21) describes how Nechtan, king of the Picts, had asked Abbot Ceofrid of Jarrow to send him architects to help him build churches in the Roman manner.
5. It is not excluded that the features encountered at Portmahomack represent the remains of a demolished seventh-century horizontal water-mill, similar to the beautiful example excavated at Nendrum, Strangford Lough in Ireland (McErlewan and Crothers 2007).

Part 2

Age of Fame

CHAPTER 4

The monks arrive

The Tarbat peninsula, now fertile and intensively farmed, was once a savage and varied terrain. Low-lying areas north of the Bay of Nigg were then flooded, making a narrower isthmus connecting a long eastern ridge to the mainland. There is a hint of an Iron Age fort, but no prehistoric settlement has yet been brought to light on this peninsula by formal excavations.[1] So the large area opened at Portmahomack poses this question: who, if anyone, lived here in prehistoric times? Two leaf-shaped flint arrowheads and a barbed and tanged arrowhead came from several acres of excavation, suggesting no more than late Neolithic hunting expeditions.[2]

Suggestive of something more special was the carved stone ball found among the rubble of the seventeenth-century church (Fig. 4.1). Beautifully fashioned from hard stone, these stone balls are perfectly spherical and often decorated. More than 400 have been collected so far. They are found *only* in eastern Scotland, and there is nothing quite like them from any prehistoric period, anywhere else. Their distribution on the map (Fig. 2.2) is uncannily similar to that of Pictish sculpture (another unique and superlative art form), but most scholars think they are much older than the Picts; current opinion is that they were made at the end of the Neolithic and beginning of the Bronze Age (about 2000 BC). With their shapely grooves and protrusions, the balls are sensual, and some people suppose them to be erotic in intent. Others note the extraordinary variety of forms, and believe them to be emblems of particular families. Others see them as coshes, strapped to a stick, like the clubs of North American Indians or South Sea Islanders. Others have suggested they were used in a game, in which the balls were hurled along the dunes in a pre-echo of *boules* or golf, each contestant having his own distinctive ball. In general, scholars currently prefer to see them as amulets or talismans, sacred objects from the huge, complex, high-investment world of British early prehistoric religion.[3] The stone ball from Portmahomack is thus an oblique indication of Bronze Age ritual activity by the sea shore. That activity, as we shall see, included burial from the Bronze Age onwards.

But was there a settlement there? A saddle quern was seen in 1948 built into the north-west gate post of the churchyard gate abutting Tarbatness Road,[4] and this has raised the possibility of prehistoric cultivation nearby. Certainly in the flat ground south of the church we found numerous examples of ard marks, not criss-cross as perhaps would have been expected from prehistoric ploughing, but thin parallel lines (see Plate 3b);[5] and in the northern quarter was a scattering of plough pebbles, thought to have been thrown out of turfs cut for later building.[6] The imprint of a slight, but perfectly circular building was defined at the south-east corner of the excavations, cut

Fig. 4.1 Carved stone ball from St Colman's church, late Neolithic/early Bronze Age.

by later constructions of the ninth–eleventh centuries – perhaps this was the modest farmstead of Tarbat's prehistoric occupants (see Fig. 3.11). Such traces hardly come up to the popular gathering expected at the best landing beach in the Firthlands. Orkney archaeologists, for example, have defined a settlement from the second–fifth centuries

Fig. 4.2 Filtration pit, for purifying water with charcoal. Scale 1m.

AD at Mine Howe that featured round houses and pottery with comb decoration and moulds and crucibles making pins and spear butts within an enclosure containing a deep and massive stone-built well. That is more like it. But Fraser Hunter has pointed out an extensive gap in settlement evidence in eastern Scotland between the third and fifth centuries AD, so we are not alone. Hoards suggest that the Iron Age peoples, the Caledonians, and in the Firthlands the Verturiones, were pacified by massive bribes of bronze and silver in the period AD 160–250, but in the next two centuries they had to go out and fight for it.[7] By the time Columba made his journey up the Great Glen in AD 565, Bridei, king of the Picts, was occupying a hillfort near Inverness, and his peers were no doubt fortifying theirs. In such restless times, there may have been land going begging. There was no prehistoric pottery from the excavations, and the ard marks and the plough pebbles, and indeed the building on the south-east side, can all relate to the earliest monastic activity. The earliest buried soil, under the church, in Sector 2 and in Sector 1, where it was cut by ard marks, was a lean silvery grey sand, the lower horizon of a podsol, a soil that had lost most of its fertility (context 1384). The possibility can be entertained that Tarbat by the sixth century was unwanted land, the kind of waste that a king might be happy to grant to an itinerant community of spiritual eccentrics.

Monastic Settlement

At the base of the valley was a marsh that had began to form, according to radio-carbon dating, during the Iron Age between 550 and 370 BC. It was still forming when the monks arrived and chose to settle on the sandy ridge where the church now stands. They had dunes and the sea to the north of them and the marsh to the south. Top of their agenda was therefore the supply of fresh water, and they devoted some ingenuity to the task. They took rainwater off the hill and led it into stone-lined cisterns (see Plate 5a; also Digest, A6, for numbered data). They built a wicker-lined well, and they dug a shallow pit down by the water table, which they filled with finely divided charcoal (Fig. 4.2). The water came up through the charcoal clean and clear, filtered like the finest Bourbon. A gully found under the church was 1.3m deep from its own old ground surface and appeared to have been lined with timber – or it could have been a tree-trunk pipe. Cereal grains had arrived in it between 540 and 650 AD (F129; for dates, see Digest, A3). Animal bone in this period was mainly cattle. There was a small square hearth associated with slag that suggested metal-working, and a piece of worked bone and afragment of iron from the podsol (F535). This indicated some modest and preliminary agricultural and light industrial action on the slopes leading down to the marsh. But for our first sure sighting of the early community we rely on the remarkable sequence of burial, excavated inside and outside the church.

THE MONASTIC CEMETERY

The strata underneath the church could be defined in six 'horizons', the first three natural – three successive buried soils – and the last three artificial – builders' levelling or floors relating to successive churches (for data references within the church, see Digest, A4). Fifteen radiocarbon dates have been obtained and calibrated, and made more precise by using sequences of graves that had cut each other, so that their order of digging was known. The burial rites were surprisingly varied: some bodies had been buried with nothing, some with a shroud pin, some in coffins and some with large flat stones supporting the head (head support burials) or surrounding the whole corpse (long cists).

From this we learnt that there were two distinct periods of burial (Figs 4.3, 4.4). The first, from *c.* 550 AD to *c.* 900, were mainly middle-aged or elderly men, often buried in long cists, or with stone head supports (Figs 4.5, 4.6). The second period ran from *c.* 1100 to 1600, and included men, women and children, sometimes with shroud pins and coffins. This result indicated with unusual clarity that two cemeteries had succeeded each other at Portmahomack, the first belonging to a community mainly of men, the second to a succession of families; the first to a monastery or something very like one, and the second to a parish church. There was, moreover, a gap between them: in the tenth–eleventh centuries, it seemed, no one was buried.

The dead and buried monastic community could itself be divided into an early and a later group. Three of the earliest graves were not actually found in the church, but down the hill adjacent to the workshops in Sector 2. These were aligned north-east/south-west, the head being towards the south-west (F515, F516, F517). The most northerly had a lid and a double wall of slabs; the next had a fine cist of large single slabs, and the third, the body well decayed, had no cist. The central burial of the three gave a radiocarbon date in the range AD 430–610. There is no doubt that the later

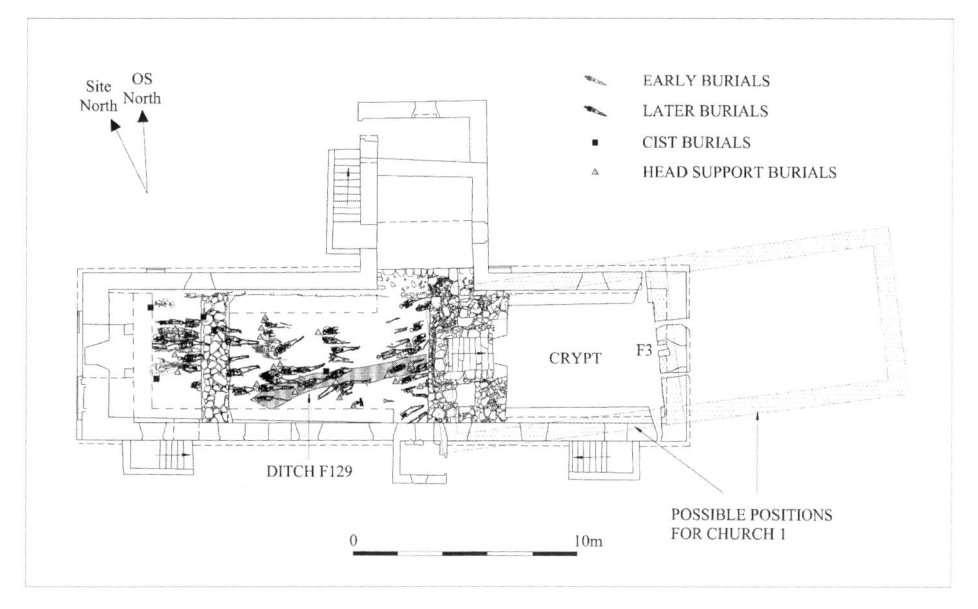

Fig. 4.3 Monastic period burials, divided into the early (Phase 1, below Horizon B) and later group (Phase 2, below Horizon C), with cist and head support burials distinguished. The early gully F129 is also shown.

monks would have been aware of these graves, particularly as one was graced with an earth mound covered by a row of stone slabs. The curbed edge of the later tawing platform (see Chapter 6) followed the line of their south-west ends.

The earliest burials rediscovered under the church, eleven of them, were concealed beneath a layer of pinkish sand (Horizon B), and were all buried in cist graves, well furnished with large slabs of local sandstone. Another dozen burials, not in cists, formed part of this group (Phase 1), making twenty-three in all. Their dates ranged from the sixth and seventh centuries. Interestingly, these people included the monastic period's only women (three of them), one among the earliest, dying between AD 535 and 605. Five of the bodies had their heads to the north-east or south-west. Most of these graves were found on the west side of the top of the hill, under the west end of the present church. A southern boundary for the cist graves seems to have been formed by the timber-lined gully (F129).

The burials of the next phase (Phase 2), fifty or more, had been generally cut into the pink sand and sealed by a brown soil above it. They included twenty-four head support burials and one on a layer of charcoal (Burial 147). Their radiocarbon dates placed them within the eighth or ninth century, and they were mostly men, young, middle-aged or elderly. Sarah King, the osteologist who examined this monastic group, found that they had narrow faces and nasal apertures, medium-sized eye orbits and broad palates. They were relatively short by modern standards: 5ft 7in for men, 5ft 3in for women. Almost all suffered from one or more types of dental disease, including calculus (plaque), caries (cavities), dental abscesses, ante-mortem tooth loss and periodontal disease. The monastic teeth were very worn in comparison to the

(a) Age and sex distribution sixth – ninth centuries

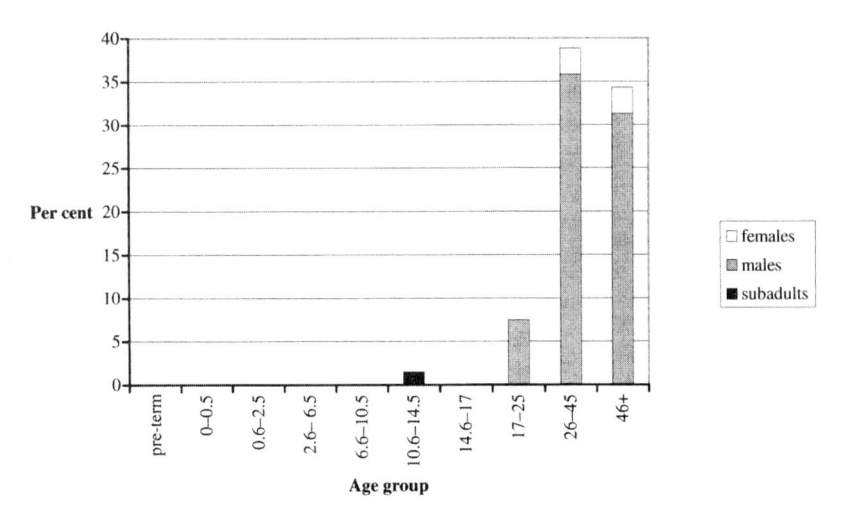

(b) Age and sex distribution twelfth – sixteenth centuries

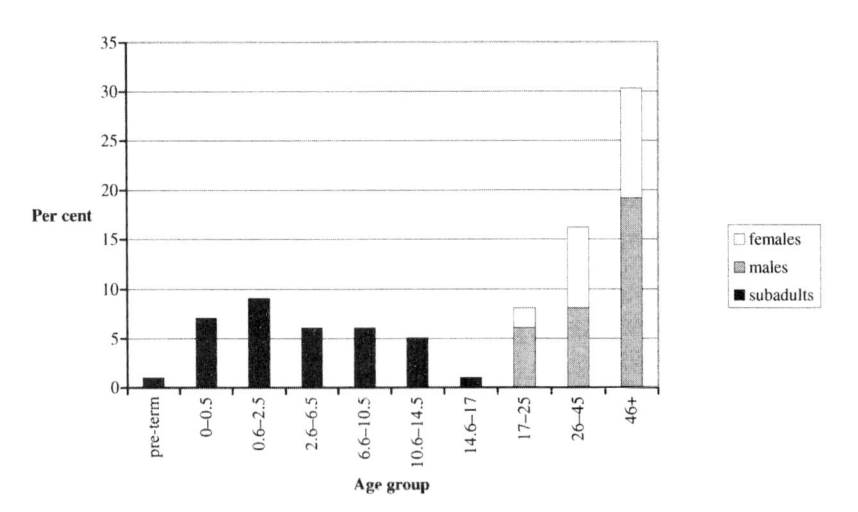

Fig. 4.4 Sarah King's identifications of age and sex from (a) Phases 1 and 2, sixth–ninth centuries; and (b) Phases 3 and 4, twelfth–fifteenth centuries. (Source: Sarah King)

teeth from the later parish community, suggesting that the first monks had a coarse diet that needed a lot of chewing. They had also suffered from age-related diseases, such as osteoarthritis of the joints and spine, and facets from much squatting. There were three cases of spondylosis (a condition of the lumbar vertebrae that may occur

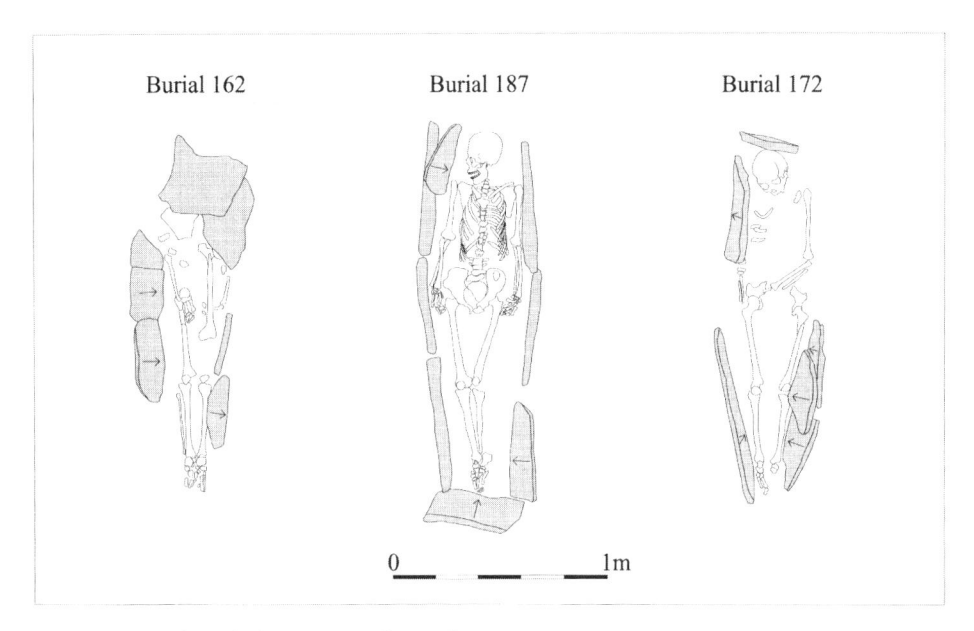

Fig. 4.5 Cist burials from Portmahomack.

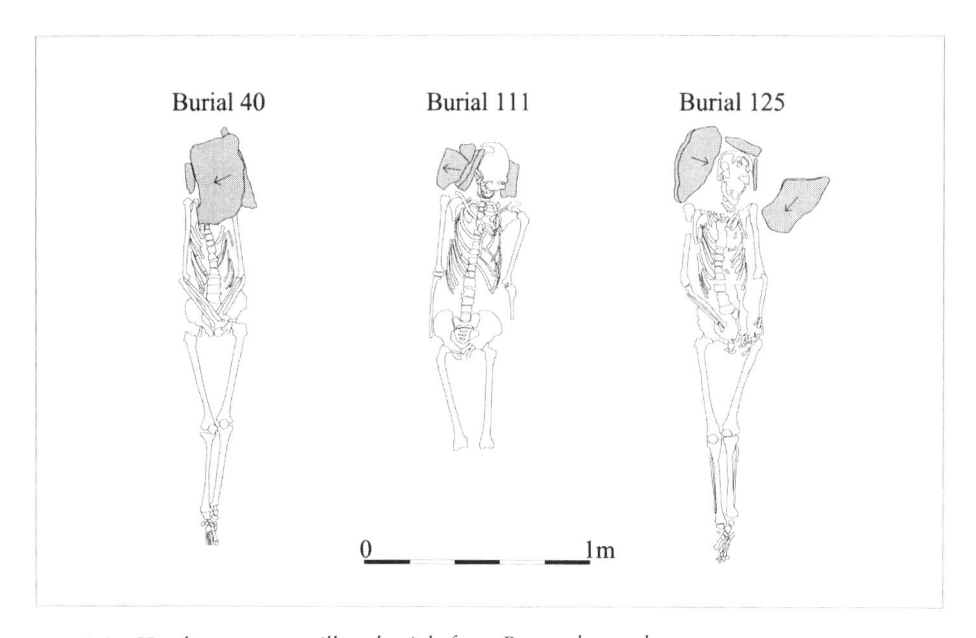

Fig. 4.6 Head support or pillow burials from Portmahomack.

as a result of bending and lifting in an upright posture) and three cases of compression fractures of the vertebrae (possibly as a result of a vertical force injury). There was evidence for hernias, suggesting much lifting, and a disproportionate amount of battering to the left clavicle and right proximal fibula (lower leg). We may safely say that many of the early monks at Portmahomack had 'done their back in'. The evidence from the cemetery, the workshops and the sculpture that we are about to explore provides ample indications of the probable cause of the problem: they were lugging enormous stones about.

Three individual monks had received major blade wounds, cutting them to the bone (Burials 152, 158, 149). One had suffered a face-to-face encounter with a long sword between 680 and 900 (Burial 158) – but survived it. Another who died of his wounds (Burial 152) had three sharp cut-marks to the skull: one wound approximately 72mm in length extending across both parietals with radiating fractures, a second wound bisecting the lamboid suture on the left side, and a third blow on the right side of the occipital. The specialist commented, with forensic detachment:

> As two of the cuts were on the back of the head, it is likely that the assailant attacked from behind. Given that one of the fractures was on the crown of the head, the individual may have been below the assailant at one point (e.g. kneeling). As injuries with larger weapons are more likely to produce terminal fractures, it is possible that a weapon such as a large sword may have been used to produce these fractures.[8]

The victim of this attack expired between 810 and 1020 – arousing strong suspicions of Norse aggression – and indeed this skull has made an appearance on television in *The Blood of the Vikings*. But who really attacked Portmahomack, and when, are matters that will be considered in their place.

This sequence suggests that the Portmahomack cemetery began in the sixth century or before and endured to the ninth, and contained mainly men – a picture that fits well with a monastery founded at the time of Columba and terminating in the time of the Norsemen. But we need to explore how far our sample represents the whole; medieval cemeteries are known or suspected in which men and women were buried separately, and this is thought to perpetuate a practice begun in early Irish monasteries.[9] So the women may have been buried elsewhere, although still in the vicinity, a possibility enhanced by a gradual awareness that the early burial ground at St Colman's was a part of something much larger and in use for much longer.

With the stimulation of anecdote, old rumour and new searches consequent on our dig, stone-lined burials are now known to have been found all along the ridge overlooking the Firth, both north and south of Tarbat Old Church. The Revd D. Campbell, compiling the *New Statistical Account* in 1845, reported:

> There is, above the village of Portmahomack, a green hill, called Chapel Hill, where there were discovered, on levelling the ground for new buildings, a number of human bones deposited within rough flags of freestone . . . Several chests, composed of rough freestone flags, were dug up a few years ago, at a place in the neighbourhood of Portmahomack, by labourers employed in levelling the ground for new buildings. Each chest contained an entire skeleton, of a size unusually large, and, from the position of the bones, it appeared that the bodies had been doubled.[10]

In 1957 the *Third Statistical Account* noted that many fragments of human bones had been found at Chapel Hill during building and gardening. The author, James R. Cheyne, liked this for the site of the earliest church, and it may be so.

But down the coast in the opposite direction, at Balnabruach, burials have also appeared from time to time. Two long cists were reported during a drainage operation in 1977. The skeletons were both extended, a woman in her late 30s lying north–south and a man between 16 and 25 in a grave above, aligned east–west. There was also a short cist, which the attendant archaeologist dated to the Bronze Age. Surviving bones from three of these graves gave radiocarbon dates of fifth–fourth centuries BC and third–fifth centuries AD. Second- and third-hand reports suggest that such burials, or their slabs, were encountered all along the shore line south of the church.[11] Other searches of old finds have revealed encounters with burials on the east coast of the peninsula too. The coast had, it seems, been attracting burials long before the arrival of any monks. This theme is taken up again in Chapter 9.

In summary then, there is a good case for the ridge along the west coast of the Tarbat peninsula being used for burial before the monastic community was established, perhaps as early as the Bronze Age and certainly within the long Iron Age from the fifth century BC to the fifth century AD. There is a likelihood that during monastic times there were numerous other burials, with slabs, north and south of the church, on this same ridge. These, of course, may well have included women, and have continued after the ninth century. However, on the summit within the present church, an area that should represent the heart of the monastic cemetery, the great majority of burials were of mature men dying between the sixth and ninth centuries. These may not represent the whole community or its whole existence, but perhaps they can be seen as its leading members during their period of control. In this central area there is a stratigraphic argument for a gap of 200–300 years before burial began again, and it did so within the walls of a parish church. This part of the story will be taken up again in Chapter 8.

Stone-lined burials of this kind are known from all over Europe in the centuries following the Roman Empire, so we are not surprised to find them in Portmahomack. The best sequences on the continent are certainly associated with Christian churches, and many of these have an evolutionary change from the grander to the more peremptory version of the rite. At Saint-Laurent in Grenoble, Renée Colardelle excavated a sequence of stone-lined burials, starting with sarcophagi of Roman type and ending with graves marked by random stones. All these surrounded a stone church which evolved in the opposite sense to the graves, becoming more elaborate as the graves became simpler.[12] At Castel Seprio in north Italy the church of Santa Maria foris Portas began in the eighth century with a founder tomb built in mortared stone with a massive slab lid on which was an image of a sword raised in relief; cist graves followed and then tombs furnished sparsely with a few upright slabs[13]. Nearer home, similar kinds of tomb are found in Wales, for example, at Llandough, where 1,026 burials dated from the seventh–tenth centuries included three cists and five head support burials.[14] Pictish Scotland took to this kind of burial with special enthusiasm. Of 145 burials excavated at The Hallow Hill, near St Andrews, 122 were in long cists and another 13 in graves edged with boulders, dated between the sixth and ninth centuries AD.[15] Comparable burials have been found the length of Pictland, from Fife to Caithness.

It is natural to assume that these burials refer to Roman practice, and are Christian in meaning. Magnar Dalland notes that the cist cemeteries at Avonmill, Hallow Hill, Four Winds and Catstane came into use in the mid-fifth century, 'a short time after Ninian had begun his mission to Whithorn'.[16] The authors of the report on Lundin Links describe it as 'a small Christian community' and give its dates as AD 450–650, but they nevertheless feel that the origin of the rite should be sought in British south-east Scotland between the second and fourth centuries AD.[17] As we have seen, two probable long cists from Balnabruach in Easter Ross date to the third–fifth centuries AD, and, in the same region, Bronze Age people, Iron Age people and Viking people also buried their dead using slabs of stone when the occasion demanded. Cist burials may be covered with kerbed stone cairns, both round and square, dating broadly to the first millennium AD, and it may be that, in a country where slabby burials were common, no Christian meaning was necessarily intended.[18] Something, however, is labelling the east coast of north Britain with this burial practice – something shared in Wales but not in England. Whether this is ethnic or religious or traditional or pragmatic – stone is used where stone is found – are matters best left on one side until the evidence as a whole has been reviewed. In the meantime there is no doubt that the majority of graves found at Portmahomack were of people who professed Christianity. Over 200 pieces of Christian sculpture have turned up in and around the church, deriving from a dozen grave markers, a sarcophagus and four monumental free-standing vertical cross-slabs. These will be described, and their intellectual context explored, in Chapter 5. For the moment we can observe that on any current theory they all date to between the sixth century and the ninth – the time that the monastic cemetery was in use.

We can, therefore, claim to have an early Christian population that was managing water in its early days and was later crippling itself carrying (and erecting) heavy stones. A few women were members of the original party, but the group apparently soon felt it could dispense with them. This was a community that did not rely on procreation for its survival, so there must have been a continual supply of imported adult males ready to break their backs at Portmahomack over three centuries. The demographics of such an artificially renewed population are hard to predict. We have seen only a fraction of the cemetery, so, assuming it was spread over the hill that carries the present church, we could multiply the number of dead by ten, to make it 600, which would be two persons dying every year. Taking a hypothetical life span of 60, we could suggest a constant population of about thirty, few enough when we reflect all they had to do. The nominal community could have been bigger than that, since, as we shall see, there is good reason to suppose that many were ceaselessly travelling (see Chapter 10).

A Stone Church?

If one important reason for shifting large amounts of stone was making sculpture, another was to build a church. It is not credible that Christian Picts had no churches, but the problem is to find them. The obvious place to look in Portmahomack was beneath the present church, but, although the search was thorough, later walls hid earlier ones. The most important lead was given by the east wall of the crypt, which

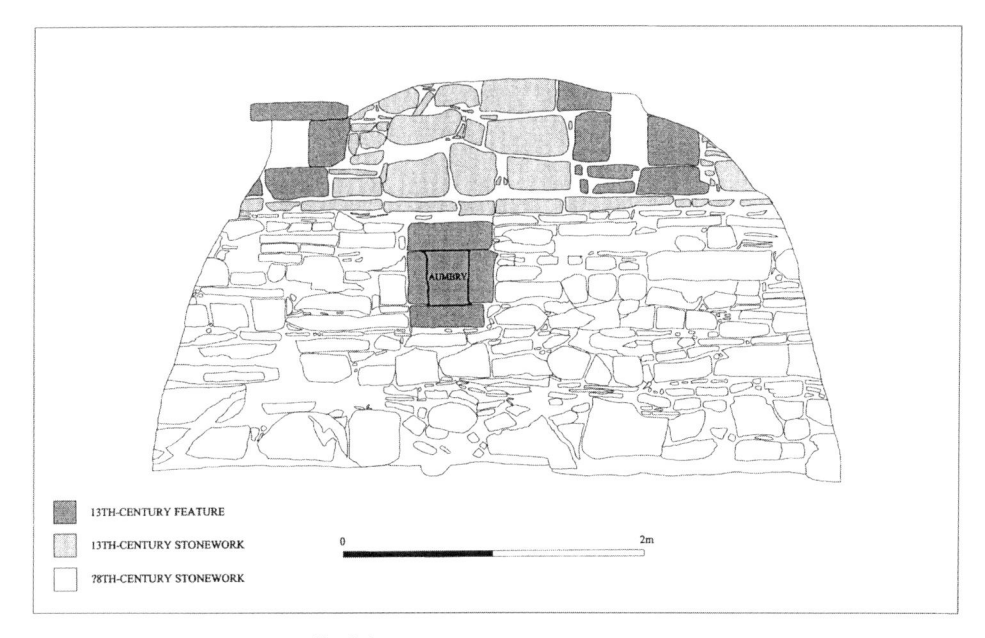

Fig. 4.7 *Elevation east wall of the crypt (F3).*

was out of alignment with every church structure that followed. It was, therefore, a candidate for a pre-existing wall that had been incorporated into a later church. The later church-building began in about the twelfth century and endured in the same place until today (see Chapter 8). No other walls were seen in the churchyard or under the church that have to belong to the monastic phase. So we are looking for a single stone building to go with this wall.

Several arguments can be deployed, and the reader's patience is requested to hear them out, since the matter concerns the only known church in Pictland. There are plenty of certainties about eighth-century Tarbat, but this is not one of them. The questions to be addressed are:

- Was there a Church 1?
- Did it run east or west from its one surviving wall?
- How was it adapted by the church-builders who followed?
- What form did it take?

To answer these questions to an acceptable degree of plausibility it will be necessary to take into account the heights of walls and the old ground surfaces, the way walls joined together and the probable form of early churches in Celtic area. Of all these things, we have only a partial knowledge (for a summary of the relevant data, see Digest, A3).

WAS THERE A CHURCH 1?

There was a large amount of sculpture of Christian character datable without much controversy to the sixth–ninth centuries. Its makers should have had a church, and it

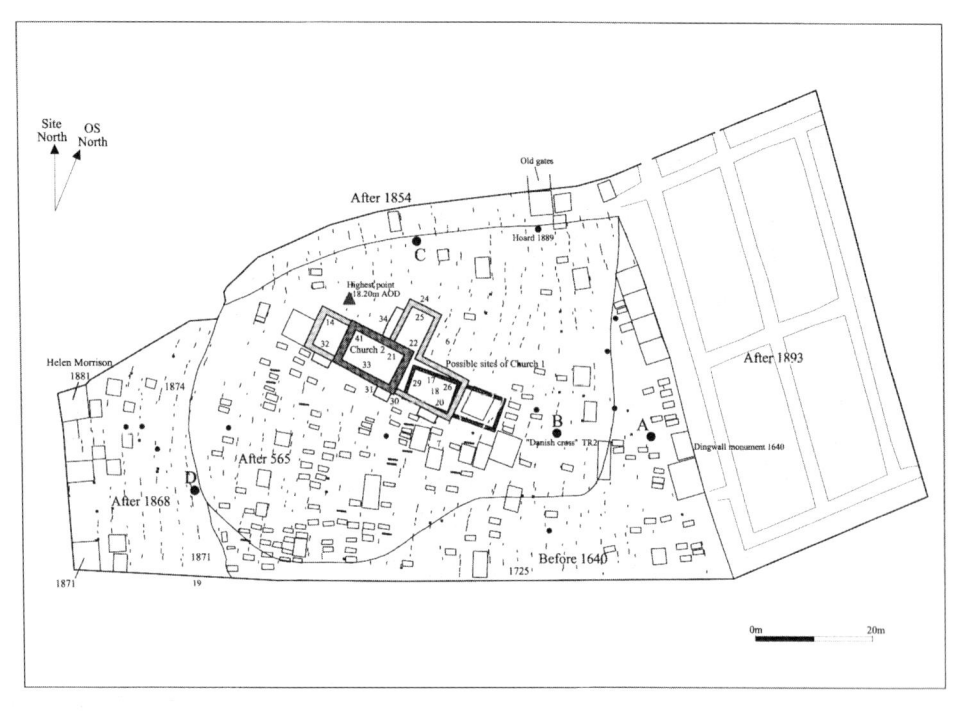

Fig. 4.8 The churchyard, showing its development from an oval original, with two possible positions for the early church. Also shown are the probable locations of the four monumental crosses A–D to be discussed in Chapter 5.

is the way of churches to keep to the same spot. This is a reason for supposing that the first church lay under the present one – that is, where we had the chance to look, rather than elsewhere on the hill. The first church may have been a construction in timber, since this is the form that an early Celtic church might be expected to have taken, although there was no evidence for it. Post-holes would not have evaded our excavators, but there were none that formed a pattern. Some indication for the presence of a church, and for its position, is provided by the burials. The earliest of these were found at the west end of the present church (and further west still), but burials of the monastic period continue all the way under the east wall of Church 2. Moreover, their alignment conforms increasingly to that of the skewed east wall of the crypt, the closer they approach it. It could be concluded that a stone church was built somewhere towards the east end of the hill during the life of the cemetery, but not at its earliest phase. Another hint is that the gully seen among the early burials is best explained as taking water away westwards from a construction of some kind, one that generated a lot of water from a roof.

The architecture of an early stone church on the east of the hill is mainly implied by the alignment of the east wall of the crypt (F3; Fig. 4.7), an alignment that varies by 7 degrees from those of the other north–south walls encountered, including the west wall of the crypt and the walls of Church 2, the parish church that succeeded it in the twelfth century (Figs 4.3, 4.8). The crypt as we have it today is a thirteenth-century design (Church 4), with an internal vault added in the seventeenth century (Church 5). Neither of these constructions can now be removed, so we are working blind, or only from hypotheses inferred from measurements. The east wall had an aumbry built into it, which may have been integral, although it was not quite central, as seen. Above the level of the aumbry, it could be seen that the crypt had been rebuilt in blocks of yellow sandstone, and the rebuild included four windows to admit light from the outside into the east end. This yellow sandstone ashlar is the signature of the thirteenth-century church, which also added a chamfered plinth all the way round on the outside at or above its own ground level. So the evidence for an early church is indirect, and without too much stress the crypt can be seen as an original construction for Church 4 in the thirteenth century – and just that. But we must persevere, and explore the possibilities, however frail, for the form of an early church, assuming that it existed.

DID CHURCH 1 RUN EAST OR WEST FROM ITS ONE SURVIVING WALL (F3)?

If the crypt wall (F3) implies an earlier building, we might consider two options: that it ran west from F3 or that it ran east (Fig. 4.3). If it ran west, we will be obliged to fit our early church somehow into the shell of the present crypt, and work out how it was entered. The westward location would give us the satisfaction of agreeing with nineteenth-century assertions that this 'vault' was a chapel of St Columba (see Chapter 1), and would also neatly explain why the present crypt was put where it was. During restoration, it was observed externally that the lower foundations of the north wall set off to meet F3 at right angles (Int. 18). This would mean that the north wall of Church 1 lay deep beneath the present north wall. The east wall (F3) also contained the aumbry, which we could surmise as an early feature, and expect it to have been, then as now, on the inside.

The current *west* wall could be part of the same early church, and indeed they are of similar build (large uncut stones at the base, rising in smaller pieces) except where the later west doorway has burst through (Fig 3.6). However, the east and west walls of the crypt are not parallel; which, if they form part of the same early church, they should be. A wall on the line of the present west wall also presents us with difficulties of access. West of the crypt, the old ground surface in monastic times was at about 17.40m AOD, but the floor of the crypt and the base of its walls lay a good deal lower than that – some 2.40m lower. Assuming that the Church 1 walls were buried no more than a metre into the sandy subsoil, the floor for Church 1 must have lain somewhere between 15m and 16m AOD. If the aumbry was to be above knee height, then the middle of this range is preferred, say 15.5m AOD. If Church 1 ran westwards from F3, therefore, much of it was underground at the time: *it was always a crypt*. It could not have been entered from the west without steps, which would have been required to bring a person down, up to 1.4–2.4m from the old ground surface onto its floor. In this case, it would have been advisable to have the steps indoors, so that water did not pour down them into the church. This, in turn, implies a more extensive building above ground, running at least 2m to the west.

A solution to these problems is given by supposing that the west wall of Church 1 actually lay beneath the east wall of Church 2. This provides room for a flight of steps inside the west wall of Church 1, in the same position as the steps are now, although a shorter flight. This Church 1 is 11.25m long, so, assuming a width of 7.5m (as the present church), this putative Church 1 is in the proportion 3:2 (ratio 1.5), which has some resonance with early practice (see below).

If, on the other hand, Church 1 ran east, then the building would have projected over the churchyard east of the present church. There is a north–south wall, east of and parallel to the east end of the present church, which at first looked promising. But this is only 5m away, has the wrong alignment (strictly north–south) and seems to belong to two burial vaults marked by stone posts.[19] Here the ground also drops rapidly into the valley, so that a church 11.25m long (as above) would surely still show above ground. It would at least have shown itself to antiquaries visiting in the eighteenth and nineteenth centuries, who observed the broken remains of eighth-century sculpture at this point (the 'Danish Cross') – but none reports the ruins of a chapel. There is no sign of a doorway in F3 (which in this case would have served as the west wall of Church 1), and we would have to abandon the aumbry as a primary feature, since it would then be on the outside of the building.

It has to be said that neither model offers a winning case; the westward church is difficult to access, and the eastward church requires us to abandon the aumbry. Both models oblige us to propose three additional walls for which we have no evidence.

How was the Church Adapted by the Church-Builders who Followed?

The longer story of St Colman's church will be recounted in Chapter 8, but there is some additional circumstantial evidence from the way that the hypothetical Church 1 re-emerged as a thirteenth-century crypt. The last people to see Church 1 reasonably intact were those who built Church 2. If Church 1 ran west, then, we argue, the Church 2 builders would have founded their east wall on its west wall. They could presumably have seen at least this wall, and felt that for spiritual or practical reasons it should form their foundation. When these medieval churchmen added a chancel (to make Church 3), this chancel would have over-sailed the area of Church 1, which we have to assume was filled with earth at the time. This chancel was chopped away in its turn to insert the west wall and steps of the thirteenth-century crypt (see Chapter 8). All this strongly suggests that the existing west wall of the crypt is a primary build of the thirteenth century. It is, therefore, of no consequence that it does not run parallel to F3.

If Church 1 ran eastwards from F3, then at the time Church 2 was built its ruin would have lain partially underground and about 12m away. Church 3 extended its chancel over virgin territory. In this case, the ruin of Church 1 had no attraction for the twelfth-century church-builders, and they ignored it. It was the thirteenth-century builders of Church 4 who rediscovered Church 1 or at least took one of its walls back into commission, rebuilding it and placing upon it their new east end. The implication is that this wall was visible, but the others were not, or were not needed.

Is it possible for one century to avoid a ruin and the next to adopt it? Of course. The monumental mood can change swiftly, so that yesterday's superannuated ruin becomes today's revered heritage. It is not excluded that, having created the crypt, the thirteenth-century churchman created the relics, the aumbry to put them in and the historical narrative to go with them (see Chapter 1). Unfortunately, this thinking aloud does not supply the trump card in deciding which way the early church ran. If it ran west, its north, south and west walls were eventually demolished to make way for the crypt. If it ran east, its east, south and north walls were (or had already been) demolished.

At this point the exasperated reader might be thinking: why on earth does he not just go and look? I agree that such an expedition would be worthwhile, but excavation in a Scottish churchyard is neither cheap nor easily allowable. The excavation would need to be about 20 × 20m in extent to avoid being misled by drains, vaults and other anticipated funereal constructions. It would have to go deep (2m+), since we suspect that the walls were almost entirely demolished before the nineteenth century. It would also first involve the excavation and recording of hundreds of skeletons and the removal of many ancestral lairs. If Church 1 did indeed run east of the present church, there one day, when time and money and permission allow, its traces may be contacted about 2m down.

However, for the time being we have marginally better circumstantial evidence to visualise this lost church underneath the present church of St Colman. It can be hypothesised to measure 7.5 × 11.25 m. Only the interior of its east wall, with an aumbry, is still showing, all the other walls having been levelled to their foundations and buried under later walls. Its west wall might originally have contained the door, and would have been entered at a level of 17.4m AOD. Steps would immediately have taken the incomer down a flight of steps to a level of, say, 15.5m AOD. Alternative entries would have been possible through the north or south walls, towards the east end. The upper part of the east wall at least was above ground level and may have had openings to admit light.

Looking ahead to the demise of the monastery, we can also see that such a structure is consistent with its destined afterlife. The medieval builders of Church 2 beheld a ruin and brought its west wall into service as a foundation. They also gathered up larger pieces of eighth-century sculpture and put them into their foundations. They filled in the body of Church 1, and extended a chancel over the top of it. Or this 'chancel' was itself a broadening of the steps to allow wider access to the older church. In due course, the later thirteenth-century-builders of Church 4 took the whole of the ancient foundation, which they could still see, into their new design, making of it a crypt that has survived to this day.

What Form did the Church Take?

I end this chapter with a brief evocation of the kind of architecture that other studies might lead us to expect. Early Celtic church buildings survive in greater numbers in Ireland than in Scotland and have been the subject of more comprehensive examination. Traditionally, the sequence begins with circular 'cells' in drystone corbelling, as at Skellig Michael, which are adaptations of Iron Age buildings – brochs and wheelhouses. The earliest churches were seen as rectangular versions of these: corbelled drystone constructions on a rectangular plan, as the Gallarus oratory, with a small door at the west end and a square-headed window in the east wall. By the eighth century the church was more clearly rectangular in plan and used mortar as well. Chancels were added in the ninth–tenth centuries, connected to the nave by arches, as at St Kevin's, Glendalough, and this scheme endured until the twelfth century.[20]

More recent studies have questioned some of this sequence. Peter Harbison thought that the Gallarus oratory could be as late as the twelfth century, and the comprehensive review by Tomás Ó'Carragáin has emphasised that differences in construction can be regional rather than chronological.[21] Five types of pre-Romanesque church were distributed in different parts of Ireland, and all were significantly absent from Ulster. Ó'Carragáin's survey confirmed several features as generally diagnostic of Irish pre-Romanesque churches: all were constructed with plinths, building blocks are large, and spalls (stone chips) are uncommon; the door is always in the west wall, most early churches have a window in the south wall, but a significant minority were lit only by an east window. *Antae* (external projections on east or west walls) occurred in 89 per cent of his drystone Type 1 churches. Six out of nine aumbries occur in his Type 2 churches (early mortared). All pre-Romanesque churches appear to be designed as single-room rectangular buildings.[22] Single-phase bicameral churches are very rare.[23] However, corbelled drystone beehive huts and clachans need not be indicative of an early date but may be adopted in the eighth–tenth centuries. Their use was in deliberate contrast to the sacred character of churches.[24]

On the Irish model, an insular church of the sixth–ninth centuries would, therefore, have been single cell, rectangular, drystone or mortared, corbelled or roofed with timber beams, with a west door and an east or south window, may have had antae and could well have had an aumbry. Early churches in Ireland could remain ruinous for long periods. On the practical side, their rubble construction did not lend itself to recycling in coursed walls, but ideologically the interior of a roofless chapel did attract burial in the Middle Ages and later.

Early upstanding churches are rarer in Northumbria and France, but both these areas feature early crypts or partially subterranean constructions. In France the best-known examples are the Hypogeum of Mellebaude at Poitiers (sixth century), where a crypt was entered by a flight of steps flanked by ornamented side walls, and the crypt at Jouarre (seventh century). Both these subterranean buildings were dedicated to burial. In Northumbria, an early church could be provided with a lighted crypt by half-burying it in a hillside, as at Lastingham. More formal crypts with two flights of steps to provide circulation were constructed at Hexham and Ripon. These are associated with the need to provide protected public access to relics, as developed in Rome. Thus a sixth–eighth-century church, drawing on French or Northumbrian models, could already have included the idea of a crypt, especially to house a special relic.

The evidence for early churches in Scotland itself has been beset by poor dating and confused by documentary expectations. These latter suggest that early constructions would have been in timber, wattle at first and then in oak board from the early eighth century, as at Iona, while (following Bede) after 710 churches in Pictland would have been constructed in stone (*iuxta morem Romanorum*).[25] The difficulty is that no early church building has actually been identified in Pictland and very few in Dal Riada. Scholars to date have been obliged to use the exiguous documentation and a number of basic architectural features to characterise early church buildings. Among these were rubble construction, simple rectangular naves, with or without square chancels, monolithic-head windows and doorways with inclining or converging jambs. Beehive cells and rectangular chapels are found in the west – for example, at Eilean an Niaomh. The remains include chapels 20 × 12ft (5 × 3m) with simple lintel head windows.[26] The chapel at Skeabost, Skye (also said in the *Origines Parochiales* to be dedicated to Columba), is 21ft (6.4m) long and has a flat-headed window 2ft high and 6in wide (61 × 15cm) in the east end. The west end is blank.[27] Some indication of how architecture arrives into the Romanesque period might be given by St Oran's Chapel Iona, which is supposed to have been built by Queen Margaret about 1074. Measuring 30 × 16ft (9.1 × 4.9m) internally, it has two narrow windows near the east end, but no window in the east wall, and a west door with a Norman arch.[28] Also on Iona, the early church at St Ronan's (eighth–twelfth centuries) was unicameral, clay bonded and whitewashed.[29]

The church on Egilsay, Orkney, has a nave, chancel and circular tower of a single build in coursed masonry oriented exactly east–west. It has round-arched windows and doors. The date should be earlier than Kirkwall (begun 1137), and may be as early as 1000, given resemblances of the tower to that at Clonmacnoise. The place name Kirkwall implies that Norsemen found a church already there. The church on the Brough of Birsay features a nave, chancel and apse, all apparently built at the same time, with stair turrets in the corners of the chancel arch; it is assigned to about 1100. That on the Island of Wyre, Orkney, is probably from the twelfth–thirteenth centuries, as is Linton Chapel, Shapinsay.[30]

Similar touchstones for second millennium churches can be found further south. At Birnie, in Moray, the Norman east–west church is built in dressed freestone masonry, and was constructed before 1184 as the first Bishop's seat (Moray). The Bishop's seat subsequently moved to Kineddar, then Spynie, then Elgin. The church also contains a very rare and interesting specimen of the ancient square-shaped Celtic bell, which may possibly indicate that the present church was preceded by a Celtic monastery.[31] Two other extant churches may include fabric of MacGibbon and Ross's 'Celtic' period: Monymusk Church, findspot of the Monymusk Reliquary, and Lybster, Caithness. The latter has a nave 17ft 10in × 10ft 11in (5.4 × 3.3), in which the north wall is 3 degrees south of true west and north of true east, supposing the variation to be 24 degrees west of north. North and south walls are 3ft 11in (1.2m) thick, and west and east walls 4ft 2in (1.3m) thick. It was constructed in irregular courses, has a west door with inclined jambs and a slab lintel. The chancel has been added or rebuilt, and was entered by a doorway with a form like the west door.[32]

The debate in Scotland has continued to swing this way and that. In 1986 Eric Fernie showed that Scotland's prime candidates for early churches (those surviving at Abernethy, Brechin, Egilsay, Restenneth, Edinburgh Castle and St Andrews) may all be dated c. 1090–1130. He finds the variety in their structure to be typical of this period and notes architectural references to both Ireland and (at Egilsay) to the North Sea lands. In 1994 Neil Cameron suggested that there was a well-established tradition of stone church-building before the twelfth century. In general, he means the eleventh – for example, the foundations at Birsay attributed to the church built c. 1060 for Thorfinn, Earl of Orkney. But, as he points out, the monolithic stone arch from Forteviot implies that building churches in stone must have been achievable in Scotland in the eighth–ninth centuries.[33]

It is interesting to compare the ratio of length to width in the earliest of the churches collected by MacGibbon and Ross (Table 4.1). It can be said that those that are undated, but expected to be early, have ratios around 1.5, while those that are known to be Romanesque have ratios larger than this. The ratio of length to width may thus provide a crude indication of early date.

These thoughts provide us with some comfort that a partially subterranean Church 1, measuring 11.25 × 7.5m and pre-echoing the present crypt, would not have been out of place in the Ireland or North Britain of the eighth century. Following the Irish tradition, it would probably have had a door in the west end and a window in the south or east wall, and an aumbry might well have been a feature of such a church. Following the Northumbrian tradition, it might have been cut into the side of a hill, with the west end subterranean and the east end lit by natural light, and entered by a less perilous south door. Some kind of drainage arrangements

Table 4.1 Length/width ratios of some early churches from external measurements

Site	Length (ft)	Width (ft)	Length (m)	Width (m)	Ratio
Portmahomack Church 1			11.25	7.5	1.5
Portmahomack Church 2			12	8	1.5
Skeabost, Skye	21		6.5		
Howmore, South Uist	17ft 7in	11ft 6in	5.4	3.5	1.5
Tigh Beannachadh, Lewis	18ft 2in	10ft 4in	5.6	3.2	1.75
Dun Othail, Lewis	17	11ft 3in	5.2	3.5	1.5
St Columba, Balivanich, Benbecula	33ft 6in	14ft 6in	10.5	4.5	2.3
Island of Wyre, Orkney	19ft 2in	12ft 10in	5.9	4	1.5
Lybster, Caithness	17ft 10in	10ft 11in	5.5	3.4	1.6
Egilsay, Orkney, c. 1000	29ft 9in	15ft 6in	8.8	4.8	1.8
Brough of Birsay, c. 1100	28ft 3in	15ft 6in	8.7	4.8	1.8
St Oran's Chapel, Iona, c. 1074	30	16	9.1	4.9	1.9
Birnie, before 1184	42	18ft 6in	12.9	5.7	2.3

Source: MacGibbon and Ross (1896).

carried water off the roof westwards, implying (since it would have been a lot easier to let it soak away to the east) that it was desirable to collect it, using a timber-lined drain. Judging from its surviving wall, Church 1 was built in good quality pink and blonde sandstone from the Middle old red sandstone beds on the east side of the peninsula, and perhaps using the Geanies quarry, the same stone that was used to make carved stone memorials.[34] The walls were rubble built, with large stones at the base and smaller ones as the wall rose. Then, or on its recommissioning in the medieval period, the wall face was tooled flush. There was no evidence for a timber predecessor. In any case, it may be that, as with the beehive huts, timbering was not chronological in its application, but regional or even ideological. Building in stone was ritually special (as with stone circles), while building in timber was a more secular option. Timber churches, could, on this reading, be expected to post-date the first stone churches, the property of builders for whom ritual aspects had been relaxed.

The number of people who could stand inside this space to say the Divine Office was about thirty, or about twenty kneeling. On the basis of such tentative calculations as have already been made, it was, therefore, probably large enough to house the whole community in prayer together. Such a building could also be used to host the burial of a founder, or a special relic or both. But at this period the aumbry might have found a more appropriate use as a cupboard to guard the Blessed Sacrament – the ritual bread and wine in their containers of precious metal. On the hill outside the church were the burials of centuries, many marked by simple grave markers. By the eighth century, a large cross-slab stood immediately east of this church, with another down the slope towards the lowest point of the valley, and the edge of the monastic enclosure. Another stood looking out to sea at the northern edge of the enclosure, and a fourth at the western edge. All this will be argued in Chapter 5.

The scene on the hill therefore changed with the years. In Period 1 (sixth–seventh centuries) the investment was mainly in cist graves. If there was a church, if there were grave markers then, we have no direct pointers to them. By Period 2 (the late seventh into the eighth century) there was a stone church and the community was increasing in size, to perhaps thirty, and was all male. There were many grave markers. In many burials, stones were placed either at the side or on top of the head. Before the end of the eighth century, there were great stone monuments in place, both around the church at Portmahomack, and on the edges of the Tarbat peninsula that now forms the greater monastic estate. All this was to come to an end, with the workshops burnt, the sculpture smashed, and defenders meeting death at the edge of a sword. The church building was no doubt burnt or ruined at the same time and lay surrounded by the remains of its monuments for up to two centuries. Then the place, respected by a new generation of clerics, who no doubt knew something of its history, was adapted for the parish church of Tarbat. A simple rectangular church was erected to the west of the buried ruin and soon equipped with a chancel. The developments of the thirteenth century, no doubt bolstered by the researches of the monks of nearby Fearn Abbey, included the full revival of the old church building, and its adaptation as a reliquary church for St Colman, revered hero of the early days of the Christian mission in north Britain and Ireland.

The early monks of Britain and Europe were intrepid and hardy, not so much the contemplative recluse, more the soldier of Christ. Like soldiers, they expected to suffer and took a pride in resisting pain, staying alive and winning. In this context one can perhaps better understand why these groups contained few women, relying as they did on that peculiar form of inebriated obstinacy that is reinforced by male bonding. In this, although they might not have liked the comparison, they bore some resemblance to the Viking war bands who were eventually to displace them. The monks, however, fought with words, and ultimately books.

If the early years at Portmahomack (*c.* 550–650) seem slow, they were probably hard years, and three or four generations were required to evolve from experimental commune to major players. Nevertheless, their skeletons tell us that that these few lived long; the animal bones tell us that they lived on beef and, presumably, on the many by-products of cattle: milk, blood and marrow. Plough pebbles, ard marks and a deposit of grain in a lined drain also say that arable cultivation was practised. The territory of the community was marked out by a modest enclosure ditch (the inner enclosure ditch, F176/F179). No doubt trips were involved: back to Iona or even to Ireland. But, if so, it was hardly via an arterial route: although pottery imported from the Mediterranean and then from southern France was reaching Christian establishments all around the Irish Sea in the sixth and seventh centuries, not so much as a sherd has turned up at Portmahomack in ten years of digging. The nearest that this particular commodity reached is Craig Phadraig (near Inverness). By the eighth century this pottery was no longer in circulation, so it does not work as a sign of networking.

Our first period thus features a small group, living relatively long, without imports or commodities, needing little and making less. Perhaps many communities of this kind lived and faded, in an undemonstrative fashion, in which case they will be very hard to find. But not Portmahomack; here the development of the site in the eighth century was to be massive and high profile. Large buildings were erected beside a paved road, and a community of craftsmen sprang into being: carving stone, making church vessels – and preparing vellum for gospel books. The community had risen from its knees and decided to address the world.

Notes

1. A dun or small hill fort at Easter Rairiche. See Chapter 9 for the argument for the early form of the peninsula and the broader prehistoric landscape.
2. From context 1384, the buried soil beneath the monastery in Int. 14, Sector 2.
3. The stone ball came from a secondary context and thus could be a collector's piece – cf. the impressive collection gathered at Dunrobin Castle Museum across the Dornoch Firth. The best study of the balls is still Marshall (1977; updated in Marshall 1983). Mark Edmonds (1992) reviews the possibility of a regional symbolic use in his article entitled 'Their use is wholly unknown'.
4. Davidson (1946: 30).
5. E.g. the ard marks under the late Bronze Age soil at Old Scatness are criss-cross (Guttmann *et al.* 2004: 55).

6. Distribution of plough pebbles along terrace wall in context 2701; turf building material, originally cut from an old ploughland and dispersed from use in walls and roofs (e.g. context 2649, towards the end of the metal-working debris sequence).
7. For Mine Howe, see Card and Downes (2003: 16–17). See Hunter (2007) for the proto-Pictish gap.
8. Sarah King in Field Reports, vol. 7.
9. As suggested by the women's cemetery at St Ronan's on Iona (O'Sullivan 1994: 360).
10. NSA 460.
11. Original information from Bob Gourley, Archaeology Section, Highland Council. The bones were obtained for dating courtesy of Daphne Lorimer, Orkney Archaeology Trust. For the dates see Chapter 3. For examples of neighbouring excavated short cists from Aberdeenshire and Edderton, see Ralston (1996). The pit for the Edderton cist measured 1.8 × 1.3m and was constructed of four slabs and capstone about 1 × 0.5m. Human bones within dated to 1680–1430 cal BC. Also information from excavation contractors, courtesy of Jan Dane.
12. Colardelle (1986; 1996).
13. Carver (1987).
14. Holbrook and Thomas (2005).
15. Proudfoot (1996); thirty-eight graves in a circular enclosure on Newhall Point headland across the Cromarty Firth opposite Invergordon included eleven with head support stones, described by the excavator as 'an enduring burial tradition in early medieval eastern Scotland' (Reed 1995: 789).
16. Dalland (1992; 1993). The *floreat* for Four Winds was AD 480–650; for Avonmill AD 400–600. Thomas (1981: 275) says long cists are symptomatic of the Ninianic conversion.
17. Grieg *et al.* (2000: 606, 611). Note dates of long cist burial under a barrow at Redcastle AD 400–560 (Alexander 2005), long cists at Thornybank, Midlothian, ranging between AD 230 and 680 (Rees 2002); and long cist at Innerwick, Dunbar, dated AD 400–660 (Rees and Finlayson 1997). According to Ashmore (2003: 39): 'Burial in long graves and cists occurred throughout much of Scotland from some time between the first and fourth centuries, along with other practices such as burial in short cists and under cairns.'
18. Ashmore (1980); Close-Brooks (1984); at Kilphedir, south Uist, a woman in a cist grave under a square kerbed cairn was dated AD 620–780 (Mulville *et al.* 2003: 25).
19. One is labelled Ross, the other uninscribed, but there are memorials in this lair to the MacKenzie, Corbett and McDonald families
20. MacGibbon and Ross (1896: 9).
21. Harbison (1970); Ó'Carragáin (2003a).
22. Ó'Carragáin (2003a: 90, 102, 45, 87, 76, 74, 80).
23. Hare and Hamlin (1986: 134)
24. Ó'Carragáin (2003a: 140)
25. HE V. 21.
26. Ó'Carragáin (2003a: 73–9).
27. Ibid. p. 68, fig. 32.
28. Ibid. p. 220.
29. O'Sullivan (1994).
30. Ó'Carragáin (2003a: 136, 127, 140, 113, 124).
31. Ibid. pp. 220, 218.
32. Ó'Carragáin (2003a: 162)
33. Fernie (1986); Cameron (1994); Alcock (2003: 285).
34. B. Grove, pers. comm.

CHAPTER 5

Carvers and thinkers

The use of stones to decorate and label the landscape was an ancient practice in Scotland. Large erratic boulders were hoisted vertically, to stand alone or in circles or rows, where they formed part of the ceremonial vocabulary of Neolithic and Bronze Age people. Enormous slabs were manoeuvred in position to make burial chambers, the distant ancestors of the cist burials of the Picts. Smaller stones were stacked into large cairns. Whatever the meaning of the chambered tombs, the cairns and the recumbent stone circles, there were plenty of examples in the Moray Firth area, and the Picts knew them. The chances are that they not only knew, but understood, the long purpose of these places better than we ever shall. Moreover, important prehistoric stones remained potent in historic times. The Pictish stone at Strathpeffer was a landmark for the Munros and the Mackenzies, a meeting place for armies in the Middle Ages. Bronze Age standing stones figure in the topographical mythology of Macbeth.[1] A stone effigy commemorating the Brahan Seer, a latter-day shamanistic prophet of the Black Isle, was constructed at Chanonry Point as late as 1969.[2] This is a landscape and a people that know what monumental stones are about. The stones had character in their shape and colour, and, once free of their bedrock, seemed to have the property of life and motion.[3]

At some time in the fifth–seventh centuries the Picts began to mark large boulders and the walls of caves with incised carvings using a unique set of symbols. These symbols, which are the way we can recognise their work, comprise a choice of animals and a group of geometric shapes. Most of the animals – for example, the red deer, the salmon and the wild boar – are easily identified and brilliantly executed with single incised lines. They stand alone or in pairs and probably had a very wide variety of meanings – from simple mood adjectives such as 'courage' or 'peace' to more symbolic meanings – the name of a person or a people – progressing to more allegorical roles when performing in the Christian menagerie, as we shall see. At least one of the animals is a 'composite', a beast with animal traits, but not itself real. It looks a bit like an elephant, and more like a dolphin, but with legs and a tail – it is a multi-talented poetical creature, in which different 'animal' attributes were combined (Fig. 5.1).

The geometric symbols are symmetrical and elegant and seem to refer to artefacts. The Celtic archaeologist Charles Thomas showed that many of them could be read as representations of objects known in the late Iron Age: spears, swords, shields and even a chariot and horses.[4] These are the kind of things that might be found in prehistoric and protohistoric graves, so that a combination depicted on a stone becomes a memorial that does instead. Thomas went on to propose that the symbols (like grave goods)

Fig. 5.1 *The Craw Stane at Rhynie, Aberdeenshire, featuring a salmon and the Pictish beast. (Source: Tom Gray)*

made statements about the rank and status of the person commemorated on the stone, and the person who remembered them. But the symbols are found alone and in combinations of two, three, four and sometimes more, and they are also used on the Christian cross-slabs. This led Ross Samson to see them as a way of depicting names – like Egyptian hieroglyphs. If each symbol was a syllable, a phoneme, a noise, then the name would emerge from these syllables when run together in combination.[5]

The symbols were incised with wonderfully sure lines on natural boulders and cave walls, and in each case the untreated surface of the rock is used. The shape, the 'personality', of the stone appears to have been important to these carvers. The symbols were also used to 'rebrand' some of the stones in prehistoric monuments. At Crichie in Aberdeenshire, the 'Pictish beast' and the 'crescent and V-rod' are associated with a stone circle, while on the Bronze Age standing stone at Edderton, across the Dornoch Firth from Portmahomack, a salmon and a 'double-disk and Z-rod' may be seen carved halfway up its wider side.

There is some evidence that unshaped symbol-slabs were used to commemorate the dead on round and square barrows, a burial practice that should reach back towards the beginning of the millennium, but direct dating is hard to come by: the stones associated with the burials have often been displaced.[6] Looking at the forms of the symbols, Isabel Henderson, the twentieth century's foremost authority on Pictish art, proposed that they had their origin in the Moray Firth area.[7] In a refinement of this idea, Gordon Murray found that there were different 'origin centres' for different symbols: the crescent and V-rod in the far north, the Z-rod in Aberdeenshire and the Pictish beast in Angus.[8] But this less successfully explains their remarkable uniformity. By current consensus they first appear in the seventh century, or not much earlier than the sixth, and linger until the eighth century or later in Aberdeenshire. That new and exotic symbol, the Christian cross, made its appearance sometime after the mid-sixth century. However, the cross was generally carved, not on natural boulders, but on shaped, smoothed rectangular slabs, in a great variety of sizes.

The Pictish symbols appear together with the Christian symbols by the eighth century and may have continued into the ninth. Lloyd Laing has suggested that symbol-bearing relief sculpture was being erected in the north as late as the tenth century,[9] although, as we have seen, this was not the case at Portmahomack.[10] These new monuments took the form of shaped rectangular slabs, varying from modest grave markers to huge slabs 3m high. The monumental cross-slabs carry, not only the cross and Pictish symbols, but a feast of ornamental and pictorial scenes. They had their descendants too, tall crosses, now without symbols, and laden with heavier more conformist iconography from the churches of Ireland and Alba. Their dating is not, as you might say, set in stone, but it is the stones and the symbols on them that have hitherto provided most of the reasoning. Perhaps the key factors at present are these: the marking of Pictish symbols on rocks carries a prehistoric meaning, and they probably began to appear before Christianity arrived in Pictland. The prehistoric practice continued, especially in Aberdeenshire, alongside the erection of new Christian monuments, carrying the cross. The carvers of the Moray Firth region can claim to be the leading artists of the Picts in their period of greatest originality.

We are now ready to examine the sculpture of Portmahomack and to do what we can to put it into context. How was it made? What forms did it take? What did it mean? Where was it erected – and why? We have over 200 pieces of sculpture, found in two groups: 40 large pieces in the church and churchyard that belonged either to small stone grave markers or to one of three monumental cross slabs (Cross-Slabs A–C); and 160 smaller pieces dumped beyond the churchyard and thought to belong to one monumental cross-slab (Cross D). Elsewhere on the peninsula there were three monumental cross-slabs, at Nigg, Shandwick and Hilton of Cadboll (these are discussed in Chapter 9). None of the Tarbat stones is prehistoric, and we have no certain reports of unshaped stones carrying Pictish symbols such as throng the shores on either side, as at Edderton, Golspie and Burghead. So, although the Tarbat peninsula was surrounded on all sides by signifiers of prehistoric belief, its own monuments were all made in a predominately Christian context.

Sculpture permeates every aspect of the monastery and its landscape, and so makes frequent appearances in this book. The rediscovery of carved fragments in the churchyard, which led archaeologists to Portmahomack in the first place, featured in Chapter 1. The role of the symbols in defining Pictish territory was a factor in the project design described in Chapter 2. The excavation of broken pieces from the monastic workshops is recounted in Chapter 3. The cemetery, which was the original location of the grave markers, is described in Chapter 4. In this chapter I shall review how the sculpture was made and what was depicted on it. Sculpture reappears in Chapter 9 in a discussion about how the major monuments were arranged in the landscape, with particular attention to the sites of Nigg, Shandwick and Hilton. These three great monuments lead us to expect similar cross-slabs at Portmahomack, and we are not to be disappointed. But the Portmahomack collection has other kinds of stone memorial too. More than 225 pieces of carved stone are known so far from the Portmahomack assemblage, and among them five main forms of monument may be distinguished. They are listed, with dimensions, in Digest, A5.

Forms of Sculpture (Table 5.1)

Two flat red stones with scratched crosses are seen as simple grave markers (TR24, TR25; Fig. 5.2). The discovery of similar incised crosses in early Christian contexts on the west coast of Scotland does suggest that such peremptory things could serve as formal memorials.[11] Ten small rectangular flat slabs, carrying the images of crosses incised or in low relief, are interpreted as grave markers. These, too, have close parallels in early Christian sites on the west coast. The unfinished base – for example, of TR33 – suggests that the grave markers stood upright in the ground at one end or the other of a grave (Figs 5.3, 5.4). There are five fragments thought to belong to architectural elements, comprising thin stone panels (TR13, TR17, TR28/35) and a grooved post (TR27). These may have derived from a *cancellum*, the stone fence used to separate sacred space, or they may have been parts of a shrine or panelled sarcophagus. Of the panel fragments, only TR17 (at 25mm) is thin enough to be accommodated in TR27. There was at least one massive stone thought to have been the lid of a

Fig. 5.2   The simple scratched cross on TR24. Height 47cm. (Source: Tom Gray)

Fig. 5.3 The grave marker TR33, found inside the church. Height 52.4 cm.

TARBAT: TR21   IONA   EILEAN NAOIMH   GOVAN

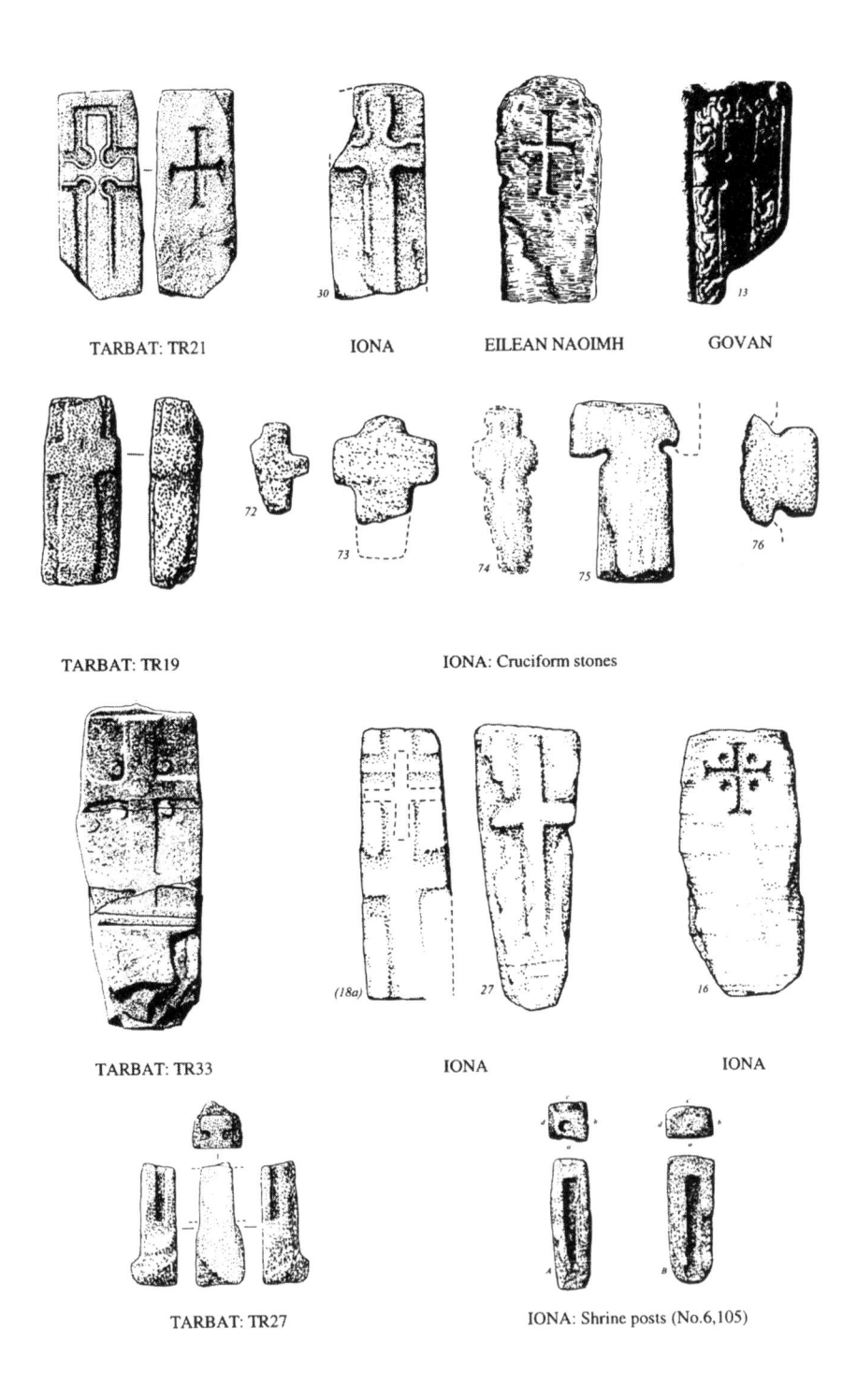

TARBAT: TR19   IONA: Cruciform stones

TARBAT: TR33   IONA   IONA

TARBAT: TR27   IONA: Shrine posts (No.6,105)

Fig. 5.4 Examples of grave markers at Portmahomack and on the west coast of Scotland.

Fig. 5.5 The Calf Stone (TR28/35, detail). (Source: Tom Gray)

sarcophagus (TR22; seen *in situ* in Fig. 3.5). This large block of stone has an animal frieze in recessed panels along one side, seemingly a wild boar and a lion – a third animal being too fragmentary to identify. The running animals show that the block was used in a horizontal position, and the underside of the frieze side has a continuous rebate, like the seating of a lid. The height of the stone appears to vary from one end to the other, suggesting that the top surface slopes with respect to the grooved base.[12] One short side has a cross in low relief. The stone may have been used as an architectural block, in which case it would have had to be placed at a quoin or as an impost for a chancel arch (so that the two adjacent faces were visible). Compared with the greatest of all Pictish lidded monuments, that from St Andrews, this is a simple affair.[13]

Lastly, but of prime importance, there were numerous fragments that had once belonged to monumental cross-slabs, comprising a base with broken tenon (TR1), a top section of a cross-slab (TR20), an inscribed edge from a cross-slab (TR10), a centre panel from a cross-side (TR2), and two central bosses (TR5, TR6). Probably also deriving from cross-slabs are 66 pieces of double-bead moulded border, 11 pieces from panels bearing key pattern, 53 fragments of interlace with strands with a central median line, 2 pieces of tight knotwork and 26 fragments of spirals. Animal ornament features on 6 panels and a human face is depicted on TR201 (Plate 6a), and less certainly on TR223. Also recorded and plotted were another 61 fragments of plain worked stone (see Digest, A5).

The sculpture was incised, or carved in low or high relief, and, in general, the smaller the piece the simpler the technique. The two pieces TR24 and TR25 were little more than scratches on the flat surface of off-cuts. The grave markers, which

Table 5.1 Forms of monument at Portmahomack

Type of monument	Finds
2 simple grave markers	TR24, 25
10 incised, tooled grave markers	TR15, 19, 21, 29, 30, 31, 33, 34, 41, 225
5 fragments belonging to architectural panels	TR13, 17, 27, 28, 35
Sarcophagus lid, carved in relief	TR22, 102, 218
Cross-slabs, base with tenon, carved in relief	TR1
Top section with cross on one side, apostles on the other, carved in relief	TR20
Centre panel with cross, carved in low relief	TR 2
2 central bosses, carved in relief	TR5, 6
Edge panel, with Latin inscription, carved in relief	TR10
66 pieces of double-bead moulded border, carved in high rounded relief	TR 42–90, 93–101, 103–13
11 pieces from panels bearing key pattern, carved in relief	TR8, 49, 61, 62, 63, 69, 72, 73, 86, 87, 88
53 fragments of interlace with strands with a central median line	TR 37, 38, 91, 92, 148, 150–99, 224
2 pieces of tight knotwork	TR14, 149
26 fragments of spirals	TR7, 9, 23, 36, 114–46
6 parts of panels with zoomorphic ornament	TR 204–6, 208–9, 216, 221, 222
2 parts of panels with human face	TR 201, 223
61 plain surfaces	–

measured about 50 × 20 × 5cm thick, were deeply incised with geometrically laid-out crosses (e.g. TR21). The grave markers were made by cleaving the slab, pecking the surface to make it flat and pecking along a scratched pattern line on the surface to make a line, which was then deepened. They were in fact deeply incised, the analogy to high relief, and may have represented a technical debt to the local pre-Christian proficiency exhibited, for example, in Dunrobin 1. The cross-slabs, by contrast, originally rose to sizes in the order of 300 × 100 × 20cm and were carved in relief, sometimes flat, but, in the case of the well-preserved fragments from the workshop, with a rounded profile. Some pieces from cross-slabs bore traces of black and red paint.[14]

SOURCE OF STONE

With one exception, the stone for carving is thought to have been obtained from the peninsula, which has long been famous for the quality of its sandstone beds: 'At

Tarbat-Ness and around it, and in almost every corner of the parish, there is an inexhaustible fund of freestone, easily wrought, durable and of a beautiful colour,' remarked the *First Statistical Account* of 1791, and, more specifically:

> There is a soft freestone at Pitkery, of an inferior quality, in the east end of the parish, but little used; a pretty good freestone at Balintore, a good deal of it used for building; but at Catboll, in the rocky part of the coast, there is a remarkable good freestone, little inferior to any in Scotland.[15]

During his nineteenth-century visit Hugh Miller observed that TR6 and TR8 were cut from pale olive-green sandstone speckled with mica – a stone similar to certain tough flags associated with the shale and fish-beds of the old red sandstone on the southern (eastern) side of the peninsula, chiefly near Geanies. Petrologically, he found TR6 to be identical with both TR1 and TR2. TR7 was cut from the warm yellow sandstone of the tall coastal cliffs near Rockfield village. Shandwick and Hilton of Cadboll, like TR6 and TR8, are of greenish stone. Miller found another stone in the base or pedestal of the Shandwick stone that had anthropomorphic ornament and was of 'warm reddish stone different from all the others'.[16]

In the 1990s geologist Nigel Ruckley used macroscopic examination of fragments and quarry samples, in harness with magnetic susceptibility and thin sectioning. His verdict was that TR10 (the inscription) and TR20 (the Apostle Stone) could have come from the same geological formation, one they shared with all the other monumental stones sited elsewhere on the Tarbat peninsula: Nigg, Shandwick and Hilton of Cadboll (this also applies to the additional flaked fragments recovered at the Hilton chapel in 1998). The sculptor Barry Grove, who made the replicas of TR1 and the Hilton stone, has affirmed that stone of this quality is present on the east side of Tarbat, among the Middle old red sandstone, particularly near Geanies, so endorsing Hugh Miller's verdict of a century ago. Ruckley found the two stone bosses, TR5 and TR6, to have affinities with TR2, and the small fragment of pattern forming TR7 was not thought to have a geological match to TR20. TR2, TR5, TR6 and TR8, on the other hand, appear to belong to stones other than TR20 (the Apostle Stone). Of the pictorial stones, only the Calf Stone was truly local, being made from an old red sandstone of the type found on Portmahomack beach. By contrast, the grave marker TR21 was probably imported. It is composed of clast-free colour-laminated fine-grained sandstone. Although the quarry at Shandwick has reddish laminated sandstones with mica-rich bedding planes, TR21 bore no resemblance to the range of stone in the quarry and does not seem to come from the Tarbat peninsula.[17] These preliminary results suggest that the Tarbat assemblage can be classified into at least four different stone fabrics. The largest and most important cross-slabs, including TR1, TR20 and those at Nigg, Shandwick and Hilton of Cadboll, are made of a fine sandstone likely to come from the Middle old red standstone sources on the east of the peninsula in the neighbourhood of Geanies. The two bosses TR5 and TR6 and the panel TR2 come from another nearby source. The small grave marker TR21 seems to be exotic, and may have been pre-carved elsewhere. The Calf Stone TR28/T35 is the only piece certainly carved from the coarse old red sandstone seen on the beach at Portmahomack itself.

The quarried stone, cut to size with the final product in mind, would have been taken off the cliffs, and in the case of the large cross-slabs this represents a considerable feat of engineering. The replica for TR1, about one-third of the whole, required eight burly diggers to lift and carry it to a vehicle parked by the beach. A full-sized slab, contained in a suitable timber frame, would require two or three dozen persons to carry it to a boat or ox-cart. It would make sense to trim the slab as far as possible on the beach to reduce the weight. The carving might then be done with the slab already erected, and thus with the principal moments of peril to its security already passed.[18] The base of the stone would be fashioned into a tenon, and the tenon inserted in a slot in a large circular slab, a collar stone, which could then be weighted down with stones and buried.[19]

Subjects for Carving

If we leave aside the simpler crosses, of which there will be more presently, the way that the complex picture schemes of the cross-slabs were devised is as intriguing as it is unknowable. The participants must have included, at the least, the patrons who marshalled the manpower, the thinkers whose ideas would represent both local identity and international religious theory and the carver in whom resided the skills for turning them into pictorial stone. Quite a seminar in fact, and, if the voices were evenly balanced, the outcome was certain to be wholly original. The originality of these cross-slabs is in fact startling, reminiscent of the great variety of burial rites in the high-investment cemeteries of another culture.[20] But, as we shall see, lively discussion on commissioning might not be the only reason for such variety.

At least four sources of inspiration can be proposed: the inherited prehistoric ornament of Britain, the language of the Pictish symbols, the everyday sights on the peninsula and the teaching of Christianity. Twentieth-century art historians have tended to raise the Christian sources above all others, and this is still the case for the authors of the current master study on Pictish Art, George and Isabel Henderson. However, as they acknowledge, the majority of Pictish ornament as well as its symbols had their origins in the Iron Age, so references to the beliefs of that era would not be unexpected.

The messages and symbols of Christianity may not now be familiar to all modern readers, so it might be worth recalling some of their character and importance. For the European Dark Ages, Christianity was the big new idea and the major political issue of the day. It offered a unifying philosophy for the new kingdoms then forming in Europe out of the remains of the Roman Empire. Christ was seen, not only as a great moral teacher, but also as the purveyor of the deeper wisdom of the wider (Roman) world which the new-age politicians were anxious to belong to, or which they wanted to reconcile with their local agenda. But in these early times there was no overall political control, and each community, each nascent kingdom, potentially had the freedom to express its own ideas about this world and the next.[21] And in Pictland they did this in stone.

The chief symbol of Christ was the cross on which he was executed by the Roman governor in Palestine (then the Roman Province of Judea) on charges of sedition. Three hundred years later, the Emperor Constantine aligned with

Christianity and adopted the cross on his battle standard and the Chi-rho as his monogram. For Christian philosophers the cross not only signified the triumph of Christ's teaching over the brutality of secular imperialism; it was the instrument of redemption and held the promise of everlasting life in paradise after death. The early Jewish writings collected as the Old Testament were considered as a forerunner of Christ's teaching and the source of prophecies about him, and certain of its ideas and stories became important for the new European Christians. They especially liked King David, not exactly a moral monarch but one who had a direct link to God and generally got his own way on earth: an agreeable role model for the new, post-Roman, kings. Other stories feature great escapes in dramatic circumstances through faith in God: Daniel was thrown into the lions' den, but the lions just licked his feet; Jonah was swallowed by a whale, but came out alive.

In these early times in Scotland the ideas of Christianity were still forming, and there was some leeway for local experiments. But what we learn from the sculpture is how quickly the people of the Tarbat peninsula could embrace the new learning from the far end of the Mediterranean – in all its complexity. We cannot yet explain or understand everything we see on these stones. But we can be confident that *they* could. We are in the presence of great artists of broad learning and deep religious belief. They stood side by side with pragmatic politicians aware of the world they lived in, its perils and prudent alliances. They looked back to a Pictish ancestry and forward to a Christian Empire.

The sculptor has it in mind to marry three professional areas of skill: the layout, which presents a series of frames within an overall symmetrical form, the ornament, which decorates the frame, and the iconography, a picture that transmits a story, a message or a sermon or some mixture of these. The large flat sides of a cross-slab are laid out like the pages of a gospel book, but taller with respect to their width – A4 as opposed to quarto. The proportions are broadly in the ratio of 1:3, but we have very few complete slabs to be sure of this. One side of a cross-slab is given up primarily to a cross, while the other shows Pictish symbols and figurative scenes. The smooth surfaces are divided up into panels that may be square or in the ratio 1:2 (see, for example, the back face of Shandwick). The frame may be in continuous strips, like the back face of Hilton and TR1, or be formed of panels, like the back face of Nigg. Panels within the frame may show Pictish symbols or pictorial scenes, or be wholly dedicated to ornament.

The ornament used is like a vocabulary, and its principal descriptive phrases are key or fret pattern, interlace and spirals, while TR1 features a notable border of inhabited vine scroll. These all feature in the broader Tarbat group of sculpture and find wide application in insular art, being noted in Ireland, Western Scotland, Southern Pictland and Northumbria.[22] *Fret pattern* is composed of interlocking ribs of stone forming a geometric maze. Where the pattern is arranged in squares, it recalls the lands of keys and may be referred to as key pattern (e.g. Fig. 5.8).[23] The majority of the Portmahomack fret pattern is formed of ribs 10mm wide[24] and is well represented in the area – for example, on Rosemarkie 1 and 2 and Shandwick. The fret pattern on TR6 is not found on any other Pictish stone, but it is closely related to patterns that occur on Nigg and Hilton of Cadboll, as well as on folio 2ᵛ (a canon table) of the *Book of Kells*.[25]

The *interlace* pattern on TR2 is quite similar to that found on the central panel of the cross-head on the Nigg slab.[26] But the principal interlace in the Glebe Field assemblage (and confined to it) consists of ribs 20–30mm wide with a central median line along the strand (e.g. Fig. 5.9). This *double-beaded interlace* seems to belong generally to the later period (late eighth–ninth centuries) and to denote Anglian influence.[27] *Spirals* are much used on Nigg, Hilton of Cadboll and Shandwick, and at Portmahomack there are numerous examples (TR128, TR130, TR144 and TR145).[28] *Peltae* forming C-shaped connections between spirals and terminating in smaller spirals of their own can be found on Nigg and Shandwick as well as on numerous monuments elsewhere.[29] In general, spiral and peltae connections are found on carved stones throughout Pictland, Dal Riada and Ireland, and the motif seems to be a typically 'Celtic' one, not generally appearing on Anglo-Saxon monuments. It has its roots in Iron Age ornamental metalwork, and spiral designs are also prolific on 'Celtic' metalwork from the sixth–ninth centuries, appearing on both secular and religious objects.[30] At Portmahomack a fondness for spirals in particular connects the stone-carvers with the metal-workers (see Chapter 6).

It is highly likely that the layout of spirals and interlace involved some learned symbolic geometry. Michelle Brown shows how the design of areas of spiral work on some pages of the Lindisfarne Gospels is based on a square quartered by two ruled diagonal lines forming an X. A compass mark is made at X and a circle is drawn.[31] The central motif for Carpet Page f. 94ᵛ is based both on a grid of sixteen units square and a circle of eight units. Further grids and circles are used to guide spirals.[32] Some metalwork (for example, the Hunterston brooch) seems to have been laid out on the same principles, and the tidy symmetry of the Tarbat ornament demands a similar geometrical discipline. An example is provided by the square lower panel of Shandwick (obverse), with its four segments of twelve spirals apiece. In the next chapter, I make similar claims of mathematical learning for Portmahomack's architects (see Chapter 6).

Carved stone bosses with decorative relief (cf. TR5, TR6; see Fig. 1.3) can be found on the cross-heads of St John's and St Martin's crosses at Iona.[33] They have obvious ties to metalwork, especially to the raised metalwork bosses found on Irish shrines, characterised by a central jewel or smooth metalwork stud and surrounded by filigree wreaths. The specific relationship with the metalwork bosses on reliquary shrines might be significant, as it has been suggested that certain cross-slabs, especially those with a particularly 'metallic' appearance, might have functioned as types of public reliquaries reflecting the appearance of specific metalwork shrines more privately located within ecclesiastical centres.[34]

The Glebe Field assemblage is also distinguished by a large number of edge-pieces or borders, which indicate the angle between two faces of a cross-slab (Fig. 5.10). There is a small group of five pieces that have a single moulding that is broad and shallow, 40–60mm wide (TR100, TR101, TR109, TR111, TR113). This matches the top edge of the Apostle Stone (TR20), which is 50mm wide. Some of these border pieces join to key pattern, others to spiral pattern, so some association between these few Glebe Field pieces and TR20 may be assumed. However, the majority of the border pieces have mouldings 15 or 30mm wide.[35] These are not matched by the other Tarbat cross-slabs, but can be seen on the Dupplin shaft (back face), where the inner narrow moulding is used to contain the panels (Fig. 5.11).[36] So it looks as though these pieces come from a different monument, and perhaps even one of a different type: a cross-shaft, as opposed to a cross-slab.

The *types of crosses* in the Portmahomack collection range from the simple scratch marks of TR24 and TR25 (Fig. 5.2), to the elaborate saltire cross to be proposed for TR20 (Fig. 5.7). Simple incised crosses occur in profusion on Iona.[37] The incised and low relief crosses seen at Portmahomack occur in similar forms on similar grave markers at the known monasteries of Iona, Whitby, Hartlepool and Govan. The two-bar Patriarchal cross of TR33 suggested to Kellie Meyer that the ceremony of *Adoratio crucis* was probably practised there. *The saltire cross* proposed for TR20 (see below) finds some echoes in illuminated manuscripts (the Book of Kells and the Book of Deer), which use the diagonal form to divide a page.[38] The form is associated with St Andrew, but the origin of the association is obscure. Meyer derives the form from the *chi-rho*, the initials of Christ's name in Greek, as re-employed by Constantine for the Roman imperial standard.

The Latin inscription on TR10 is the longest so far known from Pictland (see Fig. 1.4). It is composed in insular majuscules and rendered in low relief. The lettering is closely connected to that of the Lindisfarne Gospels, suggesting that a similar codex was present at Portmahomack.[39] The inscription has been read: [I]N NOM[IN]E IHU X[PI] CRUX XPI [IN] COM[MEM]ORA[TIO]NE REO[. . .]LII [. . . D]IE HA[C . . .], translated as 'In the name of Jesus Christ, the/a Cross of Christ in memory of Reo[. . .]lius . . . on this day . . .' Allen and Anderson note the suggestion that the person referred to was Reothaide or Reodaide, whose death is recorded under the year 762 or 763 at a place called 'Ab. Ferna', but this association has been discounted.[40] This piece of stone is now seen as part of the large cross-slab that included TR20.

The *vine scroll* may be treated as an iconographic as well as an ornamental theme, since it refers to the Eucharist.[41] For this, or for decorative reasons, the vine scroll decorates priestly vestments such as the stole and chasuble. The scroll that appears as a border on TR1 closely resembles that on Hilton of Cadboll, so it is possible that both drew on a similar set of embroidery.

Pictish symbols are clearest on TR1, where they are rendered in relief along one edge. Four symbols may be identified, which are (in descending order) the crescent and V-rod, the sword or 'tuning fork', the snake and Z-rod and the Pictish beast. The analogy in execution and location between the symbols and the Latin inscription on TR10 suggest that both had similar function, the memory of a named individual.[42] The Pictish symbols are seen further in Baroque magnificence on Hilton and Shandwick. We can note at this stage that, whatever the symbols mean, these four cross-slabs, similar in many other ways, each carry a different set of symbols (Fig. 5.6). If the symbols are names, then a different person was celebrated at each monument.

A number of animals, real and imaginary, were fashioned by the Portmahomack carvers. For Meyer, the family of cattle portrayed on TR28/35 is a 'holy family'

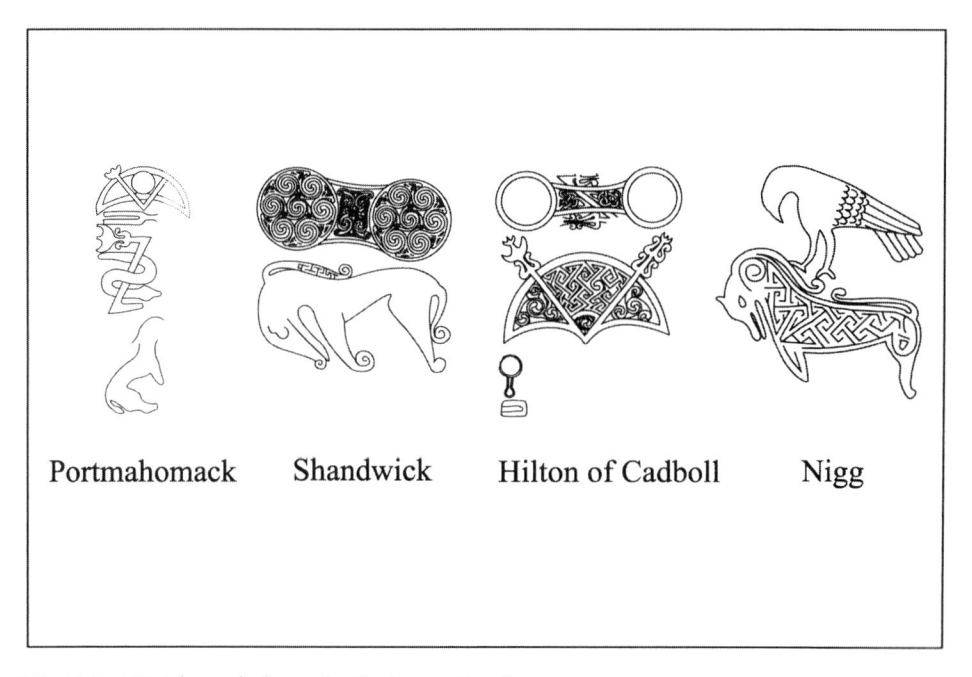

Fig. 5.6 Pictish symbols on the Tarbat peninsula.

representing the old and new covenants. A frowning animal head (TR206) might represent an architectural label stop as at Deerhurst. The Hendersons suggest that it might have served as the terminal knob for a stone chair back, as depicted on the slab at Kirriemuir 1.[43] Beasts chosen for their fierce temperaments were celebrated as having been tamed by Christ. Serpents (TR2), which signify death, are overcome. The 'dragon' on TR20 may also have been brought into the service of the cross. The lion and the boar that occupy adjacent niches on TR22 are noble beasts, denoting royalty. A bird (on TR218) echoes the theme of nobility, since the falcon, eagle or bird of prey has been shown to have been adopted by the Byzantine and European aristocracy in the seventh century.[44]

Animals perform allegorical or metaphorical roles at Portmahomack in other more elaborate iconographic schemes. Distressed animals menaced by composite beasts (as on TR28/T35) are seen as signifying aspects of the world's terror, which Christ can control.[45] On TR1, the damaged figurative scene is interpreted by Meyer as Daniel in the lion's den, a strong redemption theme (see Fig. 1.2). The scene on the upper register of the back face of TR20 features two lions disputing or sharing the half-carcass of a deer, while a bear slinks to the top right (Plate 2b). For Meyer this is a reference to sheep in peril in 1 Samuel 17: 34–7, a text that also mentions a bear; the scene would be followed by David rending the lion's jaw. For the Hendersons, the tableau illustrates Genesis 15: 9–11, where Abraham obeys God's command to make an offering of a heifer, a goat and a ram, dividing them 'per medium'.[46]

The lower register of TR20, back, shows four clerical figures. For the Hendersons these recall the apostles on the Cuthbert coffin, and the identification of apostles is

Fig. 5.7 Model of the form of Cross C, by Elizabeth Hooper. Estimated size 3 × 1m.

endorsed by the recognition of St Andrew from his heavy dishevelled hair, as portrayed on a sixth-century mosaic at Ravenna.[47] The left-hand figure has lower shoulders, so may be seated; and a nimbus, so may be Christ. But the right-hand figure stands at the edge of the stone, so this would imply a representation of Christ and six apostles. However, our reconstruction prefers twelve apostles in a row, for the reasons given below.

The Portmahomack assemblage thus should have included a number of elaborate cross-slabs, grave markers marked with plain crosses, architectural elements with animal carvings, a decorated shrine or *cancellum* and a sarcophagus lid. Pictorial schemes are set either as 'landscape' pictures where they belong to panels of a shrine or cancellum, or 'portrait images, where they are likely to have belonged to cross-slabs. The large number of thick fragments worked in high relief suggests that the cross-slab formed the main subject of investment at Portmahomack. They featured the cross together with sophisticated metaphorical and biblical imagery. In this, and in the detail of their ornament, they resemble the surviving cross-slabs at Nigg, Shandwick and Hilton of Cadboll.

FORM AND LOCATION OF THE PORTMAHOMACK MONUMENTAL CROSSES

Let us now consider the likely number and form of cross-slabs at Portmahomack and where they may have stood. Reporting on its visit of 1903, the Inverness Scientific Society supposed the churchyard at Portmahomack to have contained three monuments, basing this apparently on the sighting of TR1, TR6 and TR7. We addressed the same question with the benefit of a much larger assemblage, and came to almost the same conclusion. We compared the geology of the fragments, their ornament and the places they were found in the ground. The investigation proceeded by testing for three cross-slabs (named A, B and C) based on the three large 'parent pieces', TR1, TR2 and TR20, and a fourth (named D), based on the Glebe Field edge-pieces. All these ostensibly derived from different monuments. The results are summarised in Table 5.2.

Slab A survives as the base TR1, and finds its principal echo in Hilton of Cadboll, which it must have resembled. Like Hilton, it is lacking its cross-side. No fragment of its vine scroll has been identified among the pieces recovered elsewhere, and it must be supposed that the upper half of TR1 and the pieces of its cross-side lie buried somewhere in the churchyard. Slab B incorporates TR2, TR5 and TR6, implying a cross-slab decorated with fine interlace and two bosses. The reconstruction for Slab C (Fig. 5.7) is based on Elizabeth Hooper's model for TR20 and probably incorporates TR9, TR10, TR14, TR40 and TR201. Its reasoning starts from the arc of stone seen on the 'dragon' side, which if drawn into a complete circle implies a diameter of about 1m and a consequent width for the slab of about 1.1m. The row of four clerics is 15cm across and thus there is room in the anticipated width for twelve or even thirteen figures side by side. The inscribed stone (TR10) is related to TR20 by virtue of the square rib containing spiral ornament that features on one side. A symmetrical place could be found for it on the opposite side of the supposed cross. Assuming a ratio of 1:3, Cross-Slab C would be 3m tall. We have only glimpses of the scenes and

Fig. 5.8 Fragments of Cross D in situ, scattered over the demolished workshops.

ornaments that adorned Cross-Slab D, but the borders suggest that it took the form of a cross-shaft. In the ongoing work of reconstruction, we therefore look for our models to the Dupplin Cross and St Andrews No. 14.[48]

The original siting of the major early medieval monuments may be deduced by the secondary contexts in which they were found (see Fig. 4.8): some had been reused in the foundations of the early church, others were found in a single deposit in the Glebe

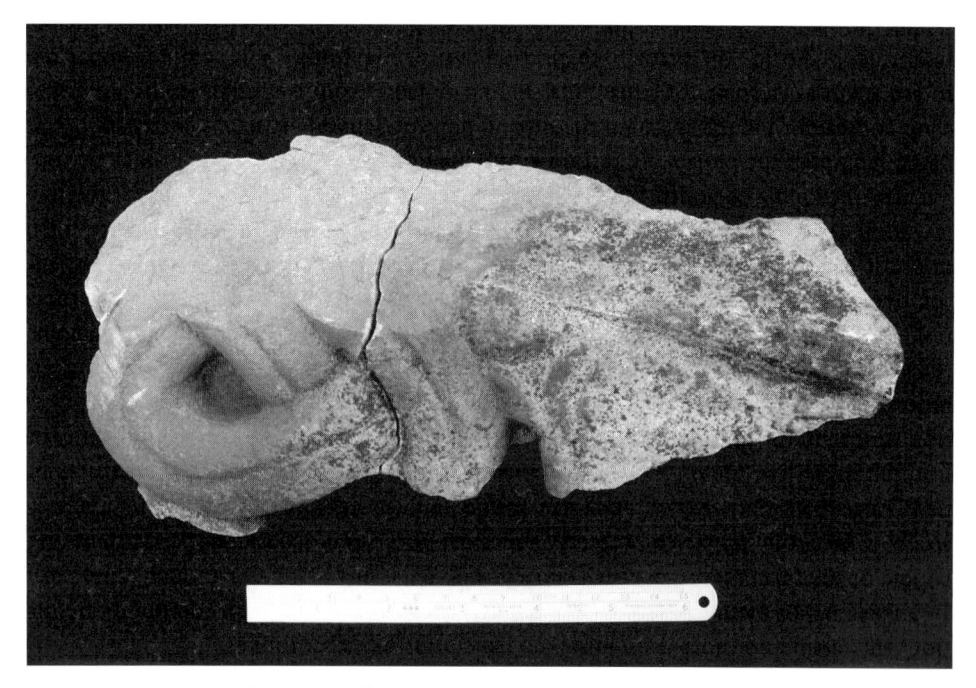

Fig. 5.9 Fragment of Cross D, showing double strand interlace. The scale is 15cm long.

Field, others in the graveyard and further afield. The degree of recycling could be estimated to some extent by the traces of earlier mortar and the amount of weathering. Our own observations could be reconciled with those of early visitors to Portmahomack churchyard (see Chapter 1). TR1 (Cross-Slab A) was found near the Dingwall memorial. TR2 (Cross-Slab B, the so-called Danish Cross) stood on a green mound east of the church. Hugh Miller junior, who checked these observations on the ground shortly after the OS Map was published, remarked of these two finds: 'The positions allotted to them were no doubt guess-work,'[49] since they were not then standing and the locations relied on local memory. However, the Dingwall memorial still stands, and the green mound can still be seen.

The parts of Cross-Slab C were well scattered, ending up in the foundations of the parish church and in the garden wall of the manse. Some pieces of it also seem to have been included in the Glebe Field dump, which implies that it was felled at the same time as the dump was formed, and that larger pieces were lying about the churchyard and available for recycling when the parish church was built at the end of the eleventh century (see Chapter 8). Other things being equal, it should have stood originally on the north or west side of the churchyard. The Cross-Slab D fragments are known only from the Glebe Field, so should have stood near to it.

THE SEQUENCE

The placement of stone crosses at the edge of a monastic precinct is a concept familiar in Ireland, as the *termon*[50] and a likely way to signal the entrance into sacred

Fig. 5.10   Corner of the shaft of Cross D.

space. This deployment represents a hypothetical moment towards the end of the monastery's life in the later eighth century, shortly after which sacred carving ceased. Does all the sculpture belong to this time? Was there an evolution of technique, of investment? A historical vision of the establishment of a Columban monastery might

Fig. 5.11 *The Dupplin Cross. (Source: Historic Scotland)*

Table 5.2 Associations with hypothetical cross-slabs

Parent piece	Location	Geological associations	Stylistic associations
TR1 Slab A	East of Slab B	TR4; TR6 (Miller); TR7?	TR17
TR2 Slab B 'Danish Cross'	East of Church	TR5, 6, 8	
TR20 Slab C	West of Church	TR10, 20; not TR7; TR9, TR14, TR40	TR7, TR12, TR18, TR32, TR39; TR201 (face of apostle)
Slab D	West of Church		TR42–119

Fig. 5.12 Fragments from the Portmahomack corpus being studied at York.

feature ill-equipped pioneers whose first efforts at memorials would be primitive. In that case, the uncut stone pieces carrying crude scratched crosses (TR24, TR25) would be among the first to be placed on graves. But the earliest sculpture is not necessarily the simplest. Other arguments might suggest that the earliest memorials would be of high quality, associated with the mother house and worthy to provide an example for those that came after. The earliest burials, for example, are constructed as cists with large slabs, while the later use more peremptory tokens – small stones set beside the head. Such early exemplars might be expected to carry incised geometric crosses or hexafoils on well-finished slabs,[51] and hollow-armed incised crosses: TR30 and TR31 might be considered candidates. Grave marker TR21 carries a particularly suggestive 'dug-out' cross on its nether side – suggestive in view of the many parallels known from Iona and its neighbourhood.[52] The fact that this stone in particular is foreign to the Tarbat peninsula, or even to the Moray Firth area is not without significance. There is a logic in some of the very earliest cross-slabs having to be imported into an area that had yet to see them. This reasoning would separate the products of the carvers by function rather than by date. The smaller crosses marked graves, some humbly, others with trappings of seniority or sanctity. Set apart from these are the monumental cross-slabs, which have a more public role. They appear to carry names, and may remember the recently deceased. But it is argued in Chapter 9 that the grand cross-slabs commemorate holy persons long dead, displaying anecdotes and allegories relating to their lives: in brief, they are history, or hagiography, designed to deepen the local roots of the Christian project.

The results from the excavation of the Glebe Field show that Cross-Slab D, and arguably Cross-Slab C, must have been carved before 830, and perhaps before 780. It seems probable that the whole assemblage had also been fashioned by that time. On the basis of the ornament, the symbols, the inscription and their obvious grandeur, it can also be proposed that the four cross-slabs at Portmahomack, together with those at Nigg, Shandwick and Hilton of Cadboll, are broadly contemporary products of the later eighth century. They represent a level of investment and a sophistication of thought that leave us in no doubt of the importance of the peninsula in this, its age of fame.

Notes

1. Aitchison (1999: 185).
2. Mackenzie (1977).
3. The Petty Stone, which marked the boundary between the estates of Moray and Culloden and weighed at least 8 tons, was in 1799 disobligingly lifted by a sheet of ice and deposited 260yd (*c.* 240m) into the Moray Firth.
4. Thomas (1961; 1963)
5. Samson (1992); see also Henderson and Henderson (2004: 59–75).
6. Ashmore (1980).
7. Henderson (1958); see also Henderson and Henderson (2004).
8. Murray (1986).
9. Laing (2000).
10. As shown in Chapter 3, the Portmahomack cross-slabs should have been carved before 830, and probably before 780.
11. Fisher (2001: 28).
12. Henderson and Henderson (2004: 40).
13. Foster (1998); Nadine Alpino, University of Kiel, on a visit to the Centre on 23 July 2002, proposed TR22 as an altar. However, the rebate on the base, which appears to be primary, and the slight taper do suggest that this heavy monolith was the lid of a coffin.
14. Seven pieces were noted as having traces of red pigment (TR149, 160, 162, 163, 164, 171, 181). These were all examples of interlace. They were distinguished from 'reddening by heat', and no example featured both. Unlike the other coloration, this can be attributed to painting on the original monument.
15. *FSA* 652, 381.

16. Miller (1889: 441).
17. Ruckley and Carver (1998).
18. This is the view of the sculptor Barry Grove, who experienced both procedures when making the Hilton replica, one side being carved recumbent and the other with the stone installed and upright.
19. James (2005).
20. Carver (2001).
21. See, e.g., Brown (1997) and chapters in Carver (2003b).
22. What follows has been much informed by studies of sculpture from the Tarbat peninsula by Kellie Meyer.
23. See Henderson and Henderson (2004: 23, ill. 16) for the difference between key and fret terminology.
24. It corresponds to *ECMS* II, pattern no. 974; cf. Kinneddar 14, *ECMS* III. 149.
25. *ECMS* II, nos 1020 and 1022; Meyer, pers. comm.
26. *ECMS* II. 281, no. 708; III, fig. 74.
27. E.g. Whithorn 5, 6, 7 and locality (*ECMS* III. 481–91); Govan 1 (*ECMS* III. 462); St Andrews 31, 15 (*ECMS* III. 363), Abernethy, Kirriemuir 3, Benvie, Glamis, Drainie (Kinneddar) 10.
28. *ECMS* II, nos 1078, 1079.
29. E.g. St Vigeans; pattern nos. 1051–5, 1066–71, in *ECMS* III. 389–90.
30. Youngs (1989).
31. Brown (2003: 295).
32. Ibid. pp. 295–7, 223.
33. Fisher (2001: 132–3).
34. Henderson (1993: 216).
35. Allen and Anderson call this a double-bead moulded border (*ECMS*, vol. 1, p. 86).
36. Henderson and Henderson (2004: 191, ill. 278).
37. Fisher (2001).
38. Henderson and Henderson (2004: 218).
39. Higgitt (1982: 310–15); Henderson (2004: 216).
40. *ECMS* III. 95.
41. Henderson and Henderson (2004: 29, 138).
42. cf. Samson (1992).
43. Henderson and Henderson (2004: 211–12).
44. Akerström-Hougen (1981).
45. Henderson and Henderson (2004: 85).
46. Ibid. p. 142.
47. Ibid. pp. 146–7 and n. 131; Bailey (1996: 58–9); Meyer considers the identification of apostles as likely, and refers to the association of this motif with baptismal sites following Lang (1999).
48. *ECMS* III. 319, 358.
49. Miller (1889: 438n.).
50. Davies (1996); Ó'Carragáin (2003b).
51. Fisher (2001: 27–32).
52. Ibid. pp. 28–32.

CHAPTER 6

Architects and artisans

In the sacred precinct of the monastery on the hill top, we have seen a rise in the quantity and quality of archaeological evidence in the late seventh and eighth centuries (Period 2): an increase in the number of burials, the possible building of a stone church and the erection of large carved stone monuments. Beyond this centre, in our Sector 2 and Sector 1, there was also change at that time: redevelopment on a massive scale. The movement of earth and stones was prodigious and not easy to break down into phases. However, contradictions can be minimised by assuming that most of the redevelopment began at the same time, towards the end of the seventh century (Digest, A3). The first action was probably to dam the streams that ran through the marsh in the valley bottom (Fig. 3.14). The dam was constructed of dumped clay and stones, and capped and faced with large blocks of sandstone. Immediately to the east of the dam, the water soon started to back up, creating a pool some 50m across. Water from the pool was led over or through the dam by means of a couple of culverts; the more northerly was well fashioned with faced stone sides, a smooth flat sloping stone bottom and a lid of broad thin slabs. At the western face of the dam it was provided with two opposing slots, into which a stone slab could fit, thus providing a sluice (Fig. 6.1; see Digest, A6, for numbered data).

Meanwhile a drystone terrace wall was constructed east–west along the valley side and adjoining the dam, protecting the land further up-slope to the north from flooding (F149). Leading to this wall from the north was a road (Road 1), paved with sandstone slabs founded on a causeway of sand, gravel and stones, and provided with roadside ditches (F469, F471, F472). Where the road met the terrace wall, it had a special deep foundation of large, roughly horizontal slabs (context 3619). A person standing on this platform would look down onto the culvert flowing at this point between edges of broad upright slabs of sandstone. Beyond the culvert was a box resembling a cistern, about 2m square also formed by slabs edge-on (Fig. 6.2; see also Plates 4a and b). It seems probable that these arrangements were intended to provide and conserve water, according to season, and that it was water that the paved road gave access to. The dam and the pool, and the dumping in the pool of numerous hand querns, implied that a water mill was built at the same time – but it did not materialise in our excavations. If it existed, it should lie further down the slope towards the sea (see Chapter 3, p. 62).

The date of these operations was given by radiocarbon: the latest layer of the marsh and the earliest layer of the pool came in at 590–720, and bone from under the west terrace wall at 630–780. These are consistent with a start at the end of the

Fig. 6.1   The culvert (F431) leading from the pool.

seventh or the beginning of the eighth century. The new water-management system had replaced the old, the wells, gullies and cisterns of which were soon buried by a levelling operation. Sand, gravel and turf was taken from the top of the hill and dumped at the bottom. What had been created was a dry, well-drained zone with a road running through and constant access to fresh water. On either side of this road there developed an artisan quarter, dedicated to the processing of cattle hides and the making of vellum. Let us call this the Northern Quarter.

Further south on the other side of the valley there were also developments that can be similarly assigned to our Period 2. The early inner enclosure ditch was filled in and another one (the outer enclosure ditch) was dug 10m or so further out (southwards), enclosing more land. It is likely that operations here had begun with a comprehensive stripping of all the turf, since the traces of up-cast from the new ditch lay directly on the subsoil (F154, at first thought to be a rampart). The ditch had been cut through sand and boulder clay to a depth of nearly 2m, and it was equipped with a wattle-work revetment halfway up to stop it fouling up with sand from the sides. It collected and held water to the top of the boulder clay and was presumably intended to distribute it to the rest of the monastic community and its animals. On the inner edge of this new ditch, and over the top of the previous one, another artisan quarter, the Southern Quarter, got going. This one was making objects of glass and precious metals.

Fig. 6.2 The road leading to the terrace wall, culvert and cistern.

These two quarters, roughly contemporary in radiocarbon years, were part of a late-seventh-century major investment by people who had come to stay, flourish and expand. Their achievement was to be glorious, but brief. By the later part of the eighth century both quarters had come to an end. Visiting each of these busy areas in turn, we shall see evidence of design talent and technical know-how everywhere, some of it familiar from other sites or neighbouring countries, and some recognisable only from modern craft analogies. And in some cases we are obliged to draw judiciously on the imagination.

THE NORTHERN QUARTER

On some unsettled Tarbat day in the late seventh century, with seagulls screaming overhead, we can imagine senior members of the community standing at the edge of the cemetery admiring the creation of their artisan quarter. They stand near the mounds and stone kerbs of burials, which are not to be disturbed but provide a northern limit to the new production zone. On the levelled surface on the west side of the new road, a crust of fine white sand was laid down (context 2353). At the north end was a tank or stone-lined trough (S4) running north-west/south-east, 5.1m in length, with a covered culvert evacuating liquid to the south-west (Fig. 6.3). Originally another culvert had introduced water from the north, but at some stage this had been blocked off with a much-decayed sandstone plug. The areas on both the long sides

Fig. 6.3 The tawing tank (S4), looking east.

of the tank were tightly paved with stone and pebbles. The slabs of the tank were stained green, and its sides were rotted and flaking. Something wet, possibly wet and nasty, was happening here, raising thoughts of latrines and washhouses. In the absence of chemical residues, the eventual interpretation depended heavily on the context given by neighbouring activities, the nature of which was to emerge from evidence recovered further south.

Adjacent to S4 and separated from it only by a fragment of further paving was the zone that came to be recognised as that of a large timber building S9 (Fig. 6.4). This area was very disturbed by the digging of later periods, notably the huge medieval rubbish pit driven through its centre (F13). However, the association of wall fragments and post-pits with an elaborate hearth and a distribution of very particular objects (including those retrieved in later phases) together create a credible structure.[1] The key features are a fragmentary wall and a ditch, both providing a curving boundary to the north, and a southern wall that gives a rather fuller account of itself. These walls consisted of pieces of rubble set in a matrix of silty sand. Dark soils and ash over the south wall implied a turf superstructure, some of it burnt in the great fire that came later. Between these two walls clustered twenty-one post-holes that could have been structural, many showing evidence that the post had been removed. The hearth was slab-lined, with a kerb on either side (and probably on the north side too originally). In addition, flat stones on either side provided adjacent working surfaces. Numerous stake-holes around the hearth tell of structures to suspend or to smoke something, or perhaps for a lume to guide smoke upwards. Burnt daub was found in

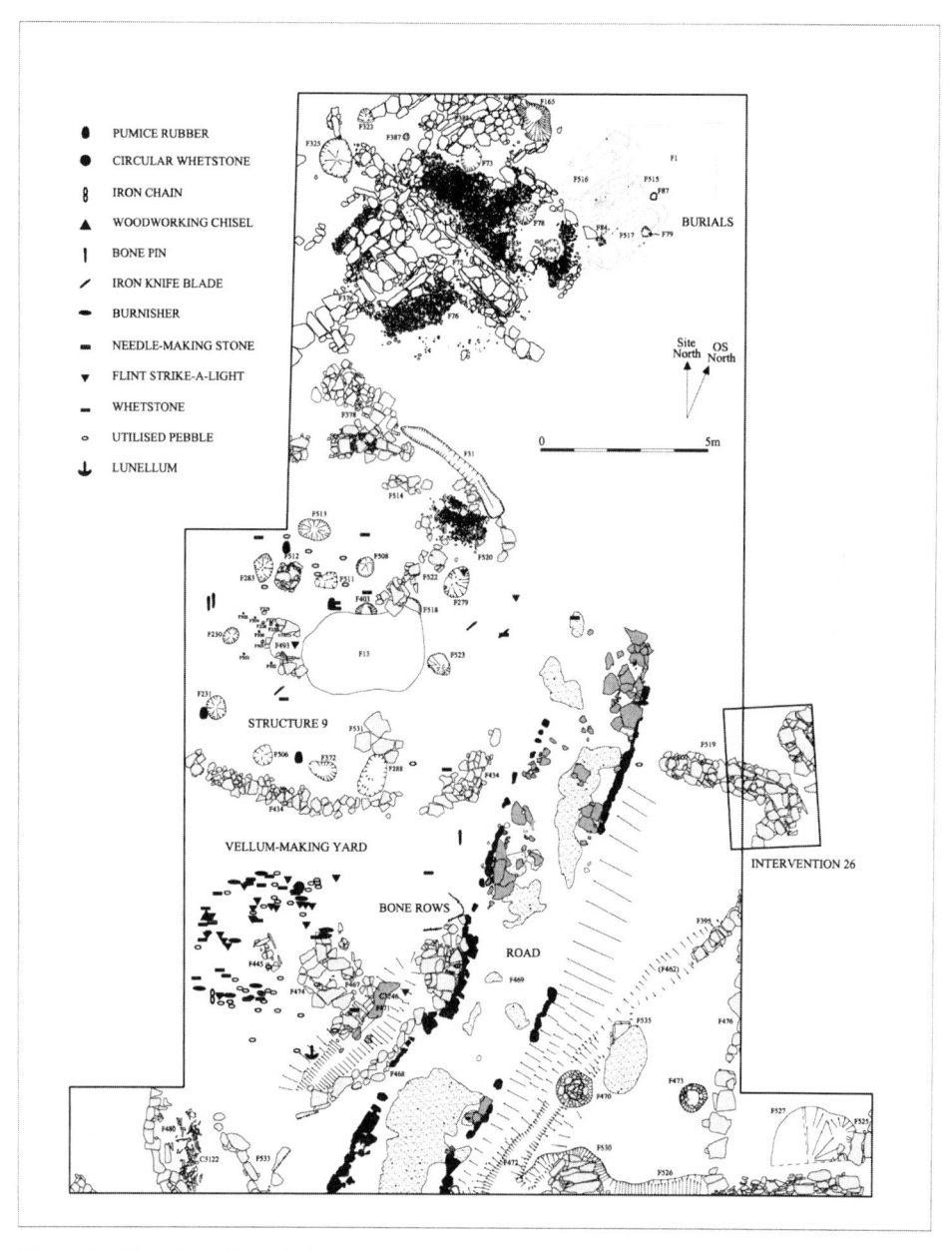

Fig. 6.4 S9 and yard, finds distribution.

the area. The building was too battered by later features to be sure of its plan, but reasons will soon be given for seeing it as bow-ended, with the round end facing east.

Immediately south of this building was a 'yard', a space defined between the road and the west terrace wall. This area also had a central hearth, formed of four large slabs of stone forming a three-sided burning area open to the south-west, with originally a fireback to the north-east. Apart from a fragmentary area of hard standing,

Fig. 6.5 Cattle bones (metapodials) set in rows at right angles. Scale 1m.

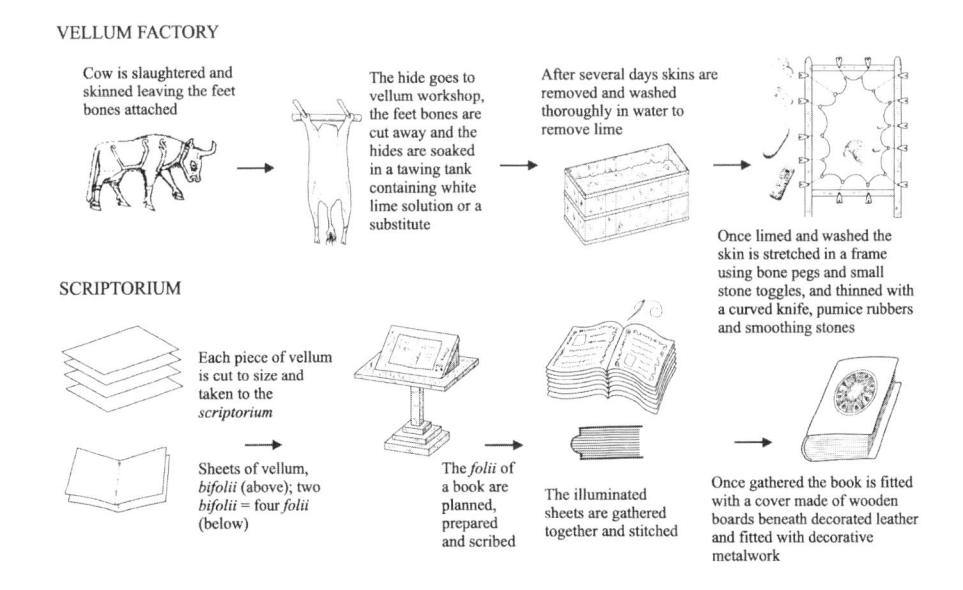

VELLUM FACTORY

Cow is slaughtered and skinned leaving the feet bones attached

The hide goes to vellum workshop, the feet bones are cut away and the hides are soaked in a tawing tank containing white lime solution or a substitute

After several days skins are removed and washed thoroughly in water to remove lime

Once limed and washed the skin is stretched in a frame using bone pegs and small stone toggles, and thinned with a curved knife, pumice rubbers and smoothing stones

SCRIPTORIUM

Each piece of vellum is cut to size and taken to the *scriptorium*

Sheets of vellum, *bifolii* (above); two *bifolii* = four *folii* (below)

The *folii* of a book are planned, prepared and scribed

The illuminated sheets are gathered together and stitched

Once gathered the book is fitted with a cover made of wooden boards beneath decorated leather and fitted with decorative metalwork

Fig. 6.6 Model of the vellum-making process.

this zone was also defined by a layer of well-trodden sand, rich in finds. The use of the building S9 and its yard comes alive with the character and distribution of these objects (see Plate 7a). Scattered inside the building were 6 pebbles, 3 pumice rubbers, 2 iron knives, 8 whetstones and 2 ivory pins (from later contexts). Its hearth had early fills that included winkles and a later fill containing a flint strike-a-light. Dropped in the yard were a crescent-bladed knife, a pumice rubber, a circular whetstone, a fragment of iron chain, a wood-working chisel (with ferrified wood flakes), 10 burnishing stones, a needle-sharpening stone, 19 flint strike-a-lights, 18 whetstones, 42 white or red pebbles and numerous cattle metapodials. Some of these bones had been sharpened to a point, and they were sometimes found parked in rows, making a V or two sides of a square (Fig 6.5; see also Plate 5b). There were also pits containing winkles and dog whelks, and two piles of ash that microscopic analysis revealed to have contained the tiny shells of *spirobis*, a shellfish that lives on seaweed.

By drawing comparisons with modern crafts, Cecily Spall deduced that the people who occupied S9 and its yard were engaged in preparing vellum, a parchment made from calf and cattle hide widely used in insular gospel books or codices of the early Middle Ages (Fig. 6.6).[2] The hide, which comes in still attached to the feet (the distal metapodials), must be washed and scraped of its blood and gore, and then preserved by soaking in an astringent liquid. Leathers are often tanned in oak bark, but parchment, needing to end up white, is soaked in an alkaline solution, such as alum (aluminium potassium sulphate) or lime (calcium oxide – obtained by burning limestone). In the absence of local limestone, the alkali used by the Tarbat community was taken from the sea shore – the shells of winkles and whelks and *spirorbis* clinging to seaweed. When burnt in a reducing atmosphere (for example, by being smothered in turf), the calcium carbonates in the shells can be reduced to lime. Into this solution the hides were given a preliminary dunking to loosen the hairs and partly to rot the flesh. We imagine the washing, sluicing and splashing, and then the dunking in lime taking place in S4. The skins would then need to be scraped and thinned using a variety of knives, kept sharp by whetstones. This part of the operation probably took place within the building S9. There the vellum-workers could also use heat, to keep the skins supple, and perhaps to singe the hairs that did not fall off so quickly by lime action. The stone and clay lump north of the hearth (F512) would make a good hard surface for scraping, defleshing and dehairing. The thinner, cleaner skins could then be returned to the tank for more serious immersion leading to their preservation.

Hides soaked in this solution are not tanned but tawed, preserved white. After a sufficient load of skins had been tawed, or when the solution had lost its potency, the tank could be emptied via the culvert and the process could start again. The tawed skins would be passed back through S9, for more finishing, and then out into the yard for stretching and pouncing. To make parchment, a hide is stretched on a wooden frame, by means of thongs attached to the corners and the edges. However, parchmenters do not make a hole in the hide, since the hole will draw under tension into a great gash. Instead the corners are wrapped around a little pebble, and the corner bound with a leather thong. The other end of the thong is secure to a peg (in our case a cattle metapodial), which is then rotated like a guitar peg. In this way the hide is put under balanced tension, until it is as tight as a drum. Then the surface must be prepared for writing. It is rubbed with a variety of abrasive stones to smooth the surface, and scraped or shaved with the curved knife – the *lunellarium* – the shape of which allows the surface of the hide to be pushed down without getting itself cut. If there is a gash, the expensive hide (the skin of a calf or cow) can be rescued with needle and thread. A fire was evidently of importance here, too: maybe for the creation of seaweed ash (two piles were found). But heat could have been important for drying and hardening the parchment. Twenty flint strike-a-lights show that the hearths were frequently relit. A covered heating duct or flue was introduced at some stage in the life of the yard, along the line of the roadside ditch (F468/F475).

The lined-up rows of bones, pushed into the ground, may have been waiting their turn to be used as pegs, or, in the case of the rectangular setting, have indicated the form of the frame. Bone-rows have been seen before but fitted to more numinous explanations. At Bornais, Niall Sharples felt that the rows of cattle metacarpals and metatarsals were patterned within arcs and alignments that 'would have taken some considerable thought' and thus ought to carry a symbolic meaning.[3] Jacqui Mulville and her colleagues felt that the practice was a signal of some changing relationship with animals; animal bone was buried in pits in the earlier Iron Ages, but from the third to the fifth centuries selected animal bones were arranged in the ground in settlements, especially around hearths.[4] Our explanation is perhaps more prosaic. But the making of vellum itself has a ritual purpose, and there are reasons to feel that the crafts we encountered at Portmahomack are part of a whole ritualised industry. In that environment we need not be surprised if we can occasionally demonstrate, in the ground as in the scriptorium, the use of patterns and numbers for the greater glory of God.

If we feel confident to designate the west side of the road as the Parchment-Makers' Hall and yard, the east side remained more inscrutable. It was certainly a demarcated area, since a row of large stone blocks ran down the hill, east of and parallel to the road, and about 5m away. These were latterly covered in turf to make a bank (F476). At the upper end the occupants were much exercised by the creation of ducts, either underground or jacketed in turf and supposed to be for the conveyance of hot air – but where and for what remained elusive (F467, F379 [=Int 26/F22], F395). As on the west side, one of these ducts had been built into the base of the roadside ditch (F395). Since the area was exceptionally rich in bones and particularly cattle bones, an essential sister activity serving the parchmenters may be supposed: the slaughtering and skinning of cattle. This process would naturally produce a great deal of blood and meat as well as hides and bone, and it may be that the area was connected with the preparation of food. One thinks of blood pudding (blood and salt), preservation in brine, sausage-making and the drying and smoking of meat. Few things are more important to a hungry growing community than the comprehensive use of every part of its greatest capital asset: the cow.

In the eighth century the northern quarter was thus dedicated to making parchment from cattle hides. The cattle were slaughtered on the east side of the road, the meat preserved and the hides then delivered to the west side. Here they were scraped, trimmed, thinned, preserved and smoothed to take writing. This was not a scriptorium, but a *parchmenterie*, the smelly end of the business. The clean folios were delivered further up the hill, to some building within the precinct where other, more learned, more senior folk made them into illuminated manuscripts.

According to radiocarbon dating, the cattle-hide workshops flourished for about 100 years, from the late seventh to the late eighth century. The passage of time can also be observed, if not measured, in the dumping of innumerable layers of yellow-grey clay-silts, almost certainly derived from the burning of turf or peat in the hearths, and thus given the short-hand term here of 'ashy-silts'. They were dumped mainly in the lower half of the site, where, no doubt intentionally, they raised the ground level by about half a metre and waterproofed the terrace walls. There were surfaces within the ashy-silts on which people worked, as could be seen on the west side by alignments of metapodials high in the sequence. A cattle scapula found among them on the west side was probably used to shovel them about. When the end came, in the late eighth century, there was fuel in the hearths, and rows of bone pegs were parked on the surface awaiting use.

THE SOUTHERN QUARTER

Across the valley to the south, the flat, open well-drained land had once been an arable field, but was destined to be the home of a new industry. The first thing to strike the eye would be the large building S1 (Fig 6.7; see also Fig. 3.1), but nearby would be a number of probably outdoor activities, captured only as a scatter of objects in dips and hollows where they had been spared from ploughing (see Chapter 3). It is best to explore S1 first, since it sets the standard for its neighbourhood.[5]

S1 is one of the best-preserved buildings that has reached us so far from early historic Scotland. In its original form, it consisted of a symmetrical set of post-pits surrounded by a perimeter trench, and including both a hearth and a flue (Figs 6.7, 7.5). The post-holes form three clear groups, a semi-circular group of six in the east (E2–7), a rectilinear group of 6 in the west (E1, E8, W1–4) and a pair to the north (P2, P4). Situated in a gap in the perimeter wall, this pair clearly related to the entry to the building. The post-pits were very busy, with signs of recuts and disturbances that were by no means easy to understand. However, Madeleine Hummler's analysis demonstrated that, in nearly all cases, the post-pits had contained a single upright post on a sandstone pad that had later been replaced by a double post, an upright and a buttress. Two phases of use were thus reasonably certain (Digest, A7). There was evidence that a number of posts had been removed – that is, pulled out rather than being left to rot *in situ* (not without making a mess of the post-pit). There were also a number of posts that, for reasons connected with the architecture, seem to have been still later additions. On this basis, the building may have had three phases: an original design, which was later subjected to extensive refurbishment and then to repair and eventually dismantling.

In the location that S1 was to be erected, the subsoil slopes downwards to the north, so the likelihood is that the old ground surface did likewise. The level of the

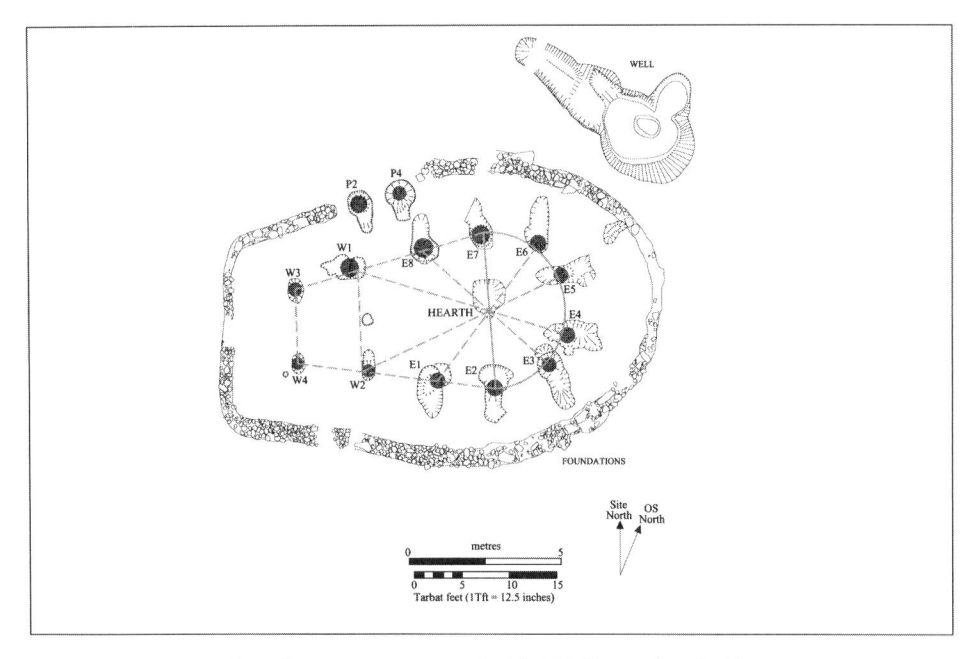

Fig. 6.7 S1, in its first phase – serving as a Smiths' Hall – and well, S8.

Fig. 6.8 S1 – a post-pit being dissected.

Fig. 6.9 Objects from the neighbourhood of S1 associated with metal- and glass-working: moulds for floriate escutcheons. These objects measure 1–3cm across.

padstones and the bottom of the periphery wall were higher on the south side than the north, so the implication is that all the features were dug to the same depth. However, given the depths, it seems very probable that the construction, as elsewhere, was preceded by a stripping and stacking of the turf.

The first phase of the building reveals its original design, a startling symmetry offering us more than just competence in construction. The world of metrics is a dangerous world, but in this case must be addressed, since it is so evident that this building, in its original form, was laid out as a conscious scheme. The east end is circular and the origin of the circle is at a point immediately south of the hearth, marked by a little lobe that not impossibly signals the former site of a small wooden marker. Arranged at equal intervals around this circle are six posts (E2–7). To this circle is attached, on its west side, a trapezium formed by the two western posts of the circle (E2 and E7) and six posts still further west, E1, E8 and W1–4, so the original design of the building has twelve posts in all. These posts also act in pairs dividing the building into bays, and the pairs have been designated as Row 1 (on the diameter at E2–7) to Row 4 at the west end. The act of attaching a trapezium to a circle inspires thoughts of geometry, but examining the lengths and ratios involved would be easier if we could find a suitable unit. All archaeological measurements were made in metres, a nineteenth-century standard from which no ancient numerical nicety can be expected to emerge. Looking at

Fig. 6.10 X-ray of glass stud inlaid with metal. (Greatly enlarged. Original is 10mm across.)

the plan in inches, the measurements are remarkably whole: 400in for the greatest width, 200in for the radius of the east end, 250in for the length of the west wall. However, other lengths are less satisfactory: 162.5in for the span of Row 2. Nor do any of these measurements presage a whole number of feet, assuming 12 inches to the foot.

On the other hand, if a foot of a different length is supposed, something long suspected at many sites, then all the numbers become obligingly whole. The unit that does this, which I shall call the Tarbat foot (Tf), is 12½ English inches (31.75mm). Using this unit, the radius of the east end is 8Tf to the post-holes and 16Tf to the perimeter wall; the trapezium posts are spaced at 16, 13, 10 and 8Tf, and the entrance is 4Tf across (Table 6.1).

The reader might think that it is always possible to invent a unit such that a majority of lengths conform to whole numbers. But these particular numbers, based on a not outlandish unit of 12½ English inches, seem to offer us a few more insights into the mind of the architect. The plan of the building is based on a semi-circle and a trapezium, where the base of the trapezium is coincident with the diameter of the

Table 6.1 Measurements of S1 in Tarbat feet

Length	Metres on the ground (to nearest 10cm)	English inches	Tarbat feet
Radius of east end	5.1	200	16
Diameter	10.2	400	32
Span Row 1	5.1	200	16
Span Row 2	4.1	162.5	13
Span Row 3	3.2	125	10
Span Row 4	2.5	100	8
Porch	1.3	50 × 50	4 × 4
Row 1 to Row 2	1.9	75	6
Row 1 to Row 3	4.1	162.5	13
Row 2 to Row 3	2.2	87	7
Row 3 to Row 4	2.2	87	7
Row 4–PW	2.5	100	8
Perimeter aisle	1.9	75	6
Width of perimeter wall	0.95	37.5	3
Length of west wall	6.0	250	20
Length east–west	14.4	567	45
From origin to F425	4.1	162.5	13
From F425 to F133	4.1	162.5	13

semi-circle. In the trapezium, the ratio of the shorter side (the west wall, 20Tf) to the longer (the diameter, 32Tf) is 0.625. The ratios of other trapezia formed by the posts are similar: that of Row 3 (10Tf) to Row 1 (16Tf) is 0.625 and of Row 4 (8Tf) to Row 2 (13Tf) is 0.615.

The significance of these numbers and their ratios is that they belong to the Fibonacci series that tends to the Golden Section (0.618). The Golden Section is 'the division of a line so that one segment is to the other as that to the whole',[6] and, together with its inverse, the Golden Number (1.618), has been valued by artists for millennia, not least because it has a particular role in nature. The series is named after the thirteenth-century scholar who set himself the task of calculating the rate at which a given population of rabbits would multiply. Starting with 1, then 2 rabbits, he forecast 3, then 5, 8, 13, 21, 34, 55, 89 . . . and so on, each number being the sum of the two before. The ratio of each number to the next is 2, 1.5, 1.66, 1.6, 1.625, 1.615, and it eventually settles at 1.618 . . . the Golden Number or *Phi*. Thus, given an infinity of rabbits, their population will increase only by 1.618 times what it was before. *Phi*, in short, seems to represent the rate (other things being equal) at which natural things multiply, and therein probably lies its deep satisfaction to humans. It has been found in plants and notably in shells, where the spiral is a progression of curves of increasing radii, in which each radius is a multiple of 1.618 times the one before. The existence of the Golden Section and the numbers of the series that leads to it must have been known for many centuries before Fibonacci. Its artistic properties have already been suspected among the makers of insular art, and it is a true delight to observe it among their architects. For, in what follows, I have made the assumption that these properties were known to the architects of S1, and it is legitimate to test for them. The measurements made on the ground in metres have been rounded to the nearest 10cm (since we were left with post-pits not posts), and were then converted to English inches and thence to Tarbat feet, whereupon the choice of length and the choice of ratio appear.

There are many ways of generating Golden Sections, using triangles, circles and trapezia,[7] but I am assuming that the Tarbat community followed a procedure that belonged to the ritual package of the early Christian movement (if not earlier), not that they worked it out here from first principles. The architect probably began by marking two points (E2 and E7) aligned north–south and 16Tf apart, marking their centre point (the origin) halfway along it. Alternatively, the origin may have been chosen first, with the two diameter pits (E2 and E7), aligned north–south, marked out next. A cord 8Tf long can be used to mark the site of four posts (E3, E4, E5, E6) at 36, 72, 108, and 144 degrees from the diameter. A trapezium is then laid out from the diameter (Row 1) westwards; two posts parallel to the diameter 10Tf long (the Golden Section) and 13Tf away make Row 3. Halfway along Row 3 (between W1 and W2) is a marker pit. Together with the marker pit by the hearth, and the posts of Row 2, this forms a cross in the centre of the building with arms 13Tf long. Row 4 is added, its span (8Tf) being a Golden Section of Row 2. It will not have escaped the reader that all the measurements contain the numbers 1, 2, 3, 5, 8 and 13, the numbers of the Fibonacci series. In asserting that these numbers were used, together with the Golden Sections created by their ratios, I am assuming no more than that such a beautifully planned and proportioned building must have had a rationale, and that this was an age that preferred a rationale rooted in spirituality.

All the structural markers were now in place and the posts could be erected. The posts were circular (tree poles) about 40cm (1.25Tf) in diameter, and each rested on a padstone about a centimetre thick at the bottom of the post-pit. The post was supported by packing stones rammed against the sides of the pit (Fig. 6.8). Padstones and packing stones were of local old red sandstone (the same used in the cist burials), and the veins in the stone showed that many used in S1 had been cut from the same block. These posts, of unknown height, must have been secured by a ring beam and bressemers to support the kind of roof anticipated: a dead weight of wet heather, wet thatch or stone slabs.

The perimeter wall was then built. It had been laid out at the east end as a semicircle at 16Tf from the origin, and at the west as a trapezium with a short wall of 20Tf (making a Golden Section with the diameter of 32Tf). A gap was left corresponding to the gap between Rows 2 and 3, and an entrance of two posts 4Tf apart erected at this point. The wall trench was about 15–45cm deep and 0.6m wide, with a U-shaped profile as if made by a shovel. Its trench was filled with beach cobbles and sandstone, including bits of slab left over from the post-packings. A piece of whale bone was included in the fill. The stones were settled and tightly packed with an admixture of 25 per cent sand. In spite of diligent searching, no traces of any superstructure or materials for one were traced in, on, above or near this cobble-filled trench. If it had been a soakaway for the dripping eaves of the timber-frame building, it would have been expected that some muck would have filtered into the trench, which was, however, clean. Nor did the trench have any drain to lead water away from the buildings. This trench was more probably the foundation for a wall. It is not excluded that the shape of S1 had a practical reason too: its round end faced into the east wind, the strongest and coldest on the peninsula.

There are as yet no close parallels to S1's combination of the circle and the trapezium. From an early medieval monastery we have only a semicircle of posts from Iona, Barber's *Magna Domus*, but this had a diameter of 18m – a formidable span to be roofed by west coast trees.[8] S1 demands a maximum span of only 5m. There is little guidance from the uneven corpus of buildings supposed to be Pictish. In Orkney, buildings cellular in plan, with round lobes nudged together, have been seen at Buckquoy and Red Craig, and similar constructions have been excavated at Bostaidh on Benera, Lewis, in the western isles. These seemed to be offering a type, so that in 1993 C. D. Morris was moved to announce: 'It is now a commonplace that Pictish houses are cellular in form, be they radial or axial and that they contrast markedly with those of the Scandinavian incomers.'[9] But research has surely rather more to discover on the matter, in particular the links between this kind of building and the curvilinear structures of Irish early Christian sites.[10] At Jarlshof, Hamilton proposed that the pre-Viking building consisted of vertical stones supporting horizontal courses, and this mode of 'Pictish' construction has been seen in walls at The Udal and Drimore on Uist.[11] The Portmahomack building can offer little of this. But the Pictish mainland in general has been rather slow to emulate the examples from the isles, and the best buildings to date, from Pitcarmick in Perthshire, look quite different from them.[12] With their rectangular plans, rounded at one end, they do, however, seem to offer a loose association with Portmahomack's more geometrical S1.

At the Viking house, Bornais 3, Niall Sharples assumed that the stone foundations excavated there were carried up in timber and that these supported a roof, since there was a lack of central posts. The space outside the stone wall was occupied by a turf wall, forming a jacket some 1.7m wide.[13] This may also be true of S1. The perimeter wall would then be an internal revetment to a thick turf wall, and the entrance a passage through it. As a turf building, it invites comparison with the Hebridean 'Black House' and at 110m^2 shelters a similar area.[14] Buildings recorded in the Highlands in historic times lead us to expect wooden posts fixed in the ground, or crucks ('Highland couples'), and walls of 'clay and bool' (cobbles and clay) or turf walls revetted internally with wattles. The spans achieved are 2.9–3.6m and lengths of 10m. There would be a timber-canopied lume set above the hearth, and the interior would be subdivided by short partitions. The wooden doors would have sliding wooden latches, and the windows wooden shutters hinged with leather. The rafters would be scarfed and lap-jointed at the wall heads, and cross-lapped and pegged at the apex. The roof would be covered with divots of turf, thatched over with stubble, straw or ferns. The roof would be stabilised by ropes tensioned by large stones hanging down. Thus no nails or other ironwork would be required. Cottages surviving in historic times in nearby Inver and Shandwick had walls of clay and rubble mixed with chopped straw and party walls of caber and mutt (stud and mud).[15] These structural practices increase confidence that S1, although a more precisely designed building than the majority of nineteenth-century cottages, could have employed such a superstructure and such fittings.

Inside the building, a hearth was developed to the north of the architect's origin-point. As found, it was 1.6m in diameter, and a deposit 30cm deep remained. Since construction of the building had begun with the stripping of the turf, life inside it happened on the surface of the sandy subsoil. The hearth was cut from this level, and in its original form had featured some sandstone settings or a kerb. Included in this hearth was the only primary assemblage relating to the building: 133 pieces of bone (mostly cattle, but sheep, pig, deer, horse, cat(?) and fish were also identified), a fragment of bronze, an iron rod, a flint scraper, 1 cereal grain, 2 nutshells, 3 seashells, 2 of winkle, 3 lumps of slag, 12 of charcoal. Some animal bone had been used as fuel (it burns to high temperature), and a sample of this was used to obtain a radiocarbon date of 760–900, a range that includes the date of its final use (see Digest, A3, A7). The interpretation of this assemblage would have taxed Sherlock Holmes. Cattle are involved, but their bones are also used for fuel; there is one grain, but one grain doth not a granary make. Nutshells and winkles might indicate consumables, but a building so grand belongs with feasting rather than snacking. It lies east–west but is not a church; it is monumental but not a palace. Cattle bones are certainly associated with the environs of S1. But the entrance is hardly a metre between the posts, too narrow for cattle to barge through on their way to milking or slaughter.

More light on the likely function of the building at Phase 1 may be won by inspecting the broader assemblage of the neighbourhood, which, cattle bones apart, seems to be concerned with crafts involving metal and glass objects. In S1 itself, material probably in use in this first phase was found in the post-pits of the second: 7 fragments of iron, including 3 nails, a piece of sheet, a disc and a pin; and from posthole E7 (near the hearth) a whetstone (F662/Find 455). Hammerscale slag, the waste product of forging iron, found its way into post-pits at W7, W11, E3 and E5, and iron fragments turned up in W3 and E8. Later pits at the east end captured a metal droplet, and a mould. In so far as we have an indication, the first purpose of S1, and the object of its design, was not a Great Barn but a Smiths' Hall. However, its time as a Great Barn was to come (see Chapter 7).

The assemblage recovered from the neighbourhood of S1 reinforces the impression of an artisan quarter: 10 whetstones, more than 260 fragments of moulds, 50 of crucibles and more than 60 pieces of slag. XRDF analysis showed that the crucibles were melting silver, copper, tin, zinc and lead.[16] Some of the moulds suggested circular escutcheons – one with a floriate design was closely paralleled by an example from Iona, another had a interlaced cross and a third disc carried the imprint of a spiral or peltaic ornament (Fig 6.9). These moulds seemed to be more suitable for the manufacture of glass, an idea endorsed by a number of finds from the same area: fragments of glass rod, glass droplets, lumps of raw blue glass and a fragment of shallow hard-fired clay vessel with coating of yellow glass. Showing how the two crafts might have been combined were an opaque white glass stud with geometric inlay and a blue glass stud with inlaid metal wire and polychrome glass (Fig. 6.10). These are the kind of studs that may be seen on the great surviving masterpieces of early Celtic metalwork: the Derrynaflan paten or the Ardagh chalice.

This material was spread over the area north and east of S1, and particularly in the top of the backfilled inner enclosure ditch. Here the rigorous search for structure brought little reward – but there was a hearth, and the position of S3 to the west, also over the top of the old ditch, does suggest that we may simply have lost the buildings to later ploughing. The finds were spread over an area 24m long, and there is room for one or even two buildings the size of S1, which could lie along the access of the old ditch without detection.

When the plan of the S1 building was first revealed, analogues were sought (unsuccessfully) among the Vikings, but the common verdict was 'it's so odd – it must be Pictish'. It can be defined more precisely now: a Pictish building making ingenious use of local materials, and driven as effectively by spiritual and aesthetic principles as other products of insular art. Moreover, it was, appropriately, a building built to shelter artists, makers of fine church plate.

CONCLUSION

The period covered by this chapter is given by radiocarbon dating to span a long eighth century (c. 650–820; see Digest, A3). Supported by eight nearly identical dates, this range seems to represent a very plausible interval from the beginnings of craft practice on an industrial scale to its ending. The architects and artisans who were busy outside the cemetery underpinned the artistic endeavours of those who built churches, carved monuments and illuminated manuscripts in the inner precinct. But these are no peasant providers for the refined academicians on the hill. Those who developed the landscape on the valley floor had not only to excavate a marsh and transport enormous stones; they had to understand the principles of hydraulics and the properties of materials that made the water run. The building S1 is the outcome of architectural and spiritual thinking of a different order from that of a gospel book; but it shows the importance of symbol and worship in everything done in the service of the Christian God, and, one strongly suspects, his many predecessors. The Tarbat foot, if we can accept its existence, can be found in other structures in the monastic precinct: the width of the road (2.5m, 8Tf), the size of S4 (16 × 3Tf) and even the much mangled S9 can be proposed as an architect-designed building like S1 on a diameter of 32Tf.

These buildings housed crafts fundamental to the age of Christian sanctity. The making of the components of vessels of precious metals requires a visual imagination and a strong sense of design as well as an ability to handle glass, silver and bronze – arguably a process of much greater skill than fixing the parts together. The preparation of vellum was no less ingenious, adapting local resources – beach pebbles and seaweed for example – to the process. In a way the artisans were aware, as no others in the monastery, of the magical conversion there were achieving. They began with blood, ash, bone and clay and produced clean media for writing the Scriptures and holy vessels for the Mass.

Saying Mass requires only one holy book, only one chalice, paten and pyx. Slow as they were to finish to the degree of perfection required, a fair number of chalices and books must have emanated from the Portmahomack workshops over their century of production. Why so many vessels, so much parchment? The answer must be that their peak output coincided with an expansion of the monastic network, and every new monastery required its own 'starter kit'. During his mission in Ireland it is said that Patrick 'took with him across the Shannon fifty bells, fifty patens, fifty chalices, altar-stones, books of law and Gospel books, and left them in new places'.[17] The eighth century would be the apogee of the early monastic movement in north Scotland, and it seems that one of the jumping-off points for the expanding network would have been at Portmahomack. From this auspicious beginning, Christianity was destined to endure for another millennium in Easter Ross, but not before experiencing a most significant and nearly terminal setback. At the start of the ninth century began an era of social and political turbulence in the Moray Firth area lasting two centuries. And the new era was signalled at Portmahomack by a pivotal event: the monastic project went up in smoke.

Notes

1. The interpretation of S9 and the vellum-working that follows here owes much to excavation and studies by Cecily Spall (see also Carver and Spall 2004).
2. For the full argument, see Carver and Spall (2004).
3. Sharples (1999: 30).
4. Mulville *et al.* (2003: 28–30). They cite teeth at Dun Bharavat (Harding and Armit 1990: 81); deer jaws at A' Cheardach Bheag (Fairhurst 1971: 74) and cattle metapodials at Bornais (Sharples 1999).'
5. This account is indebted to excavation in 2002 by Cecily Spall and subsequent analysis by Madeleine Hummler.
6. *Chambers English Dictionary*.
7. See Robert Knott's website at the University of Surrey: www.mcs.surrey.ac.uk/personal/R.Knott/Fibonacci/fibnat.htmlIf
8. Barber (1981).
9. Morris (1993: 295); he cites Hunter (1986: 26) and Crawford (1987: 140–6, esp. fig. 46).
10. Fanning (1981: fig. 8).
11. Hamilton (1956); Ralston (1997).
12. Ralston (1997).
13. Sharples (2005: 183).
14. Thomas (1867).
15. Houses in Ross-shire; see Stell and Beaton (1984).
16. Heald (2003: app. C).
17. Tírechán, *Collectanea*, in Bieler (1979: 122–3).

CHAPTER 7

Serving new masters

FIRE AND THE SWORD

The brunt of the attack was borne at the heart of the monastery, on the hill and in the adjacent workshops, the parts nearest the sea. Over the workshops was laid a mantle of multi-coloured deposits – white, pink, red, orange, black, the garish remains of straw, heather and timber consumed by fire at high temperature. The blanket of burning lay over the hearths, over the turf walls, over the floors of the vellum-workers' hall, into the tawing tank and it ran up in a scraggly carpet over the retaining walls of the pool. It was continuous, excepting only where it had been cut away by later features (see Plate 8a). This fire might have been an accident, since accidents do happen, especially in workshops with hearths, but the next event, hard

Fig. 7.1   Excavators defining the pebble Road 2.

Fig. 7.2 Metal-working hearth (F148).

Fig. 7.3 Small hearths for workers with precious metals, being lifted by Cecily Spall and Nicky Toop (on the right).

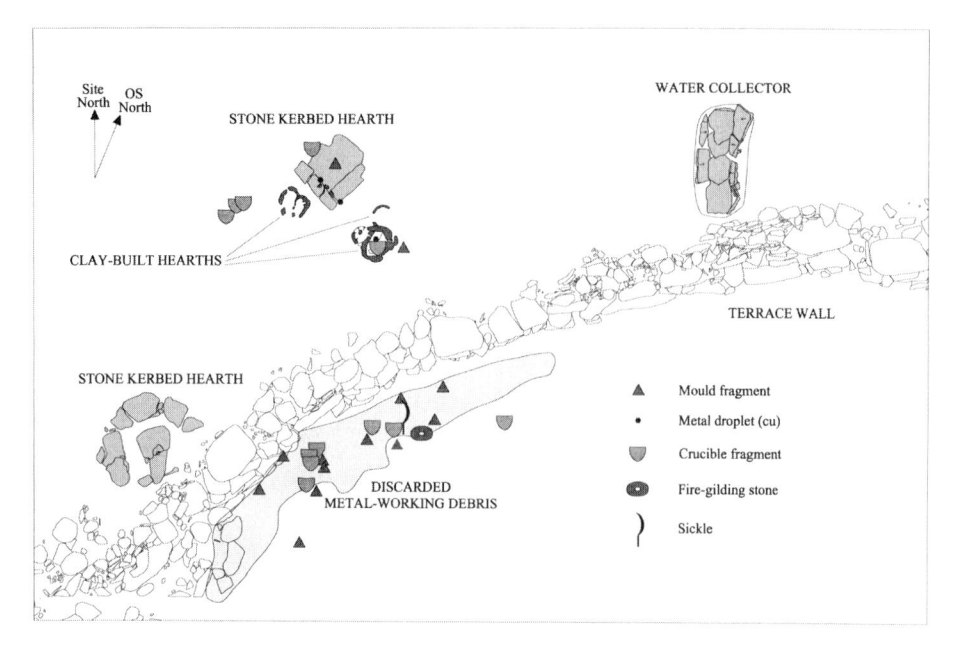

Fig. 7.4 Plan of Period 3 metal-working area beside the pool.

upon the first, makes this unlikely. Onto the charred devastation had been tipped more than a hundred pieces of broken sculpture, sharp and unabraded, some of it blackened, cracked or reddened, evidently by heat. Much of the carving, we deduced, had belonged to one major stone monument with rounded moulding, probably a cross-shaft (Cross D), which had stood at the edge of the monastic burial ground (see Chapter 5) and had been thrown down and hammered into fragments. The fragments had been strewn over the east part of the workshops, accumulating in the now filled-up road-side ditch, where they lay, higgledy-piggledy, marking the end of the monastic adventure. Higher on the church hill, at least one, and perhaps all three, other major cross-slabs were also probably demolished at this time, and pieces from them were to lie about in the churchyard for nearly 1,000 years. If the sculpture found in the workshops had been made in the later eighth century, it will have been broken up not much later, as it was uncommonly fresh. At this time, too, at least one of the monastic community died from sword wounds to the head (see Chapter 4).

This raid is argued from radiocarbon to have taken place between 780 and 830 (see Chapter 3), and initiates our Period 3. It put paid to the vellum workshops and also to the pool and its waterworks. Two pieces of carved stone, probably belonging to Cross D, were found in the pool near the terrace wall, on the latest layer of organic debris to settle in the water. The culvert and the square cistern were filled in and covered by four sandstone capstones large enough to take a lorry. The road was reborn and now probably crossed the whole valley with a supporting revetment or kerbside wall on its west side. Potholes were first filled with metal-working slag, but at a given moment a new surface was laid, of pebbles tightly rammed into sand (F18; Fig 7.1). The new surface spilled over the edges of the old road into its ditches, leaving just the kerbs showing. The dumped sculpture, which was largely the remains of Cross D, standing by the precinct gate, had been used as hard core, especially in the ditch on the south-east side. However, the ditches on both sides soon had to be recut to canalise the water ever-flowing off the church hill. The workforce evidently still knew its way around the workshops, road and pond.

Northern Quarter: The New Metalsmiths

Together these events provide too many coincidences to dismiss entirely: one must conclude that this monastery had been attacked by fire and the sword – and probably the sledgehammer. All the more interesting, then, that it was not abandoned. On the contrary, camped out almost immediately over the old workshops was a community of metal-workers, who built hearths, worked bronze and iron, and constructed numerous timber shelters of uncertain shape, implied by scores of post-sockets. They also dug shallow culverts to help with the perennial local problem (getting rid of the water). One of these had been lined and roofed with slabs of sculpture, the broken pieces of the Calf Stone, its carving worn where it had been walked upon (Plate 6b). The northern quarter was first subjected to a tidying-up operation, in which timbers were removed from the Parchment-Makers' Hall (S9), and the hot burnt areas levelled with sand. But new industrial work began almost instantly, with a hearth (F148) laid directly over a previous hearth (F493), only the distinctive layer of savage scorching separating the two (Fig. 7.2). The upper hearth was dedicated to a craft new to this area – metal-working. Crucibles and moulds, and whetstones for finishing cast objects, were broken and dropped in the vicinity. The chemistry of the crucibles shows that objects were being cast in bronze and silver, and from the sandy floor of the new workshop above the burning came a black touchstone, a carnelian gem and a possible gilding stone for mixing amalgam – all hints that gold was included in the repertoire (Plate 7b).[1] The gem had been flaked at the back where the goldsmith had levered it out, presumably from the gold setting of an antique signet ring – the metal being suitable for recycling and thus the bit he actually wanted. If these were indirect clues to a gold supply, a more direct clue on the supply of silver came in the form of a single sceat – a tiny silver coin made in Frisia (Holland) about 715[2] that had escaped the melting pot. There were some signs that glass too was worked by these craftsmen: a fragment of reticella glass, a blue glass bead with zig-zag inlay, a spacer bead and a mould from the roadside ditch. The metalsmiths' activities diversified in the form of small specialist hearths: a little circle of heat-shattered clay on a stone slab produced a bronze droplet, a crucible sherd and a fragment of iron (Fig. 7.3; for reference numbers see Digest, A6).

What kind of a business was this? As usual we are privy to the makers' end of the process, not the users', so there were few direct signals of what was actually going out. But there were some. There were two dress pins, a fragment of a plaque, a strap end, a fretwork handle and a disk with spirals – all of bronze, broadly from the eighth–tenth centuries in date and from the area, but all residual. An iron snaffle bit was also found. There was a painted pebble, a cultural emblem of the Picts, near the top of the metal-workers' dumps.

The technology – as suggested by the crucibles, the moulds and the metals worked – is equivalent to the metal-working of the monastery in the southern field by S1 (see Chapter 6). The form of the first hearth of the new industry was identical to the last hearth of the old – that of the parchmenters on the other side of the road, now buried by debris from the fire. But the objects suggested by the moulds, unspecific as they are, and the residual material, have few allusions to sacred vessels, and more to personal ornaments such as pins. But there was nothing here that recalled the material culture of the Norse. It seems that these were still Pictish craftsmen, although not disposed to die with their former employers. The smiths continued to function, but served more secular masters: the same people, doing a different job.

Some of the metal-workers' debris was tossed over the revetment wall into the open water of the pool (Fig. 7.4). Inside the terrace, new quantities of debris soon accumulated, a new series of ashy-silts, marking the slow plop of time in a workshop. There were nineteen post-holes in this south-east area, two of them of squared timber, but this did not amount to architecture. There was a squared timber also in the pool, just over the repaired revetment wall, one of a number of posts sunk in the pond floor near the metal workshop, which perhaps formed a bridge or jetty of some kind over the now stagnant water. A heavy-duty turf bank still provided a division of activity. Metal-working did, however, spread to the west side of the road, and, later on, iron-workers were to occupy the whole north part of the site into the Middle Ages.

The Southern Quarter goes Agricultural

The southern quarter was also resurrected, also on the old foundations and also with a new function. The Smiths' Hall (S1), standing at the far end of the enclosure, was not burnt down, but it was completely rebuilt: all but two of the posts were replaced (Fig. 7.5; for details and reference numbers see Digest, A7). At the east end, the six posts on the circle were superseded by six pairs of posts, the inner standing upright and the outer leaning towards it to serve as a buttress. At the west end a new row of four posts was introduced, the outer pair buttressing the inner pair. Halfway along the inner face of the west wall, a new post was implanted. The north entrance was rebuilt as a square of four double posts, those on the outside of the building being equipped with buttress posts pushing inwards. It can be noted that several of the second series of posts appear to have been rectangular in scantling. Assuming this building was constructed in a similar way to its predecessor (see Chapter 6), the entrance implies a surrounding turf jacket some 1.3m thick. This was a new robust structure, if a little out of symmetry now with the original design.

The reconstruction may have been prompted by the incidental collapse of the first building – and yet this had stood long enough to create the debris that found its way into the new post-pits. A more likely explanation for the need for buttress posts is the lateral thrust of an upper floor. An upper floor over the east end would have

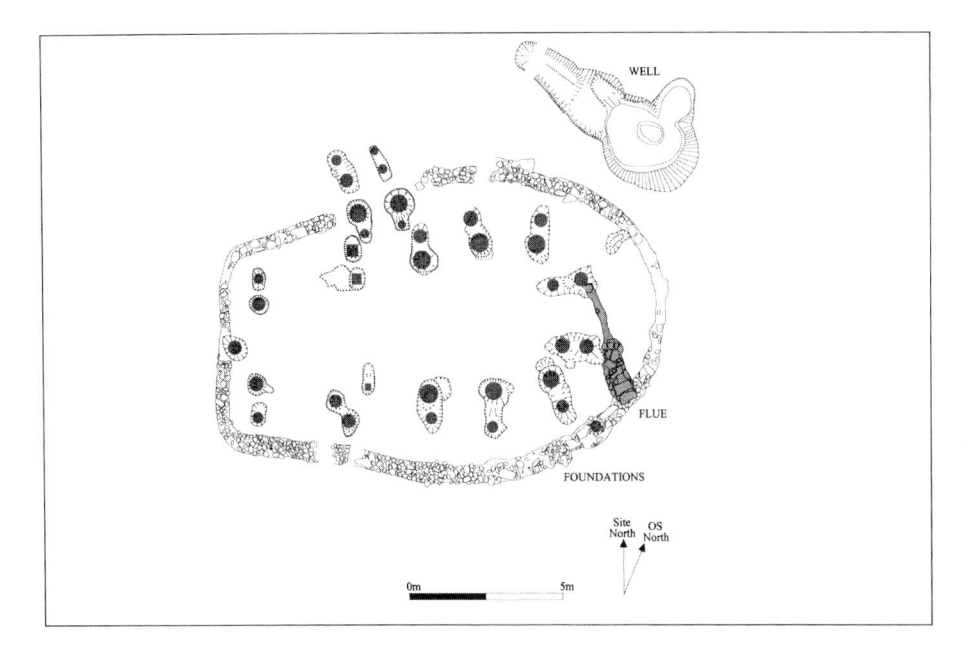

Fig. 7.5 S1, after its refurbishment as a Kiln Barn; with well, S8.

blocked out the fire from the hearth, but it is interesting to see that cutting into the periphery wall (and thus belonging to a second phase) is a flue, which appears to have been designed to bring hot air into the building from the south. This would be wholly compatible with an upper floor, and indeed immediately suggests a use analogous to examples from historic times: as a Kiln Barn.[3] It is more debatable whether there was an upper floor on the west side, but the addition of buttress posts throughout suggest that one was eventually added. The evidence from the excavation of the buttresses suggests that, in general, they leaned inwards at 60 degrees from the horizontal (see Digest, A7). Given that the spacing in a post pair was 1m, the posts would join at 2m up, implying a floor at least this high.[4]

We now have something highly functional, in which grain can be dried at the east end with a flue and malted and stored at the west end. If the central hearth still functioned, it might be possible to see a dual use of S1– as a forge during the summer and as a barn once the harvest was in, in September. But that does not account for the refurbishment or explain how a hearth and an upper floor might function together. Two phases seem to explain the evidence best: two phases, two different purposes and probably two different kinds of settlement, one succeeding the other.

Near S1 was a large hole that took the form of a timber-lined pit, with large open cuts, platforms and drains at different levels around it (S8). The primary feature suggested a well, perhaps with different points of access. Access to the Mine Howe Iron Age well excavated in Orkney was elaborate and riveted with stone and in that case was thought to have provided access to rituals connected to water cults.[5] But the untidy access platforms around a well might equally have developed as a response to a vanishing water table, or have been caused by there being too much water. Beginning as a source of water for the activities in S1, it became a sprawling soggy hole as the water rose and overflowed in successive years.

Together with the refurbished S1 we may group S5, that peculiar oval structure at the east end of Sector 1. Supported on six large posts, it contained charred grain in a central pit and in its surrounding ditch. It was most likely a grain dryer of some kind, and radiocarbon dates have it in use sometime between 680 and 900 and disused by 1030. The late date of disuse makes it a good candidate for Period 3.

The site had, therefore, changed its character. But by how much? The severity of the fire was not in doubt, but how far had it put paid to the monastery? The new bronze-workers were closely related to their predecessors by a common craft: they used bowl and triangular crucibles and clay moulds. But they seem to have been making something rather plainer than the monks had required. The iron-workers were forging and left plenty of hammerscale and slag. It would be possible to imagine that the apprentices of the community of smiths that had served the monastery in the neighbourhood of the old Smiths' Hall (see Chapter 6) were under new management, and making simpler stuff.

We can distinguish here two kinds of consequence, dubbed for brevity 'discontinuities' and 'continuities'. The discontinuities were in the production of sculpture and vellum and the use of the cemetery, the pool and probably of the church. The continuities were in the use of the road and the building S1 (but directed to a new function) and in the production of metalwork – but making different things. If we turn our backs on the churchyard, with its knocked-over grave markers and ruined church, we can see the new kind of place that the Portmahomack monastery had become – an industrially active farmstead.

A Historical Context

The new owners of this dissolved (or rather immolated) monastery were thus keen to keep the working parts working. Who were they? Our dates put this episode into a period within 800–1100, a era otherwise very little known: there was a hoard deposited near the present north gate of the churchyard around 1000; it included coins of English and French kings of the ninth–tenth centuries and a number of silver arm-rings – the ring-silver of the Norse who used them as money (Fig. 7.6; see Chapter 1). Portmahomack, it seems, was still an international port, and no doubt a party to the politics of the age. But this was the true Dark Age of Scotland, and, like all Dark Ages, it was paradoxically a time when stakes were high and enduring agendas set.

Speaking of this period, the Scottish historian Dauvit Broun remarked: 'We must acknowledge that the political landscape north of the Mounth is impenetrably obscure.'[6] Can we offer any framework on which to suspend this phase of the Portmahomack settlement? We can probably agree that there were three main players in our region: the Picts, the Scots and the Norse, each speaking a different language. The Celtic peoples intermingled at aristocratic and clerical level, to produce by the

Fig. 7.6 Hoard of silver coins and ring-silver found in the Portmahomack churchyard. It was deposited c. 1000 (see Chapter 1). The coins are about 1in (25mm) in diameter. (Source: NMS)

ninth century a Gaelic-speaking Alba. In the same century, the Norse emerged from Norway and first raided, then settled, the Northern Isles, Caithness and Sutherland. Alfred Smyth described the process as 'a violent piratical phase as a prelude to more determined and successful attempts at colonization'.[7] These attempts were, however, geographically constricted. The warlords of Moray, the Mormaers, defended their patch, and by the eleventh century the Norse had penetrated, as place names show, not much further south than Dingwall, where they had a *Thing* or assembly place. For over 200 years, the Tarbat peninsula, and, for that matter, the Black Isle, were frontier territories in a war zone. The protagonists in the struggle included, on the Norse side, Sigurd the Mighty, Aud the Deep-Minded and that unsubtle negotiator Thorfinn Skullsplitter; and, on the Moray side, Mael Brigte, Finlay and Finlay's elusive but now infamous son Macbeth.

The use of the written sources to chronicle the doings of these figures is perilous, since the sources, such as *Orkneyinga Saga*, are mostly late and laced with legend. We have some unexpected and surer information thanks to Alex Woolf's recent proposal to locate the Pictish territory of *Fortriu* in the Moray Firth region. If such a move is acceptable, then a whole lot of interesting events can move with it.[8] Constantine, who held the power in greater Pictland between 789 and 820 and was commemorated on the Dupplin Cross, was also a king of Fortriu. He must have died just before, or just after, Portmahomack was raided. If the raid took place about 800, as I have suggested, all-out war was not long in coming. In 839, according to the *Annals of Ulster*, the heathens (that is, the Vikings) won a battle against the men of Fortriu. Eóganán son of Óengus, Bran son of Óengus, Aed son of Boanta and others 'almost innumerable' fell there. This would have hit the Pictish families very hard, making way for other aristocracy, particularly from the Gaels of Argyll. In 865 the same source records the death of the chief bishop of Fortriu, Tuathal mac Artgusso. This is 'the only reference to a Bishop of Fortriu in the Chronicles', Professor Broun has remarked to me in a letter, and he goes on: 'I don't see any reason why the "chief bishop" in 865 could not have been based at Portmahomack. Would there have been any church as impressive as Portmahomack in the north by the ninth century?' Well yes, since in our archaeological reasoning the church at Portmahomack had already been demolished. But there can still be a bishop of Fortriu, and there are other candidates for his seat: Rosemarkie on the Black Isle or Burghead and Kinnedar in Moray, where high-quality sculpture has come to light.

And there is more: in 866 'Amlaíb and Auisle went with the foreigners of Ireland and Alba [= Britain] to Fortriu, plundered the entire Pictish country and took away hostages from them'. This would have been another grievous depletion of the aristocracy. The men of Fortriu defeated the Norse in 906, but by the time Malcolm I arrives in 950, the place he comes to is Moray – the 'sea settlement', and Fortriu is never mentioned again.

All this provides a plausible context for the events at Portmahomack. But it also provides a framework for those semi-mythical heroes from the Norse sagas, which truth-loving historians rightly urge us to avoid. But who can resist these stories? For example, Mael Brigte, the Moray Mormaer, was famous for the undoubtedly improbable feat of killing his enemy when he himself was already dead. He was worsted in battle by Sigurd the Mighty, who cut off his head and tied it by the hair to his saddle bow. However, on Sigurd's triumphant return north, the head bit him in the leg and gave him blood-poisoning, from which he never recovered. Sigurd is said to have been

Plate 1a)   *Portmahomack: members of the digging team relax on the beach.*

Plate 1b)   *St Colman's church, with the Dornoch Firth beyond.*

Plate 2a)   *The Dragon Stone (TR20).*

Plate 2b)   *The Apostle Stone, reverse side of the Dragon Stone (TR20).*

Plate 3a)   Excavating the nave of St Colman's church in 1997.

Plate 3b)   Ard marks in Sector 1, cut by the inner enclosure ditch; seventh century or earlier.

Plate 4a) The northern area (Sector 2) under excavation in 2005, looking north with St Colman's church on the right. In the centre of the excavated area is the kerbed road, in use during the eighth century.

Plate 4b) What became of the mill: the road foundations, culvert and cistern of the eighth century being dissected by Justin Garner-Lahire on the last day of the campaign.

Plate 5a) Features under excavation in 2007 in the northern area (Sector 2). In the foreground is a cistern fed by a gully; in use during the earliest days of the monastery (sixth–seventh centuries).

Plate 5b) Excavation of cattle bones in situ *in the vellum-working yard, eighth century.*

Plate 6a) Fragment, possibly from the Apostle Stone, found in the workshop area (TR201).

Plate 6b) The Calf Stone (TR28) under excavation by Katie Anderson.

Plate 7a) Evidence for vellum-working from Sector 2: curved knife (lunellarium), white pebbles, pumice rubbers, needles. Scale in mm.

Plate 7b) Evidence for the working of precious metals from Sector 2: crucibles, moulds, whetstone, touchstone, finishing stone. Scale in mm.

Plate 8a) The sequence captured in the south-facing section on the east side of Sector 2. The white sandy layer towards the bottom is the floor level in the eighth century. Above it lie orange and black lenses of primary burning, and above these the layers that produced broken hand-sized pieces of sculpture. Higher still are layers owed to metal-working after the raid.

Plate 8b) The sequence captured in the west section of Sector 2. The horizontal white layer is the vellum-workers' floor and beneath it layers of redeposited subsoil used to level the site for use beside the marsh.

buried about 892, presumably in Sigurd's Mound (Syvardhoch), which is recorded in the thirteenth century for Sidera (now Cydera) on the Oykell Estuary near Dornoch.

The Norse first mention Tarbat, which they apparently knew as 'Torfness', in events relating to the years 891–4. Einar the Turfer 'was the first of men to find how to cut turf from the earth for fuel, in Torfness in Scotland'. He clearly was not, since the monks of Portmahomack had been using turf as fuel and building material there for more than 200 years. Einar, who died around 910, was said to have taken over 'the island territories'. He was 'tall and ugly and one-eyed, though still the most keen-sighted of men'.[9] There is some implication here that Einar had control of Tarbat, if not further south still.

Of Einar's successors, his son Thorfinn Skullsplitter and his grandson Sigurd the Stout seem to have kept a strong grip on the Moray Firth during the tenth and into the eleventh centuries. Around 995 Sigurd the Stout was challenged in Caithness by Findlaech (Finlay), Macbeth's father, who was defeated (with the unfair intervention of a magic banner). In the early eleventh century we hear of 'Torfness' again, since a great sea battle took place there in about 1035. The victor was Thorfinn the Mighty, son of Sigurd the Stout. The Moray leader defeated at sea is named by the *Orkneyinga Saga* as a certain Karl Hundison, and the saga goes on to recount how Thorfinn the Mighty, a golden helmet on his head, a sword at his waist, and wielding a great spear in both hands, chased the defeated Scots deep into Scotland. He and his men 'went over hamlets and farms and burnt everything, so that scarcely a hut was left standing. Those of the men whom they found, they killed, but the women and old people dragged themselves into woods and deserted places with wailings and lamentations.'[10] Arnor the Earl's poet celebrated the event with a laconic strophe:

> A keen sword at Tarbatness
> Reddened the wolf's fare.
> The young Prince wielded it –
> It was a Monday.
> Their swords sang there,
> South off Oykell.
> There fought with Scotland's king
> Our valiant lord.[11]

Karl Hundison (or Hundason) is thought by many to be none other than the character that Shakespeare knew as Macbeth, son of Findlaech and murderer of Duncan, who was active in the area from about 1030 until his death in 1057.[12] Historian Barbara Crawford comments:

> The Tarbat Ness headland is likely to be *Torfness*, where Earl Thorfinn the Mighty met Karl Hundison [MacBeth?] in battle between 1030 and 1035 . . . The victory of the former allowed the consolidation of Norse settlement around the shores of the Dornoch and Cromarty Firths.[13]

It seems that, by the early eleventh century, control of Easter Ross was in the hand of the earls of Orkney, and it is not improbable that such control had from time to time been exercised by Sigurd the Mighty in the ninth.[14] Moray leaders from Findlaech onwards obviously felt they had an ancestral claim on the territories to the north, as far as Caithness. But the frontier probably established by the Norse at the Beauly River is one that has endured on the map.

For all his bad press from Shakespeare and his predecessors, Macbeth was no usurper but could claim royal descent in Moray from his father Findlaech and from the line of Malcolm on his mother's side. Duncan, who became King of Greater Scotland in 1034, was his second cousin. Nick Aitchison would actually prefer to see Duncan as Karl Hundason, the loser at Tarbat Ness, since the *Orkney Saga* elsewhere mentions a Magbjóthr but describes Karl Hundason as the next man to take over power in Scotland after Malcolm (that is, Malcolm II), which was Duncan.[15] The battle off Tarbat was part of a wider campaign. Hundason's eleven warships first attacked Thorfinn at Deerness, demanding tribute for Caithness. But Hundason was defeated and had to swim for his life. Then Karl Hundason raised an army that included Welsh and Irish soldiers, but Thorfinn responded by mustering 'all the troops from Caithness, Sutherland and Ross', which implies that Ross was already under Norse control at the time.[16]

Macbeth murdered Duncan in a blacksmith's hut at Pitgaveny, near Elgin, in 1040, and, if Duncan was really Hundason, this might be construed as the price of failure.[17] Macbeth was to rule for seventeen years, and a case can be made that these years were happy and prosperous. He made a pilgrimage to Rome in 1050, as did Thorfinn the Mighty, E. J. Cowan remarking drily: 'it is not recorded whether he booked passage with Macbeth.'[18] In Rome, Macbeth famously distributed money with great freedom, and it is not inconceivable that both northern Scottish rulers by this time would think a papal blessing worthwhile – in the manner of getting recognition by the United Nations. Now that he was a monarch of the Scottish house, Macbeth and his lady gave their patronage to a monastery in Perthshire, on St Serf's island in Loch Leven. In the eighth century, this monastery had had links with Iona. Revived in the tenth century, it was a *culdee* establishment that maintained its Cartulary in Gaelic (this has not survived, though a Latin summary has). It probably resembled the Book of Deer, a holy book with notes in the margin. From the mid-tenth century St Serf's was dependent on St Andrews, and it became Augustinian from 1150. Thus, on St Serf's island, the old world was connected to the new, and Portmahomack ought to have been remembered there.

The stories we have do not make it easy to assign modern political virtues to any of the players concerned, Christians included. Their principal instruments of negotiation were the sword and the bed. So Gillacomgain usurped his current Moray leader, uncle Finlaedh, by setting fire to his house, and was murdered in turn by his son Macbeth, who went on to murder Duncan. These were all members of the same family, and Lady Macbeth, whose real name was Gruoch, married the two murderers in turn, no doubt to secure the succession of her noble genes as well as to maintain her standing in Moray. In the 870s Einar the Turfer avenged himself on Hafdan Highleg, who had burnt his father and sixty followers in his house in Norway, by blood-eagling him, and thus, according to *Orkneyinga Saga*, offering a sacrifice to Odin for victory.[19]

Pillow politics could be an equally persuasive instrument of negotiation. Olaf the White, king of Dublin, chose three queens: first, Aud the Deep-Minded, daughter of

Ketil Flatnose, Norwegian ruler of the Hebrides; then a daughter of an Irish high king, Aed Findliath; and then a daughter of Kenneth MacAlpin, king of Scots, a marriage that, as Alfred Smyth tells us, 'fits in with the Scottish phase of the Dublin leader's career'.[20] This dynamic Olaf is thought to be the hero who was eventually laid to rest in the Gokstad ship-burial. Early medieval politicians in the Moray Firth were, therefore, concerned with being good with an axe, good on a horse, good in a boat and good in bed, without troubling themselves with such abstruse questions as whose country is that? Or what's the real name of god?

If even half of these anecdotes have a whisper of reality, this was a violent age, and the contrast with the previous centuries is marked. In the eighth century Pictland was not just the site of a few monasteries – it was a largely Christian kingdom. Tarbat was a holy island, or nearly one, marked by huge cross-slabs, endowed by wealthy Pictish patrons, their names emblazoned in symbols in the Pictish manner. The monasteries were in contact with each other, with Ireland, with Northumbria, with England and with the Continent; and, where spiritual alliance went, commerce was not far behind. This common market of its day was no doubt at least partly what irritated the Scandinavians. Their first raids took place all up and down the east and west coast, visiting destruction on Lindisfarne in 793 and on Iona in 804. These monasteries were said to have revived after their experience, and were periodically visited, if not inhabited, by Christian communities.

Portmahomack was another early target, no doubt because it was as important as these two. Its workshops were burnt, and its great monuments, symbolic of ideological restrictive practice, were thrown down. Here we do not think there was a survival of the resident monastic community. The place remained in the front line, and in a dozen skirmishes the men of Moray clashed with the Norsemen. Their monks were murdered, their bishops were killed, their skulls were split. But they fought back. Sigurd and Thorfinn and their ilk never achieved their goal of opening the passage along the Great Glen as a short cut to their possessions in the Irish Sea. Just as Alfred and Edward the Elder fought back in England, so Finlay and Duncan and Macbeth fought back in Moray. And the Tarbat peninsula, with its gem of a port and its beachhead, a frontier post if ever there was one, must have changed hands a dozen times. No one put up new sculptures or built new churches, but the metal-workers were valued – a protected profession; indeed what warrior would kill a smith? Around the year 1000 someone buried a hoard of English and French coins and Viking ring-money by the present churchyard gate, and we can see now that this is a smith's hoard waiting to be converted to the commission of the next warlords – be they Viking or Mormaer, Einar or Mael Brigte. In 1035 a battle took place on the peninsula – probably at Blar á Cath, 3km up the coast from Portmahomack[21] – and the men of Moray under Macbeth or Duncan lost their fleet and the harbour. But not for long. 'Time and the hour runs through the roughest day,' as Shakespeare hath it. There were Viking place names on Tarbat – Bindal and Cadboll – but this is not Orkney; this is not a Norse place. Without any stronger indications one way or the other, the Portmahomack Period 3 metalsmiths and farmers had equal chances of being the servants of the Earls of Orkney – or of Macbeth.

Notes

1. Major traces of silver, copper, tin, zinc and lead were found in crucibles by XRDF; Heald (2003: app. C).
2. See Blackburn (1998) for a preliminary report.
3. See, e.g., Fenton (1999: 100); Fenton and Walker (1981: 138).
4. Building A4 at Yeavering had 60-degree buttresses (Hope-Taylor 1977: 59, fig. 19.4; 60, fig. 20, N3, M6). The posts are 3ft (90cm) apart, implying a wall plate at 6ft (180cm).
5. Card and Downes (2003: 16); cf. Ritchie (2003).
6. Broun (2005: 41–2).
7. Smyth (1984: 146). An invaluable recent summary for north-east Scotland is Crawford 1995.
8. Woolf (2006). Warmest thanks to Alex Woolf for letting me know of his work, and to Dauvit Broun for discussing its implications with me.
9. *OS* 7; Anderson (1922: 377).
10. *OS* 20.
11. Arnórr Jarlaskald (*OS* 167).
12. Properly Mac Bethad mac Findlaech: Oram (2004: 18, 89); Grant (2005: 98); Cowan (1993: 125); the Karl Hundason in *OS* 'would appear to be MacBeth'.
13. Crawford (1987: 73).
14. See, e,g., Fraser (1986).
15. Aitchison (1999: 57).
16. Ibid. pp. 37, 56.
17. *Bothirgouane*; Aitchison (1999: 62).
18. Cowan (1993: 128).
19. Smyth (1984, 148, 154).
20. Ibid. pp. 156, 192.
21. NGR 925 869.

Part 3

Legacy

CHAPTER 8

Aftermath: St Colman's Church

Macbeth was killed by the Cumbrian prince Malcolm, son of Duncan, that Malcolm Canmore who established a dynasty that would rule Scotland until the death of Alexander III in 1286. Among the eight children of Canmore's second marriage – to the English princess Margaret – was David, who, with his mother, was to redesign Christianity in Scotland. From David's accession as David I in 1124, and especially after his conquest of Moray in 1147, we can expect the arrival of a new order in Portmahomack.[1] The Christian churches encountered by the reformers exhibited a fine diversity of married priests in secular, monastic and *culdee* communities:

> There were countless shrines, chapels, hermitages, possibly even small churches, bearing ancient dedications to an enormous variety of saints, the overwhelming majority of whom were of Celtic origin . . . Only a small proportion of these sacred sites were selected for permanent parish kirks and we hardly ever know why one site was preferred to another.[2]

In the course of the twelfth and thirteenth centuries this liturgical gallimaufry was visited by a rigorous transformation: 'A high degree of uniformity was imposed generally on the whole of western Christendom . . . As a result the peculiarities of many regional churches of the west, that of Scotland among them, were ironed out'.[3] So when did the cleansing fire reach Easter Ross?

Alexander Grant feels that our region was not properly incorporated into the Scottish kingdom – and thus the broader Christian Europe – until the appointment in 1215 of the first Earl of Ross, Farquhar MacTaggart: 'the frontier between Ross and Moray was still, in many respects, the effective frontier for the kings of Alba.'[4] Geoffrey Barrow points out that, although Rosemarkie was the site of the ancient see, there is no record of any bishop's church in Moray before the thirteenth century, and it was in the thirteenth century that a functioning cathedral church for Caithness was opened for business at Dornoch. The dioceses of Ross, Moray and Caithness were created by Alexander I or David I, and 'it is hard to be sure how far parish churches in any recognizable sense existed in Scotland before *c.* 1120'.[5] Farquhar MacTaggart ('son of the priest'), who defeated invading Irish Norse on behalf of Alexander II, crushed the Galloway Rebellion of 1235 and was father-in-law to Olaf of Man, was a player on the international stage. In the 1220s he founded Fearn Abbey on Tarbat.[6] His profile as first Earl of Ross seems to attract the logic that things should start with him.

These are influential thoughts for placing the new beginnings, the building of the first parish church, at Portmahomack. Was it really not until 1215 that St Colman's was founded? What happened in the century and half that separates Farquhar from Thorfinn? There are three indications that, contrary to the burden of these gappy documents, our settlement continued to flourish, and had acquired its new church by about 1100, before the arrival of the first Earl and even before King David I. First, we can assume an interest of the Scottish church and king at least from 1179, when William I ('The Lion') built a castle at the south end of the Tarbat peninsula at Dunskeath.[7] Secondly, there is no interruption to the tireless industry of the Portmahomack metalworkers. And, lastly, the earliest finds in the new church are some pieces of broken clay – unprepossessing but significant, since they are pieces of a mould used to case a bell. This has to be the bell of a church, and its radiocarbon date allows it to be as early as 1030 – though it could be as late as 1270 (see Digest, A3). On this reading, Thorfinn was scarcely cold before the builders of a new Christianity arrived.

Since most of this chapter is concerned with the church, let us first pay a valedictory visit to the workshops. We left the craftsmen in the last chapter smithing for Macbeth or the earls of Orkney. Towards the end of the eleventh century there is a change of use and mood: the pebbled road still runs down the hill, but bronze- and iron-workers now cluster up the north end. Their hearths are associated with paved areas, stake-hole clusters and post-holes. There are numerous pits for metal-workers' waste. The shelters, windbreaks and hearths are protected from flooding by culverts, one of which is lined with the broken pieces of the Calf Stone. Within a hundred years or so the site sees another change of use from industrial to domestic. It starts with a layer of rubble levelling, and continues with the digging of pits containing domestic rubbish. More gullies are dug, and windbreaks, enclosures and shelters of indeterminate shape are fashioned out of stakes and posts. Over the dam and boggy pond, a layer of rubble provides a route for farmers and cattle. Finally, green-glazed pottery from Scarborough in Yorkshire arrives on the surface of the road. We are in the early thirteenth century (for data references, see Digest, A6).

The outer enclosure ditch, which has become a tree-lined ribbon of stagnant water, was finally decommissioned. Trees and bushes were cut down and thrown into the ditch, and the soil on either side pushed back in. Now it was ready for ploughing, and rig and furrow, containing twelfth–thirteenth-century pottery and coins, ran over the top. Only a future aeroplane would know it was there. Up near the road, ploughs soon also ran over the old workshops, and later the ground became waste, providing a space for fishermen to prepare their bait.

These events therefore align quite reasonably with the documentary story. The Portmahomack workers in precious metal start work under new patrons, Norse or Moray lords, after a raid and a fire in the late eighth or early ninth century. By the tenth or eleventh century they have added a squadron of ironsmiths. At a given moment, the site goes domestic, and within a century the estate has been tidied up and directed to farming. That given moment, dated to around 1100, should mark the creation of the parish church (Fig. 8.1).

We are about to embark on a brief history of the church of St Colman from the twelfth to the twentieth centuries, and I should hasten to reassure those readers who mainly want to know about the early monastery that this is not entirely irrelevant to

Fig. 8.1 St Colman's church from the south-west.

them. Just as the survey of the Tarbat peninsula provides a geographical context for the monastery (see Chapter 9), so the later story of the church offers it a chronological context. It is important in particular in providing an overview of the social theatre that is a Christian building. Although there was little material continuity between the monastery and the parish, we can believe that their peoples were descendants of each other. The changing Christian attitudes of Portmahomack's later people provide the time depth for a long chain of ideological mutation, in which the later echoes the earlier practice (Fig. 8.2).

Over the top of the burial ground, strewn with broken gravestones, and west of what we must suppose to have been the ruins of the semi-subterranean monastic church, a new church building was erected (*Church 2*). It was built on foundations of red sandstone slabs bonded with a lime-rich white mortar resting on water-worn boulders from the beach, laid in a trench (Fig. 8.3). Discovered among the foundation stones were four grave markers (TR21, TR30, TR 31,TR 33) and a sarcophagus lid (TR22), all reused as building stone. Traces of white mortar on the Dragon Stone (TR20) retrieved from the crypt suggest that this too had once served in the foundations of Church 2. Indeed, the slabby character of the lower courses suggests that a great many more monuments from the monastic burial ground still lie hidden in the walls of St Colman's.

154 Portmahomack

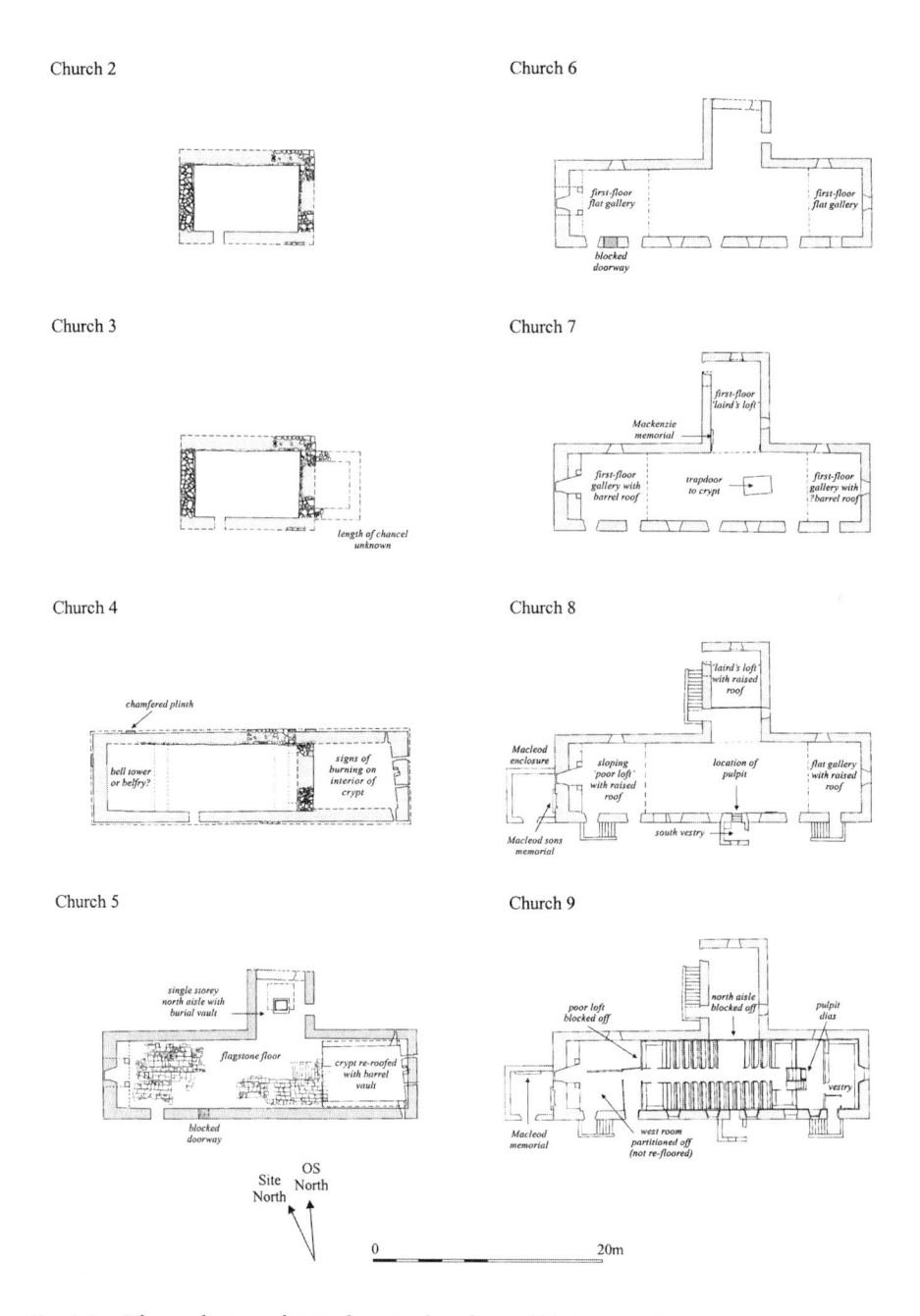

Church 2

Church 3

length of chancel unknown

Church 4

chamfered plinth
bell tower or belfry?
signs of burning on interior of crypt

Church 5

single storey north aisle with burial vault
flagstone floor
crypt re-roofed with barrel vault
blocked doorway

Site North
OS North

Church 6

first-floor flat gallery
first-floor flat gallery
blocked doorway

Church 7

Mackenzie memorial
first-floor 'laird's loft'
first-floor gallery with barrel roof
trapdoor to crypt
first-floor gallery with ?barrel roof

Church 8

Macleod enclosure
'laird's loft' with raised roof
sloping poor loft with raised roof
location of pulpit
flat gallery with raised roof
Macleod sons memorial
south vestry

Church 9

poor loft blocked off
Macleod memorial
north aisle blocked off
pulpit dias
west room partitioned off (not re-floored)
vestry

0   20m

Fig. 8.2 The evolution of St Colman's church, twelfth–twentieth centuries.

The wall of Church 2 was carried upwards with square blocks of red sandstone, to form a rectangular building 12 × 8m in plan, with a south door. It was laid in a strict east–west alignment maintained by all subsequent churches on the site (Fig. 8.2). It must have had a simple belfry of some kind to house the bell implied by the

Fig. 8.3 Foundations of the west wall of Church 2.

bell-mould fragments. Soon, probably very soon, or even immediately, two walls were added to the east end, which either implies a square-ended chancel (4m wide internally), or an attempt to join up with the old Church 1 (see Chapter 4). These projections, north and south, which make *Church 3*, were bonded with the same white mortar as before. The stone was from the upper old red sandstone beds towards Tain, which may reflect a source available to crown agents or an association with Tain, which was itself being renewed at this time. The Portmahomack building provided space for a larger community in the nave and a group of barely more than two (priest and altar boy, say) officiating in the chancel.

Church 2 was erected after the ninth century, the latest likely date of the sculpture included in its foundations: but this sculpture was generally worn and abraded at the time of its reuse. The bell-casters' pit was probably late in its radiocarbon range (1030–1270), since it was the charcoal (and perhaps therefore old wood) that was dated. The form of a single-cell building, with its 1.5 (3:2) ratio plan, would be familiar to the earlier, seventh–ninth-century, Celtic church, but the use of mortared ashlar, and the square chancel, would suit a later date better. It is not easy to be sure, since there are few dated churches in Scotland to compare with. Those simple rectangular buildings we have are generally placed in the twelfth century, and this century would suit Church 2 and its modified version, Church 3, well enough (see Chapter 4).

Church 4 was a longer, more serious communal church. The building was lengthened by 5m to the west and 10m to the east, for which purpose the west wall of Church 3 and its east wall, together with the chancel, were demolished. At the west we can suppose the erection of a belfry, if not a tower – the truncated remains of another bell-casting pit containing fragments of fired clay mould were found in this phase in the centre of the nave. At the east end there was a newly built crypt or the restoration of an old one, possibly digging out the mainly subterranean ruin of Church 1 (see Chapter 4). The new construction distinctively employed blocks of yellow sandstone ashlar, cut from quarries on the east side of the Tarbat peninsula, bonded with a grey shelly mortar. The rebuilt east side of the crypt now rose high above its sloping ground surface (then at about 16.7m AOD), and four slit window lights were included in the new build, two at each of the south-east and north-east corners.

The new church seems to fit into the mood and needs of the thirteenth century,[8] when the making of ritual was a full-time and professional business. The Parish Statutes of that time demanded that a church be divided into two, the nave built and maintained by the parishioners and the chancel paid for by the rector, and the Fourth Lateran Council of 1216 decreed that parish churches should have a resident priest. Dunbar proposes two major periods of church-building in the Highlands, the first from *c.* 1175 to 1250 and the second from 1375 to 1410. Early churches of the first period have an oblong nave and a small square-ended chancel, entered by means of a narrow chancel arch, as in two examples on the Isle of Bute, constructed between 1170 and 1200. There was Romanesque carving around the doorways. This type of simple late-twelfth-century Romanesque building would compare with our Church 3. St Mary's Chapel, Lybster, is also a small two-chambered building with a square-ended chancel and nave with a west doorway, but in Ross, Sutherland and Caithness,

Fig. 8.4 Chamfered plinth of Church 4, seen in the architect's test pit. The scale is 1m.

comments Dunbar, early architectural remains 'make a decidedly poor showing'.[9] These early churches may have been thatched with heather after local practice.[10]

The Benedictine church on Iona, built in 1200 with an aisleless choir and a single string course, was enlarged around 1220 to include an undercroft, which recalls what happened to our Church 4.[11] This was a time of great investment in the Roman Catholic Church in Scotland, and included a resurgence of the monastic movement. Perhaps special energy should be credited to the years of Farquhar MacTaggart, first Earl of Ross, who founded the Premonstratensian Abbey of Fearn, with the help of monks from Whithorn. Originally founded at Mid Fearn near Edderton, it was removed to its new site at Fearn (New Fearn) on the Tarbat peninsula in about 1238. The abbey got busy moving soil and laying drainage, adapting the old portage to drive its mill (see Chapter 9). If there was a moment by which the industrial sector at Portmahomack must have finally become redundant, this was it. From now on Fearn would call the shots on the peninsula. Our rebuilding may have been made financially possible by the assignment of Tarbat to the Abbey of Fearn, which lay in Tarbat parish and supplied its priest. By 1255 a church at Portmahomack (its first mention) is served by a canon of Fearn, and in 1274 a canon of Fearn was assigned vicarage revenues. The canons of New Fearn were still drawing revenues from the vicarage of the church of St Colman in 1529, when Pope Clement VII confirmed them.

The thirteenth-century church offered a new, enlarged space, appropriate for the ritual of the times. The congregation now stood in the extended nave (probably beneath a belfry), facing the long chancel at the east end. Beneath their feet was an earth floor disturbed by the burials of many of their ancestors. An altar, the sacramental table, would have stood at the back of the chancel, the choir either side, and the new cast of actors – priest, deacon, subdeacon, acolyte, thurifer, sacristan, torchbearer – in the space in between. New formal Roman Catholic rites most likely enhanced or replaced those of the local Christians, and the services would have been lengthy and elaborate with sophisticated liturgy and chant. The interior of the nave, where the congregation stood, would have been splendid with decorated coloured hangings, the Stations of the Cross and painted statues of the Virgin Mary and the saints. At the east end in the chancel, the priest and deacons in their colourful vestments and the boys in their cottas and cassocks would officiate at an altar decorated according to the season of the church year. During Mass, incense was burnt, and holy water, wine and oil were poured for the solemn sacrifice of the Eucharist (which was said to transform the sacred bread and wine into Christ's body and blood). These rituals of the Roman Catholic Mass had evolved from a combination of Christ's teachings, references to Jewish practice, the domestic customs of the late Roman landed gentry (which included both burning incense and sprinkling water to lay dust), together, perhaps, with some ancient local traditions. It may be that the fragments of medieval pottery found in the church excavations were from vessels used in the Mass: an aquamanile for pouring holy water for the *lavabo* (ritual washing of hands), the chafing dish for holding charcoal for the thurible (from which the incense rose). Latin was the language of worship and prayer, and the pictures and music, intended to be the best that artists could offer, were offered *ad maiorem Dei gloriam*, to the greater glory of God.

In front of the chancel, a flight of steps descended to the crypt beneath. Here would be a safe and private place to house relics and the sacramental oil, wine and hosts in aumbries and chests. It can also have served as a place for special devotions, such as Masses to be said for specific souls, in the manner of a chantry, or in favour of particular kinds of intercession, such as that of the Virgin Mary – a Lady Chapel. It was during this period that the Portmahomack community claimed to be hosting the relics of Colman, the seventh-century bishop of Lindisfarne (see Chapter 1).

One major event had marked the fabric of the church during the Middle Ages. The internal walling of Church 4, including all the walls of the crypt, show marks of significant burning, which has scorched the face of the sandstone to a bright orange. A series of dumps and lenses of charcoal was also found in this phase, in the nave near the crypt entrance. The excavator thought these might be associated with fallen roof timbers or thatch. A major fire had clearly affected the nave and reached down into the crypt. After the fire, the parishioners soon recovered, laying a mortar floor and plastering the crypt walls.

This great fire that marked most of the internal walling of Church 4 may relate to a documented incident of the 1480s. A long-lasting feud over land and cattle between the Rosses of Balnagowan and the Mackays of Strathnaver had boiled over at some point around the middle of the century. A party of marauding Mackays, well out of their own territory and on the edge of Ross ground, was rounded up and chased into the church of Tarbat, where they took refuge. They were locked in by the Rosses and the church set on fire; their leader, Angus Mackay of Strathnaver, was burnt to death with an unknown small number of his following. The Clan Aoid (Mackay) naturally did not take this without retaliation and in time formed a large war band and attacked the Rosses somewhere on the border between Ross and Mackay territory – in any case a fluid one. The resulting battle of 'Aldy Charrish' or 'Aldecharwis' has not been located. The Rosses were heavily defeated by the Mackays, losing at least eleven of their leading men, who are named in the Calendar of Fearn, which gives the date of the battle as 7 July 1487.[12]

Between the twelfth century and the sixteenth, many people were buried in the nave of the medieval church, of whom 99 were excavated (Fig. 8.5). The first group lies beneath the mortar floor, so is taken to be earlier than the fifteenth century. There are astonishingly few of them: 18, of which 9 were identified as adult males, 2 as females and 6 as children. But a high proportion of these – 5 males, 1 female and 2 children – were buried in coffins. This leads one to suppose that burial in the nave and the use of a coffin at this time was something of a privilege. Burial 43 preserved a leather shoe in a style that belonged to the late fourteenth or early fifteenth century (Fig. 8.6).

The period following the laying of the mortar floor, on the other hand, saw an explosion of burial in the nave. The demographic profile was that of a more normal population: 36 males, 19 females, 14 children and 19 infants. Only 12 of these burials had coffins and 8 had shroud pins. This population was shorter than their monkish predecessors – men averaged 5ft 6in (*c.* 1.7m) and women 5ft 1in (*c.* 1.55m) – both shorter than modern Scots, but the specialist thought they would have had similar

Fig. 8.5 Medieval burials under excavation in the nave.

faces. They suffered from most of the known medieval ailments, including rickets in childhood, caused by Vitamin D deficiency, a well-known result of swaddling babies and thus denying them sunshine. Contrary to popular belief, north-east Scotland is not itself naturally deprived of sunlight. In the fifteenth–sixteenth centuries, 62 per cent of those buried were children or infants, so acute illnesses such as diarrhoea and respiratory infections were likely to have been prevalent. However, 47 per cent of the adults, slightly more men than women, lived to be over 45 years old. The women particularly suffered from osteoarthritis and osteoporosis, and two had died in childbirth. In contrast to the monastic period, only two stone memorials can be assigned to the Middle Ages. One lies at the west end of the church and carries a sword and the initials AMRM, perhaps a member of the Munro family. The other lies (still buried) outside the east wall and carries a floriate cross (Fig. 8.7). Both these grave slabs probably date to the fifteenth or sixteenth centuries.

Burial in the nave ceased abruptly on the construction of *Church 5*, which was effectively a new building with a revolutionary design. The whole axis of service in the Tarbat church turned through 90 degrees. The pulpit, replacing the altar as the focus, stood against the south wall. The congregation now entered through a new south door beneath a belfry, and mustered on a newly laid flagstone floor facing south to hear the sermon, which formed the new religious focus. The former east crypt, no longer required for mystical association with relics and intercession, was rebuilt with a vault to contain the coffins of selected persons. The medieval arrangements were swept away, and the floor was dug out to subsoil at the level of the wall footings. The

Fig. 8.6 Fragment of leather shoe from Burial 43. The shoe rests on a piece of wooden coffin and within it lay the remains of a big toe.

barrel vault was bonded with a silty clay at the sides and a hard coarse buff mortar at the top, where timber centring used to construct the vault had left its imprint. On the floor of the crypt was a layer of the silty clay used in the sides of the vault; when rediscovered it was covered by traces of rotted planks, perhaps from a floor or the remains of coffins. A new set of steps was constructed, which debouched through an inserted stone doorframe carrying a Mason's mark. The hard buff mortar used for the top of the vault provided a signature for all the building works relating to Church 5. The stone used seems to have been obtained from a distance, and perhaps from outside the peninsula. Part of the north wall of the nave was demolished and a single-storey north aisle constructed. At its centre was a burial vault, still containing coffins in 1997. At the west end, a relieving arch was inserted inside the west wall, providing a joint platform nearly 3m wide. Its purpose was to support a belfry – an earlier version of the one that still stands. The relieving arch was no doubt necessary to let in the light of the splayed west window, but faith in its stability was short lived: a curious reinforcement contrived from two pillars was inserted directly under the soffit of the arch.

This new interior space was created as a result of the Reformation, and reflected its thinking.[13] The emphasis was now on the word of God as found in the Bible and the enriching sermon of the minister. *The First Book of Discipline* (1560) summed up the new liturgical requirements as: a bell to bring the people together, a pulpit to preach the word, a basin for baptism and a table for communion. The pulpit became the main focus, as at St Colman's. The intercession of saints was no longer sought,

Fig. 8.7 Grave cover seen at the east end outside the chancel. Drawn by Trevor Pearson.

so that there was no more need of statues, chantry chapels or altars. Confession was discontinued, but there was a stool of repentance on which sinners had to sit during services. Fornicators were required to sit on the stool for three days, and adulterers were obliged to stand on it wearing a hair shirt.

Churches were embellished with a rectangular extension to the north, known in Scotland as a 'north aisle'. Its purpose was to house the laird's family and provide him with a family burial place. In 1581 the General Assembly of the Church of Scotland forbade burial within churches, a stricture repeated four times before 1643. Thus burial was to be no longer in the nave but 'lying in the most free air'. However, burial vaults were erected by important families, and these could be within the church, as at St Colman's, under the north aisle and in a refurbished east crypt.

Holy Communion, no longer the mystical transformation of the Eucharist but a more symbolic feast, was taken by members of the congregation at a table before the pulpit. Communion plate was sold and replaced with simple domestic wares. Communion took place once or twice a year, and people travelled from considerable distances to be present. Communicants passed bread to each other, and wine was drunk from the one large cup, or, when crowds were large, two or more cups might be used. Admission to the Communion table was by a token obtained from the minister. Pewter communion vessels and tokens, denoting eligibility to sit at the communion table, have survived in Tarbat Old Church from a later period: in 1806 six communion cups, three plates for the bread and a thousand tokens all marked 'Tarbat 1805' had been bought for the sum of £5 sterling.

The ideas that led to the Reformation were affecting Scotland by the 1530s and reached their peak in our region by the 1560s.[14] Church 5 must have been up and working by the turn of the century, but the reordering of the establishment may have taken a few more years to effect. Many medieval churches were derelict by 1560, and would in any case need rebuilding.[15] At the Reformation, Tarbat Church was first assigned as a *mensa* to the Bishop of Ross. In 1626–8, Fearn parish, including the Abbey,was separated from the parish of Tarbat, to which it had therefore originally belonged. By 1634 Sir John Mackenzie is chief heritor and has the right to the north aisle.[16] The laird was increasingly significant in the control of religious thinking, as well as in the economic and social control of the local inhabitants. At St Colman's he entered via a private door in the east wall of the north aisle. The bones of his relatives lay in a special burial vault beneath his feet. The construction of the north aisle had presumably been achieved before 1623, the date on two cartouches reinserted in its walls. In 1690 an act in favour of Presbyterians was passed by William and Mary, and Tarbat may have then ceased to be Episcopal in name. It became one of fourteen churches in the possession of George, Lord Tarbat, first Earl of Cromartie and Sir John Mackenzie's heir. The Christian religion now became an overt instrument of the aristocracy, and the relationship between the local landowners and the minister was to become ever stronger over the next 300 years.

The power of the Catholic Church was broken, though Episcopalian Catholicism lingered on in the north-east, and half the Catholic priests became Protestant ministers. Although a few Catholic priests were said to be still 'haunting' the Tarbat area in the seventeenth century, after 1560 the Roman church had no jurisdiction in Scotland, and the responsibility for paying for the upkeep of the church and the salary of the minister was entrusted to the lords, and after 1690 to the local landowners or heritors (in general those who had acquired the former church lands). The Revolution Settlement of 1690 theoretically placed administrative power over the church in the hands of the congregation, but for the next few centuries the landowners and ministers (often belonging to the same families) were to be largely in control of the minds as well as the bodies of the Tarbat congregations. It can be guessed that a measure of older superstitions or independent thinking still survived. In 1714, according to Colin Macnaughton's history, Alexander Robertson, fisherman of Portmaholmag, gave the couple-tree (that is, the beams supporting the roof of the church) three wacks with an axe after the death of his father to make sure the disease that had killed him did not spread. Significantly it may also be noted that in 1735 none of the elders of Tarbat church could speak English, their language presumably being Gaelic.

There was just one exception to the stricture against burial inside St Colman's church. This was the grave of William Mackenzie, minister to the parish of Tarbat from 1638 until his death in 1642. When the grave associated with his tombstone was excavated, it proved to contain, not only the skeleton of a man (26–45 years old) but a woman (46+) and an infant under 2½ (Fig. 8.8). Other memorials survive from inside the church. Built into the blocking of the old south door are three fragments of a recumbent slab, featuring a crest with a stag's head, a skull and crossbones and the letters NDH SPOVS and CAILLI. The skull and crossbones suggests a seventeenth-century date and the stag is an emblem of the Mackenzie family. The family was acquiring land in the Tarbat area from the early seventeenth century, and Sir George Mackenzie was created Viscount Tarbat in 1684 and Earl of Cromartie in 1703. This fragment commemorated an ancestor of Sir George who is not yet identified. Names recorded for early seventeenth-century Mackenzies are Colin, Alexander, John, Kenneth and Roderick. Also commemorated was the wife of the dead man, indicated here only by the letters for 'and his spouse'. The memorial plaques (cartouches) set into the east and west walls of the north aisles both carry the date 1623. One was for Jean Leslye, the wife of James Cuthbert, one-time Provost of Inverness commemorated on the opposite wall.

A series of inspections and estimates that led to the erection of *Church 6* began in the 1720s and took some forty years to realise.[17] Curiously it involved no great redesign, but a massive amount of rebuilding: the church was largely rebuilt from the foundations using a better and more local stone from the quarries on the east side of the peninsula. The iconic Tarbat belfry, made in beautifully shaped and fitted ashlar, belongs to this phase. With its attractive 'birdcage' shape and iron bell-frame reached by a winding stair, it is thought to be the work of Alexander Stronach, the dynastic name taken by at least three generations of master masons living in Tarbat, and active between 1634 and 1790. The present church bell is inscribed: 'The Church of Tarbat. John Milne fecit J764', but a later inscription reads: 'Recast 1908'.

Provision was made for a greatly increased congregation: a flat first-floor gallery constructed at the west end would have held another fifty people; this area would become known later as the poor loft, and this is how it may have begun. At the east

Fig. 8.8 The tomb and memorial of William Mackenzie. The inscription reads:
HIC IACET PRAEC VENERABILIS MR GVIELMUS MACKENZIE TARBATENSIS ECCLESIAE QVONDAM
PASTOR QVI VT IN ECCLESIAE COMMODUM NATUS SIC IN EIUSDEM DAMNUM ANTE DIEM DE NATUS
FATO CESSIT 29 SEPTEMBRIS ANNO D 1642
PHOENIX PRESBITERVM FOELIX SINE FELLE COLVMBA
HOC TEGITUR TVMVLO PASTOR AMOR POPULI
SR IOHNE MACKENZIE OF TARBAT OUT OF HIS LOVE TO HIS PASTOR BESTOVED THIS BURIAIL
PLEACE ON HIM

end a more modest gallery, supported by two joists, may have been intended as an organ loft. There were now no fewer than five doors in the south wall. Starting from the east, the first was accessed by a staircase and led to the supposed organ loft. The next was arched and may have been that for the minister, the next two led to the nave and the last provided access to the west gallery. The congregation thus found its way through three doors, suggesting that places were allocated and society was well ranked. The laird's family continued to use their private east entrance into the ground floor north aisle.

Social segregation became more marked still in *Church 7*, the result of modifications later in the eighteenth century. The north aisle was extended and an additional storey was raised, now reached by a specially dedicated exterior staircase at the new north end. The new and commodious upper floor – the 'laird's loft' – was furnished with a fireplace to keep the occupants warm during lengthy sermons. The ground-floor door on the east side was converted into the window that can still be seen. The floor of the west gallery was raked to give its occupants a better view. The interior of the nave and aisle were plastered white.

A visitation of 1780 explains the background to these developments. It resulted in the unanimous agreement of the heritors

> to have the aisle belonging to Sir John Gordon and to which he has exclusive right, fitted up in such a manner as to answer the purpose of accommodating the parishioners in attending divine service, the said John Gordon having given his consent to this under condition that the thing is to be done at the joint expense of the heritors, which was also agreed to.[18]

It was also agreed that the west gallery, currently dedicated to the poor of the parish, shall be reallocated to the use of the heritors for the price of the seats. This agreement meant that the laird and the heritors could rise from the ground together.

Each part of the community – laird, minister, upper class, professionals and poor – was now truly consigned to its own estate. Assuming a modicum of space around the pulpit, the whole church now had a capacity of some 1,000 souls.

Further modifications were soon made, to result in *Church 8*. The wall plate of the whole church was raised by 1.07m, and supported a new roof with a shallower pitch. Access to the laird's loft was moved to the south end, with a new external stone staircase. External stone staircases were similarly provided for the west and east galleries. A vestry was constructed on the south wall, where the minister could enter, robe and step straight up onto the pulpit. The windows were enlarged. The walls were replastered up to the level of the new high ceiling. A higher wainscoting was inserted, and above it the plaster was painted a terracotta colour.

We get a flavour of a Ross-shire cleric of the late eighteenth and early nineteenth centuries (and of his sermons) in William Forbes, who was Minster of Tarbat from 1797 to 1838. His brother-in-law described him as

> a profound and scriptural divine . . . at one time in a flow of high spirits, laughing until his eyes ran over at his own anecdotes – at another sunk in the deepest gloom, which his countenance, naturally dark and sallow, was particularly well suited to express.[19]

Fig. 8.9 Recording the memorials of the seventeenth–nineteenth-century churchyard.

William Forbes's exacting standards led him falsely to accuse a parishioner of making his maid Jean Purves pregnant, leading the aptly named Archibald Dudgeon to challenge him to a duel. (In fact the guilty party was Archibald's brother.) William Forbes is remembered in a remarkable eulogy in stone, which still hangs on the south wall of the nave:

> IN MEMORY OF THE REVD WILLIAM FORBES AM LATE MINISTER OF TARBAT WHO DIED 12 MAY 1838 IN THE 72ND YEAR OF HIS AGE, AND 41ST OF HIS MINISTRY. ENDUED FROM HIS YOUTH WITH DISTINGUISHING GRACE HE BECAME THROUGH LIFE A FAITHFUL AND DEVOTED SERVANT OF JESUS CHRIST GIVING TO EACH OF THE CHILDREN OF ZION HIS PORTION OF MEAT IN DUE SEASON; AND DEALING WITH DARING SINNERS AND PRESUMPTIOUS HYPOCRITES WITH A FIDELITY, POINT AND PATHOS, WHICH WILL TELL AT THE TRIBUNAL OF JESUS TO SUPERIOR TALENTS, AND A JUDGEMENT CLEAR AND PENETRATING. HE JOINED A CORRECT CLASSICAL TASTE WHICH GAVE TO HIS DICTION A PECULIAR DEGREE OF PERSPECUITY, NEATNESS AND PRECISION, AND A TRANSPARENCY TO HIS STATEMENT OF TRUTH WHICH TOLD BOTH ON THE JUDGEMENT AND CONSCIENCE. HIS PRAYERS, RICH IN DIVINE UNCTION WERE GRACIOUSLY ANSWERED IN THE CONVERSION OF SINNERS AND HE COULD SAY WITH THE APOSTLE; 'I HAVE NO GREATER JOY THAN TO HEAR THAT MY CHILDREN WALK IN TRUTH'. HE WAS ALSO (LIKE HIS GREAT MASTER) A MAN OF SORROWS. HIS SON ALEXANDER A PROMISING YOUTH AT THE AGE OF 16 DIED IN 1833; HIS ELDEST SON WILLIAM, WHO WAS POSSESSED OF GREAT PIETY AND ABILITY WAS CUT OFF TWO YEARS THEREAFTER IN THE 20TH YEAR OF HIS AGE. BUT THESE SEVERE TRIALS, BEING SANCTIFIED MADE HIS CHRISTIAN GRACES SHINE MORE BRIGHTLY. HE DIED RIPE FOR GLORY. THE RIGHTEOUS SHALL BE ON EVERLASTING REMEMBRANCE. HIS ELDEST DAUGHTER ISABELLA DIED IN 1840; IN THE HOPE WHICH IS THROUGH GRACE, HAVING A DESIRE TO DEPART AND BE WITH CHRIST.

By now (but probably long before) the ministers were supported by the farming of Glebe land next to the church, and the provision of a manse (the vicarage). In 1801 the manse was totally rebuilt, and the Glebe enlarged from 4 acres to 6 acres and 2 roods. Geanies made over a small part of the land that adjoined the northeast part of the Glebe. The majority of the population of the eighteenth and nineteenth centuries were buried in the churchyard, in which memorials now proliferated at an increasing rate. While families tended the graves of their ancestors, they would brook no encroachment, and there was only one answer: to increase the size of the churchyard, which was to happen in 1854, 1868 and 1893 (see Fig. 4.8). Seen from the air, a circular bank shows the western limits of the early churchyard and the final circuit still in force today. After the Reformation, families claimed the right of burial in certain parts of the churchyard (lairs), and were deemed to be their sole owners. Most of the memorials erected were tombstones, upright head or foot stones carrying a name or initials and a date (Fig. 8.9). In the seventeenth century, from which we have only a few survivals, the recumbent slab was popular, carrying on a tradition from the Middle Ages. It seems to have been appropriate only to ministers and the richer classes. Some of these slabs were recycled, although the practice was frowned on. On 27 September 1789 a meeting of the Kirk Session heard a complaint from John Ross, Tacksman of Wester Geanies, about his rights in the churchyard of Tarbat. In a cheap move, Hugh Bain, a tailor in Elgin, had taken violent possession of a burial place, slipping his aunt into another family's lair, and cutting away part of the initial KM (for Katherine Munro, wife of Hugh Ross of Geanies) to make it IM, for Isabel Monro, the aunt. More elaborate markers were made in the form of tables on stone legs, columns and occasionally crosses. Symbols became popular in the eighteenth century, particularly reminders of mortality such as the hourglass, the coffin or grave-diggers' spades.

The Tarbat churchyard is representative of a number of Ross-shire families. The Rosses themselves, who held sway in the pre-Reformation centuries, are found all over the burial ground. The Mackenzies, who rose to fame after the Reformation, have a number of clusters of fine monuments, which probably represent their lairs. We can also track the resting places of Munros, Mackays, MacLeods, Skinners and many others who lived and died in Easter Ross and knew The Port and its ever-varying fortunes.

It is interesting to observe the emphasis of monumentality at Portmahomack through twelve centuries (Fig. 8.10). In the early days of the monastery, the sixth century, grave markers were few and modest. They increased in number and ultimately in size through the eighth century, those remembered being monks and priests. During the next four centuries, investment in memorials was low or non-existent, picking up in the thirteenth and fourteenth centuries for the aristocracy. A serious growth in the size and monumentality of memorials followed, with increasing attention to the lords and the ministers of the great families. During the nineteenth century, memorials were democratised, so that few parishioners were without a marked grave and the means to pay for them. This strange fluctuation must be a real reflection of the attitude of successive generations to their ancestors, and when and whether that attitude was turned into material culture for archaeologists to find.[20]

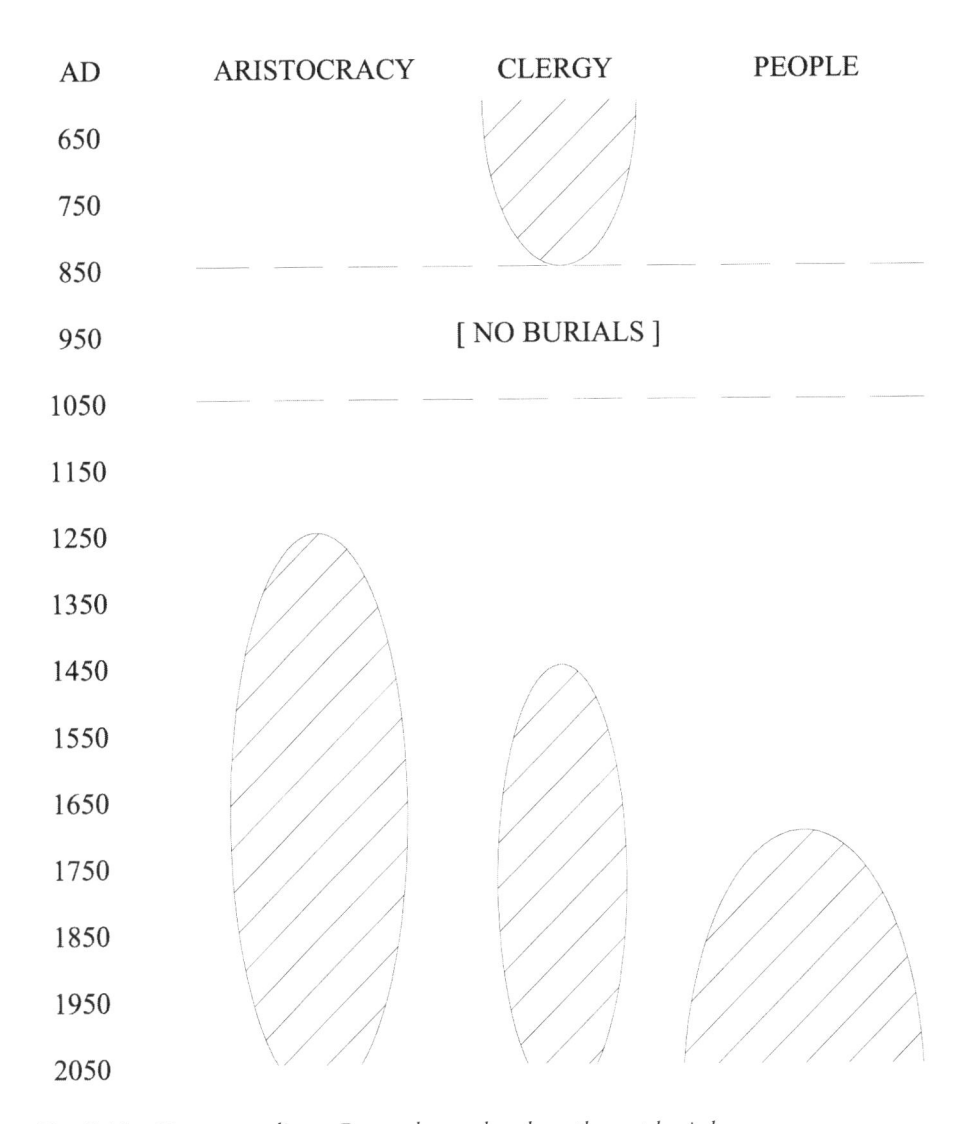

AD	ARISTOCRACY	CLERGY	PEOPLE
650			
750			
850			
950		[NO BURIALS]	
1050			
1150			
1250			
1350			
1450			
1550			
1650			
1750			
1850			
1950			
2050			

Fig. 8.10 Monumentality at Portmahomack: where the emphasis lay.

The social competition visible in the new layout of the church may have reflected a surge in the old struggle between laird and landowners, and landowners and the rest of the congregation. Land reform and improvement were to the benefit of the landowners, but not necessarily to that of their employees, many of whom were being infamously dispossessed by the Highland Clearances. Ministers played a crucial role in this, since their advice and strictures could be pivotal. In the early nineteenth century, the labourers were increasingly supported by ministers of a new evangelical persuasion, and matters came to a head in 1843, when ministers and congregation broke with the bonds of the heritors and marched out to form the Free Church of Scotland. At Portmahomack, the new Free Church building was built between St

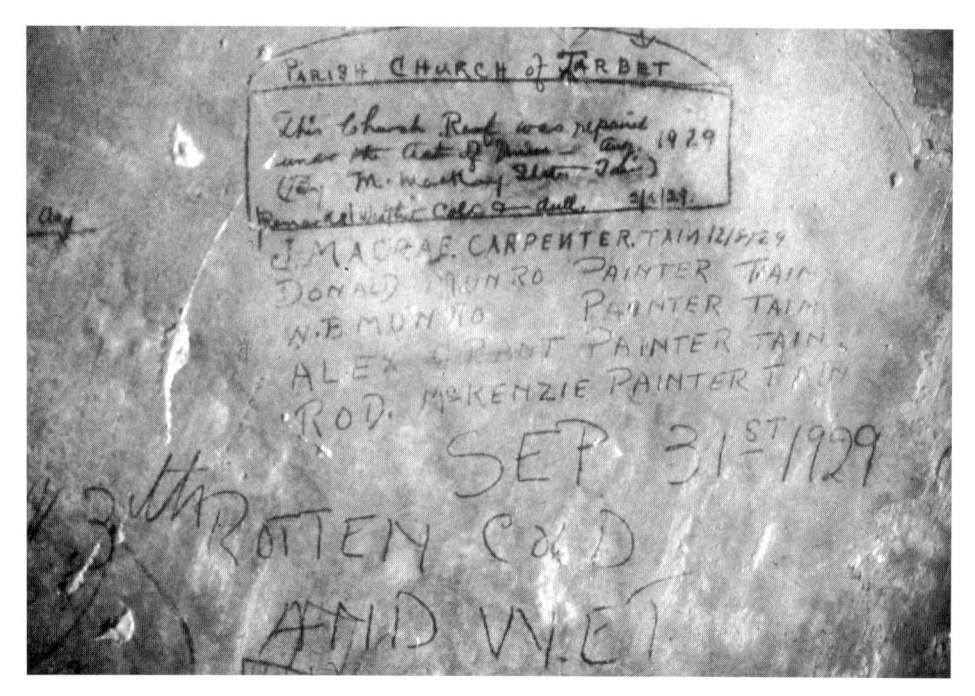

Fig. 8.11 Graffiti in the twentieth-century church.

Colman's and the beach (where its successor, dating to 1893, now stands), and most of the congregation joined it. St Colman's congregation, which had numbered over a 1,000 before 1843, had dwindled to 85 ten years later.

The old church was adapted to its new circumstances, reaching back into earlier traditions to emphasise its superior ancestry to become *Church 9*. The direction of worship returned to the traditional west–east axis. High box pews were placed at either end of the nave with smaller unenclosed seating in between. At the east end, the loft was removed and replaced by an elaborate timber staging with a pulpit and precentor's box at the front and a vestry at the back. A lower ceiling was inserted, and the openings to the north aisle, both upper and lower, were boarded up with timber panelling, which also continued round all the nave walls. The nave walls and vestry were painted in lemon yellow (upper half) and terracotta red (lower half), separated by a horizontal black stripe.

Tarbat Old Church had now become the preserve of 'high church' parishioners. In 1866 the General Assembly permitted the return of music, and Tarbat subsequently acquired an organ. The eastern platform was shared by the organ and the lectern that held the Bible. In front of it was a box from which the precentor would read out extracts of the sacred texts while the congregation awaited the minister's sermon. The sermon, which might continue for an hour or more, was delivered from the platform above. Perhaps with these lengthy perorations in mind, nineteenth-century heritors were obliged to provide seating spaces for their parishioners to the measure of 18 × 29in per posterior.

However, financial support was still forthcoming. In 1851 a grass Glebe was provided for the minister and in 1874 the land held by Minister Campbell amounted to 12 acres. In 1856 an inspection recommended extensive repairs to the church, manse and outbuildings. Church walls, the harling, the roof, stone stairs, windows and doors all needed repair. Notwithstanding the existence of the popular Free Church, the Tarbat churchyard continued to be the main place for the burial of everyone, and the churchyard was enlarged in 1868 and again in 1893.

In the twentieth century, the upkeep was to provide a continuing challenge. In 1928 the church, manse and Glebe were transferred from the Heritors to the Church of Scotland Trustees. Graffiti record a repair job in 1929 (Fig 8.11), but only seventeen years later, in 1946, the church was declared redundant, and in 1980 the now ruinous building was purchased by Tarbat Historic Trust for £1.

Church 9 was essentially the church that was restored by the Tarbat Historic Trust, who have effectively created *Church 10*. The dais at the east end has been maintained, but its superstructure has been opened up to create a gallery for the museum. The upper and lower parts of the north aisle have been reopened to create the Laird's Loft auditorium (above) and the Treasury (below). The old poor loft has been re-floored and has become the Activity Centre. In the crypt, the fabric and atmosphere of the original churches have been preserved. The lower part of the east wall, with its original aumbry, may date to the eighth century; its upper half and its windows to the thirteenth. The marks of burning in 1480s are still visible, except where the medieval walls are now hidden by the inserted barrel vault of the seventeenth century. In the nave there are glimpses of preserved walls, and the line of others marked out by paving or brass rods in the floor. The churches of the eighth, twelfth, thirteenth, sixteenth, eighteenth and nineteenth centuries run like veins through the old building that the Tarbat Trust has hopefully endowed with another 1,000 years of life.

The story of St Colman's church is the story of its people since the twelfth century, and it gives context in several ways to the early monastery that is our main concern here. The church was the theatre in which the spiritual aspirations of the community were played out – at one time dependent on their lords, at another on their intellectuals, at another on their gods. As the spiritual agenda changed, so did the scenery and the stage props within the building and outside it. The investment in monuments was never very great, and yet the resources of the peninsula did not vary unduly and the population must have stayed roughly the same size. With this in mind, the achievements of the eighth century seem little short of miraculous.

Notes

1. Oram (2004: 96).
2. Barrow (1981: 73).
3. Ibid. p. 62.
4. Grant (2005: 110); cf. Barrow (1981: 51).
5. Barrow (1981: 68, 73).
6. Grant (2005: 107–23).
7. Ibid. p. 107.
8. Barrow (1981: 72–5).

9. Dunbar (1981: 39, 49).
10. Notes by Arthur Mitchell in MacFarlane (1906–8), vol. 1.
11. Dunbar (1981: 41); Ritchie (1997: 104)
12. I have taken this account verbatim from a note kindly sent to me by Monica Clough.
13. Howard (1995: 193).
14. Dunbar (1996: 127–8).
15. Howard (1995: 168).
16. Fraser and Munro (1988: 31, 47).
17. Ibid. p. 45.
18. Ibid. pp. 46–7.
19. Fraser and Munro (1988: 55).
20. Carver (2005b).

CHAPTER 9

Ritual landscape, with portage

If one way of seeking a context for the early monastery at Portmahomack is to see what happened to the site in its later years, the subject of Chapter 8, another is to examine the landscape in which it lies, which is the subject of this one. We have already noted the 'sister sites' of Nigg, Shandwick and Hilton of Cadboll, which share the ornament, date and status of their monuments with those at Portmahomack. How did these places connect with each other? And what was their role in the peninsula? Did the peninsula itself have a special function in the region in which it lay? If there was a portage here, as the place name implies, then, whatever its sense of isolation today, in a maritime world Tarbat was a crossroads at a central place (for archaeological data, places and places names cited in this chapter, see Digest, A8).

LANDSCAPE

The spine of the peninsula (Fig. 9.1) is a chain of hills along its east side beginning in the south with the hill of Nigg (200m a.s.l.) and petering away north in ever smaller humps: Geanies (70m), Meikle Tarrel (60m) and Bindal (30m). A low-lying neck of land connects this chain westwards to the mainland, the Dornoch Firth pushing into it from the north at the Bay of Inver, and the Cromarty Firth from the south, at the Bay of Nigg. Between them is perched Loch Eye, so it takes only a little imagination to claim this as a portage route, which I will (imaginatively) try to do in a moment. At the centre of the isthmus is an E-W ridge which includes the Hill of Fearn, where Fearn Abbey was built, and represents the natural entry onto the peninsula, unless of course you come by boat.

Landing a boat was easiest at a beach. The west coast has both shelter and sand, the havens of Portmahomack in the north and of Nigg to the south. On the tricky east coast with its rocks and on-shore winds, there is just one harbour halfway along, Shandwick Bay, with a small beach adjacent at Hilton. All round the tip of the peninsula there are rocky inlets, some little more than narrow gaps in the slabby rocks, where a boat may take refuge or be held still while being unloaded or heaved out of reach of the sea – Port Uilleam, Port Mor, Port Buckie, Port a' Chasteil and Port a Chait. Seafarers running for Cromarty Firth aim between the Hill of Nigg and Gallow Hill (the north and south Sutors). Those heading for Portmahomack, Dornoch or Tain must leave the Ness to port. If they get caught on the weather shore, they must beat for the rocky creeks and such shelter as a cave affords.

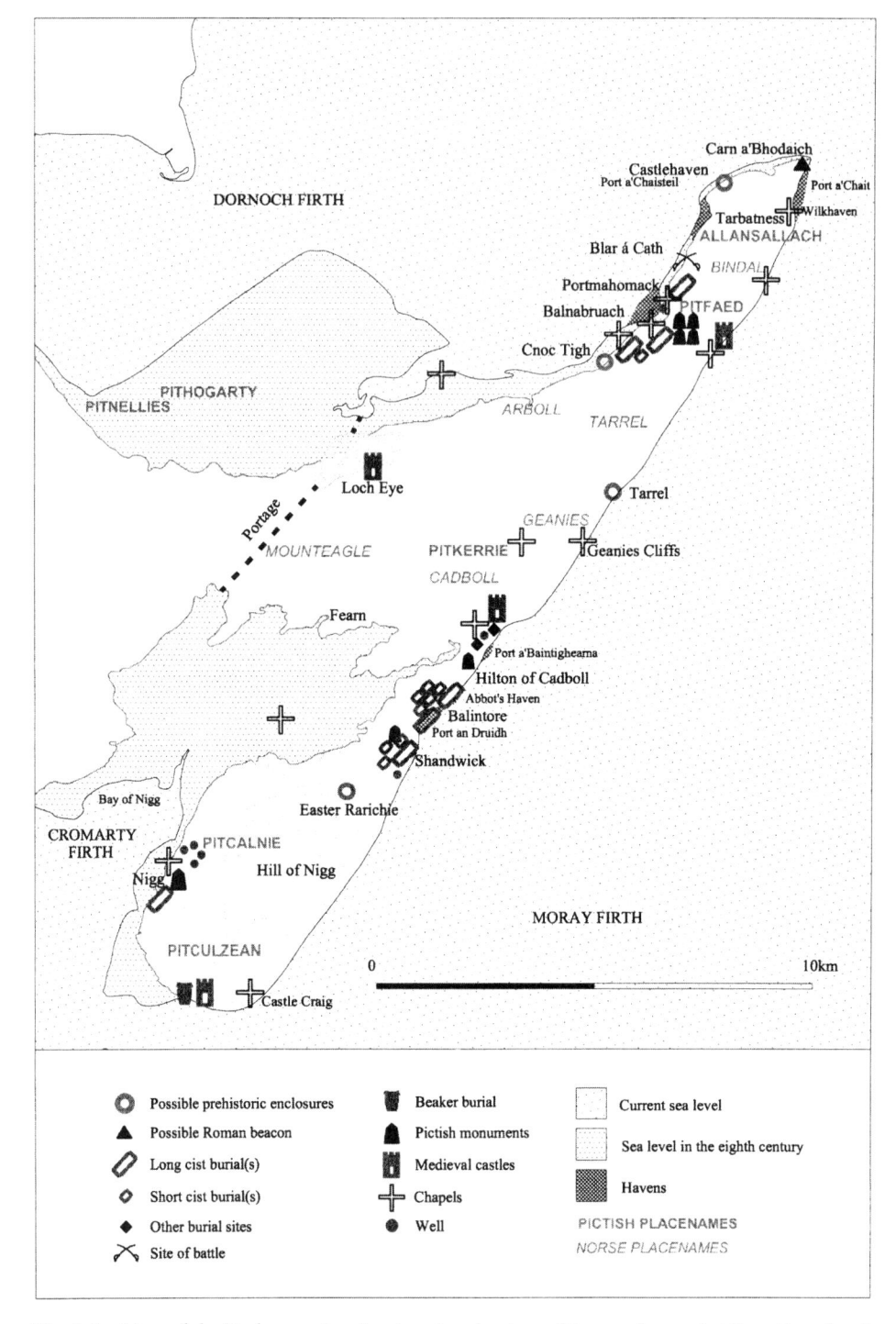

Fig. 9.1 Map of the Tarbat peninsula, showing the sites of Portmahomack, Nigg, Shandwick and Hilton of Cadboll, as well as sites of harbours, chapels and wells and Pictish and Norse place names and the line of the portage. The eighth-century coastline is conjectural.

Communication by ferry and boat was the norm until recently, and, although sea travel off the peninsula appears daunting, especially in winter, the east coast, as the west, has probably seen 4,000 years of seafaring.[1]

In the late eighteenth century there were twelve boats operating in Tarbat parish from five fisher-towns.[2] The standard boat carried seven men and a boy, was low and open, about 26ft (8m) long, and rowed with six oars, sometimes assisted by two big square sails. It was easily beached and did not require a jetty.[3] Cod fishing increased from 1670 using lugworm and shellfish as bait. Banks of shells are encountered at many sites around the peninsula, in addition to Portmahomack; they are perhaps owed to the preparation of this bait (although a very hungry person will, I believe, eat a shellfish). Around 1800 there were herrings in the firths in winter, skate and haddock further out in summer and 50,000 lobsters could be caught in one season. In 1845 the population of Portmahomack doubled seasonally with people from all over the Highlands arriving to assist with the herring curing.[4] Ice houses were built to preserve the catch at the fishing villages of Hilton, Shandwick, Balintore and Rockfield.

The land itself was (and is) extremely fertile, lying at the centre of the largest concentration of some of the best arable land in Scotland, with plenty of pasture as well as moorland. The main crop was bere barley, with some wheat for landlords, and in 1791 the parish produced 'much more corn than is sufficient for the support of the inhabitants'.[5] Ploughs were made almost entirely of wood.[6] The principal fuel was turf or peat, but this ancestral resource was already in peril from the plough. Around 1800 Fearn people were spending the whole summer finding and fetching turf and peat for fuel 'to the total neglect of everything that might improve and benefit their farms'.[7] The peninsula was famous for the quality of its sandstone, used for building and carving (see Chapter 5). In the absence of limestone, lime was obtained by burning seashells. But tenants on the whole could afford neither stone nor timber and built their houses of 'earth', remaking them every five or seven years.[8]

However miserable humans contrived to make life for each other, the resources of this remarkable peninsula were generous. How far does the early nineteenth-century description echo earlier days? We have already seen that cattle and sheep were raised, barley was grown and the good stone was used to build medieval churches, and, of course, it was carved by the Picts into some of the finest and largest monuments in Europe. Turf was used as fuel and for cladding large timber-frame buildings and heather was used for thatch. In some ways, the early settlers had all the good things that the peninsula offered, but in larger quantities.

EARLY INHABITANTS

Real prehistory is hard to find, or has proved hard to remember. In the nineteenth century a probable early Bronze Age or Beaker period burial emerged from the sand on the shore beneath the North Sutor. It consisted of two earthenware urns, one filled with ashes and fragments of half-burned bones, the other with 'bits of a black bituminous-looking stone, somewhat resembling jet which had been fashioned into beads, and little flat parallelograms, perforated edgewise with four holes apiece. Many animal bones were reported from associated layers.'[9] Other burials have been claimed for the Bronze Age, on the basis of their slabs, but I think we should look at these again (below).

For the Iron Age, the remains of what may have been a broch stand on a tongue of raised beach 650m south-west of Lower Seafields.[10] Tarrel dun, possibly dating to the Iron Age, has a wall measuring up to 3.7m in thickness and enclosing an area about 9.5 × 6.7m.[11] The fortification at Easter Rarichie is a good candidate for the later Iron Age (that is, the Pictish period). It has a sister site to the north-west, but neither has been investigated.

The Carn a' Bhodaich near the lighthouse is possibly a prehistoric cairn, but has also been suggested as the site of a Roman beacon.[12] A Roman camp has been supposed on the Black Moor about 1 mile (1.61km) from Tarbat Ness.[13] A Roman coin found in Tarbat churchyard is a 'fairly worn antoninianius of Tetricus II, AD 270–273/4 minted at Trier(?)'.[14] The claims that these imply Romans on the peninsula, treated with scepticism even at the time, are now regaining ground. Intensive survey of the Moray Firth region by Ian Keillar and Barri Jones from the air and on the ground at Tarradale in the Beauly Firth has revealed traces that would be accepted without cavil as Roman anywhere else.[15] Probably Roman or Pictish are intertidal structures in the Beauly Firth originally noticed by J. Fraser before 1699 – 'oak beams 20–30 ft long with axe marks under the sand'[16] – and investigated by Alex Hale of Edinburgh University in 1994, who found two squared, jointed cross-beams plus timber-lined pits, associated with cherry pips. The Romans sailed around the whole island of Britain following their victory at Mons Graupius, and in all probability they would have returned, for slaves, skins, furs, cattle, punitive raids or diplomacy. In any event, Tarbat Ness did not move and would remain as it had always been in the professional consciousness of anyone sailing in the northern parts of the North Sea.

Burials constitute a type of archaeological monument that is apt to be noted and remembered by antiquaries, but they have to be treated separately here because, with the single exception of the North Sutor Beaker burial, their dates are nearly always in doubt. In the absence of grave goods, as has generally been the case, the recognition of early burials has depended on finding human skeletons associated with large slabs of sandstone. But without careful excavation it is hard to know how the two relate. In general terms there are three types of burial in this vicinity that commonly employ slabs of sandstone. First, Bronze Age short cist burials, in which a crouched skeleton is accompanied by pottery vessels and other objects, encased in a box or cist made of large, usually single, slabs. Secondly, Pictish-period long cist burials, in which the skeleton is extended and the slabs line and roof the pit. We have seen examples of these at Portmahomack itself, and noted that their use is pre-echoed in the Iron Age (see Chapter 4). Thirdly, the closely related head support burials, where the skull is supported by one or more stones (also see Chapter 4). And there is a fourth kind. The Vikings used a type of cist burial in the form of rectangular, oval or boat-shaped pits lined with slabs, in which the body might be extended or crouched. In other Viking examples, the stones were laid at ground level.[17]

Sighted briefly in a contractor's trench, a 'long cist' may therefore be pre-Pictish Iron Age and a 'short cist' may be Norse. It is also worth noting that the Norse in the later Scando-Scottish period also adopted the long cist. At St Peter's Church, Thurso, a cist grave found in 1896 was covered by a twelfth-century rune-inscribed cross commemorating an Ingolf.[18] As has been proposed for Portmahomack, Pictish long cist graves often find themselves implanted in an earlier prehistoric cemetery, the graves in strings along a coastline.[19] In Ireland, too, it has been observed that early medieval people may seek out Bronze and Iron Age monuments as burial sites.[20]

A literature survey by Graham Robbins in 1998 located twenty sightings of burials on the eastern seaboard of the Tarbat peninsula, of which six contained short cists and/or crouched skeletons, one contained long cist graves and thirteen sightings just reported human bone.[21] At Shandwick, there were four or five burials in short cists, a stone coffin and two other burial grounds, one adjacent to the Shandwick cross-slab and another exposed in a quarry near the site of the Old Shandwick chapel. Among a number of other confusing pieces of information, Watson reports that 'At Clach a' Charaidh [the Shandwick stone], all unbaptized infants of the parish were buried up till fairly recent times. It is now cultivated . . . the plough used to strike the grave stones but these have been removed.' Also: 'Near Shandwick Farm-house, to the south-west, between the sea and the rock was a graveyard, the name of which I failed to find. Some of the stones are still visible.'[22] At Balintore, north of Shandwick along the coast, no fewer than fourteen burial sites have been recorded. Three burials are stated as having short cists and two others long cists.[23] At Hilton there are burials associated with the chapel of St Mary.

Other sightings remain even more oblique. Watson notes:

> At Nigg Rocks, below Cadgha Neachdain [Nechtan's path], there is a graveyard, now covered in shingle. Here the Danish princes were buried. Their gravestones came from Denmark and had iron rings in them to facilitate their landing. So local tradition. This most unlikely spot for a graveyard was not selected without some good reason, the most probable being that hermits once lived in the caves, whence the place was reckoned holy ground.[24]

Watson also records that the curate of Nigg lived at Easter Rarichie, and the field behind his house was called 'raon a chlaidh', the graveyard field. 'The plough goes over it now and formerly used to strike the gravestones, but these are now removed.'[25]

It is noticeable that these burials are all said to be located at or near the sites of Pictish monuments, and that in each case a chapel is likely to have been in association with them. This, and the lack of pottery, are strong indications of their being either Pictish or Viking in origin, rather than Bronze Age. But not exclusively. The association of the burials at Portmahomack with those at Balnabruach (see Chapter 4) proposed that they could belong to a single long-lasting cemetery strung out along the crest of the dunes, and dating from the Bronze Age to the Pictish – and I would say also, as a guess, to the Viking period. One thing is clear: the coast of the Tarbat peninsula was thick with burial sites, and, whether early (Bronze Age) or later (medieval), they focus on Portmahomack and its three sister sites of Nigg, Shandwick and Hilton of Cadboll, to which we now turn our attention.

NIGG, SHANDWICK AND HILTON OF CADBOLL

The site at Nigg consists of a promontory defined by re-entrants, which converge to form a steep narrow valley, resembling a hollow way, leading down to the shore of the Cromarty Firth. The north-east re-entrant is also narrow and steep, and a small burn runs along it. The present church, a mainly eighteenth-century building, lies north-east/south-west across the promontory, surrounded by a fenced churchyard. The original position of the great cross-slab at Nigg is not remembered, but it was said 'always' to have stood in the churchyard when it was blown down during a storm in 1727.[26] It was subsequently placed up against the east[27] gable of the church until the end of the eighteenth century, when it was removed to gain access to the family vault of Ross of East Kindeace. Allen and Anderson saw it 'in a new stone base at the west[28] end of the church immediately outside the vestry, at the top of a very steep slope',[29] and it now stands inside the church at its south-west end.

The original siting of the Nigg monument, if in the churchyard and subject to strong winds, is likely to have been in the centre of the promontory at its forward end. Without its present screen of trees, this promontory gives good views out to the Cromarty Firth. Two streams run either side of the promontory and form a single U-shaped channel where they meet about 10–15m below the neighbouring fields (that is, at about 10m AOD). The channel is currently hugely overgrown. It continues, gently sloping towards the Firth, where it splays out at a sheep wash. The route could then follow either the front edge of the 10m contour or go straight down to the water. It is debatable whether boats came up here, but it is certainly a point of access. There are signs of foundations on the promontory that were more visible around 1800 when a visitor noted: 'Behind the church is still to be seen the foundation of a large house above 90 feet in length, which goes under the name of the Bishop's House . . . One of the vaults remained entire in the year 1727.'[30] Nigg was one of the mensal churches of the bishop in question (of Ross).

The ornament and iconography of the Nigg monument are among the most elaborate of the entire Pictish corpus and have been extensively studied.[31] The monument is a rectangular slab 2.36m high (as currently restored), 1.03m wide and 130mm thick. The cross-side (now facing south-east) is infilled with fret pattern, and geometric and zoomorphic interlace. It is flanked by panels of spiral bosses and interlace bosses around which snakes coil. Above the cross is a pediment containing a vignette representing the desert fathers St Paul and St Anthony, icons of early monasticism, with their books, fed with a circular loaf by a raven and accompanied by their lions.[32] On the back, surrounded by an arched frame of interlace and fretwork panels, are images of a bird of prey and the Pictish beast, and a composite scene referring to King David, featuring a spearman pursuing animals, a figure with sheep and harp, a horseman and a figure with two cymbals from whom animals flee. This is a carving rich in references to literature at the heart of early Christian monasticism.

Shandwick was a *vik* name implying traffic on its sandy beach at least from Viking times. The Pictish monument stands on the 25m contour in open ground above Shandwick village and beach (Fig. 9.2). It is known as the Clach a' Charridh (variously

Fig. 9.2 The site of the Shandwick monument in its shelter, looking out over the Moray Firth.

'monumental stone' or 'stone of the burial ground').[33] As mentioned above, the Shandwick cross-slab is associated with one or two burial grounds and one or two chapels. In spite of intensive surveys, none of these has been securely located in modern times, but the existence of a chapel and burial ground near the cross, and a chapel and burial ground near the sea seems inherently probable. Of all the Tarbat monuments, the Shandwick cross-slab is the one most likely to be at the site of its original erection and its vista is spectacular, extending to the coastline of Moray.

In his visit of 1776, Cordiner described a 'very splendid obelisk opposite to the ruins of the castellated house called Sandwick'.[34] It was then surrounded at the base with large well-cut flagstones.[35] It had been damaged before 1811 and was blown down in about 1846, when it broke into two pieces. It was subsequently clamped together and re-erected 'on a circular stepped base that conceals some of the sculpture at the bottom'.[36] In 1988 an area 8 × 8m was excavated around the base, and a steel and glass protective shelter erected. No features were reported from the excavation.[37]

The slab is now 2.97m high, but at least another 200mm of it is thought to be buried. It is 1m wide and 190mm thick. The cross-side faces east across the sea, and takes the form of a 'jewelled' cross flanked by cherubim and seraphim.[38] Below these are two lions, one of which has a cub, being brought to life in an allusion to the resurrection. The lions and the serpents below them are seen as evoking the power of Christ. On the back face, contained in a series of panels, are represented a double-disc symbol inlaid with spiral ornament, a large Pictish beast sheltering two small sheep, and a busy scene featuring mounted horsemen, two warriors sparring on foot, a crouching archer and a dozen animals or birds all moving from left to right. Below this is a virtuoso panel expanding from four small spirals at the centre through three widening circles of eight, sixteen and sixteen spirals of increasing size. The lowest visible panels contain fret-pattern and knotwork, but are now partly hidden. Kellie Meyer sees the populated panel as a reference to the Last Judgement and a description of the other world, and the back face of Shandwick certainly lends itself to interpretation as an evocation of paradise, a paradise full of animals and the joys of hunting and fighting, reached through a transfiguration of the soul expressed as an explosion of spirals.[39]

Hilton of Cadboll is the current name of a village at the foot of the cliff immediately north of Balintore. The monumental Pictish cross-slab is associated with the site of St Mary's Chapel, on the foreshore north of the present village. The cross-slab had been taken down before 1676, since its front side, which may have once carried a cross, now carries an inscription of that date commemorating Alexander Duff and his three wives. MacFarlane reports that the cross-slab had blown down in a gale of 1674.[40] In 1776 Cordiner saw 'a very splendid monument . . . near to the ruins of a chapel in an early age dedicated to St Mary'. In 1811 it was lying near the seashore face down when Cordiner is said to have discovered that there was carving on the underside and had the stone turned over.[41] However, Cordiner says nothing of this and had apparently died in 1794.[42] By Stuart's time it was lying 'in a shed, the wall of which was believed to have formed part of an ancient chapel'.[43] By 1903 the stone had been removed to Invergordon Castle, where it stood on a modern base in the grounds at the side of the carriage drive half a mile south of the castle.[44] When Invergordon Castle was demolished in 1928, the stone was donated to the British Museum, but, following protests, was transferred to the National Museums of Scotland in Edinburgh, where it remains.

A survey of 1998 showed that the ruined chapel of St Mary by the sea lay in the deserted medieval village of Cadboll Fisher, a daughter settlement of the Abbey of Fearn, dating to the thirteenth century and later.[45] Although the place name Hilton has been adopted by the present seaside settlement, it should originally have been on a hill. This other suspected deserted village is unlocated, but the possibility remains that there was a Pictish settlement on the hill, at Cadboll Castle, North Cadboll, Cadboll Mount or Geanies, perhaps associated with another chapel of St Mary near the source of the best stone for carving (see Chapter 5). Thus the idea was floated that the Hilton monument had stood originally on the high ground at or near Cadboll, an elevated spot that would command a broad view of the northern firth.

The Hilton of Cadboll stone exhibited in the National Museums of Scotland was evidently only the upper part of the monument, since the ornament was discontinuous. Excavations by Historic Scotland in 2001 revealed a substantial lower part, which was found *in situ* on the west side of the chapel of St Mary. This was part of the original base of the monument, but not in its original setting. It was minus its tenon, and had been placed upright in a pit supported by packing stones. The excavator, Heather James of GUARD, demonstrated that this second setting of the stone could be dated to the twelfth century. Immediately adjacent was an earlier setting

Fig. 9.3 The Hilton of Cadboll replica, carved by Barry Grove (seen in the picture). It is positioned a few metres west of where the original is thought to have stood.

('setting 1') which took the form of half a collar stone set in a large pit. The other half of the same collar stone was found nearby. The pit of setting 1 had been cut into wind-blown or beach layers that contained charcoal and human bone that gave radiocarbon dates in the range of the seventh–ninth centuries. This supports the view that there was a Pictish settlement at St Mary's by the sea and that the great cross-slab was originally erected there.[46] If this position did not command the same vista as the cross-slabs at Nigg, Shandwick or Portmahomack, it would still mark a beach-side site enclosed by a ring of cliffs – a protected enclave suitable for an ecclesiastical site of the Pictish period.

The upper part of the Hilton stone measures 2660 × 1400 × 40mm and the carving now survives only on one side of it. Beside the lower portion (measuring 850 × 1400 × 210mm) the Historic Scotland excavations retrieved 11,263 fragments of cut stone, of which 3,366 were decorated.[47] Most of these were naturally seen as belonging to the former cross-side of the Hilton slab, and included fine decorated bosses, interlaced animals and the bottom of a cross with a stepped base. The well-known reverse side consists of three panels framed at the sides and base by vine scroll and at the top by a double-disk and Z-rod symbol. The upper panel contains a crescent and V-rod inlaid with spirals and fret-pattern and two isolated disks containing knotwork. The centre panel features the famous scene of a horsewoman (she is said to be riding side-saddle) accompanied by a man with a big nose (behind her), two armed horsemen, two trumpeters on foot, two hounds and a deer. A symbolic mirror and comb are placed in front of the lady's horse. The lower panel consists of spirals. It can be deduced that the cross-slab originally stood 3.51m above ground level, and that the base was at least 30mm thinner than the upper part – actually more, since the upper part had been trimmed.

At first sight the scene of a woman off hunting with her friends seems to transport us directly into the Pictish countryside, where we can stand and watch great figures of the day ride past. But those that have studied the language of art know how artful it can be. Stone carving needed to say a great many things about the other world, not just what you could see at any time in this one. The Hendersons see the hunting scene as belonging to the same ethos as Classical exemplars. As such it is a 'literary construct not a literal account', not so much a hunt, as a parade, symbolic of the good life and good leadership, rather than evidence for secularity or a conjunction between church and state.[48] The woman could certainly be the subject of this stone celebration: Boniface thought a mirror and comb were gifts fit for a queen.[49] Thus the Hilton figure echoes the queen of Carthage who rides out with horsemen and hounds, her purple cloak clasped by a gold fibula as described in *Aeneid* book IV.[50] For Kellie Meyer, the Hilton lady is taking part, more specifically, in a wedding parade.

Although the three monuments at Nigg, Shandwick and Hilton of Cadboll have much in common with the sculpture produced at Portmahomack, there is little as yet to indicate what kind of sites they stood in, and thus whether all four sites formed a linked system. Before advancing an opinion on this matter, we still have two tasks to do – namely, to gather other evidence for the ritual landscape (mainly from the later period) and to investigate the portage.

Place Names, Chapels and Wells

We are fortunate in that the place-name scholar W. J. Watson chose Ross and Cromarty in 1904 for one of his most detailed studies. The names imply prehistoric sites as well as sites named in particular languages, such as Pictish, Gaelic and Norse. Pictish and Norse names are relatively few, but this may be because the predominant language spoken on the peninsula was Gaelic, from some time in the ninth–eleventh centuries up to 1800.[51] In other words, the people of Tarbat would have been renaming Pictish and Norse sites in Gaelic for 1,000 years.

Remarkably, some Pictish names do survive, signalled by their *pit* prefix, referring to a piece or parcel of land and often suffixed by its owner or a natural descriptor. Four names are accepted: Pitculzean in Nigg (*pit* of little wood); Pitcalnie in Nigg; Pitkerrie (dark place) in Fearn and Pitmaduthy (*pit* of Macduff) in Logie Easter.[52] Other candidates are Allansallach (swampy place) near the port of Wilkhaven, and Pitfaed, which Watson says is 'of doubtful meaning' but has the same form as the other *pit* names.[53] It is of great interest to us, since it lies just to the north of St Colman's church.

Norse names defined by Watson are Arboll 'seal-steading', Cadboll 'cat steading', Tarrel 'bull-steading', Geanies 'cliffs' and Shandwick, sandy bay, creek or town. He derives Locheye from Norse *eith*, isthmus, and feels it might refer to slow running water between lochs. Similarly Mounteagle is also an *eith* name. These last two both lie on the proposed portage route (below).

Other significant places for the hunter of early settlements are the many named wells. 'Fresh water springs are to be found in every corner,' announces Sinclair, 'particularly in parts near the sea. One of them at Portmahomack is remarkable for the lightness of its water.'[54] Macfarlane knew of twenty-four wells, the biggest cluster in the neighbourhood of Nigg.[55] Many of these were renowned for the curative properties of their water, such as Tobar na slainte (healthy well) at Shandwick and a well near the Hilton chapel Tobar na baintighearna.[56] One at Nigg and another at Portmahomack were entitled Tobar a' bhaistidh – baptismal wells. Tobar ma Chalmag, Colman's well, is 'behind the library' at Portmahomack near to Pitfaed. At Teampul Eraich, near the old castle of Tarbat (that is, Ballone), was 'a plentiful spring of water which continues to bear the name of Tobair Mhuir or Mary's Well. A small cave or grotto is shewn as the abode of the priest.'[57]

These wells are naturally now somewhat clogged with the weeds of myth. The Tobar na Baistidh (baptism well) at Portmahomack was said in the early twentieth century to have been made holy by a fragment of the true cross and gifts from St Regulus and St Duthus. In the eighteenth century a local wise woman, Kirsty Beg, had recommended that the water be used to baptise the eldest son of the Third Earl of Cromarty, and the water for all baptisms 'has ever since been procured from this well'. I was informed that it was actually the town water supply (see Chapter 2), and it lies directly over the site anticipated for the monastic mill.

The peninsula was also peculiarly well endowed with chapels, many of which could date back to the Middle Ages. Geoffrey Stell noted about ten sacred sites, many of which were said to have been dependent chapels, which possibly served different localities within the medieval parish.[58] A significant proportion appear to have been private chapels closely associated with local lordships. Two or more are associated with each of Portmahomack, Hilton of Cadboll, Shandwick and Nigg. The most significant perhaps is the *Annat* in Nigg parish, a name implying the presence of relics of a founder, which shares its site with the castle built by William the Lion, King of Scotland, in 1179. The Bindal Moor hermitage and the use of the caves point to an early 'holy man' tradition of some kind. Not all these chapels need date to the Middle Ages, let alone the Pictish period, but their number and presence, with those of the holy wells, do strongly suggest a busy ritual landscape of the kind associated with a holy island. This immediately provides us with a richer context for the Pictish cross-slabs.

The arrival of the Abbey of Fearn was the most important single innovation that is likely to have redrawn or concealed any previous religious landscape. The monastery founded or repossessed the many chapels, invested in agriculture, including the importation of cartloads of soil, canalised the streams to drive a mill and stimulated the fishing industry. It also became the landlord of a majority of the farmland. Unfortunately, most of the records of the abbey were accidentally lost in the fifteenth century, so the account of the achievements of the community and, more pertinently, its thoughts on the previous sanctity of the peninsula, are sparse and inferential.[59]

Portage

From the shape of the land, and the place name, Tarbat, we expect there to have been one or more portages on the peninsula, where boats or ships were dragged overland from one maritime thoroughfare to another.[60] Although this may not have saved much time, and probably had to be paid for, it was no doubt Hobson's choice in foul weather or contrary winds, when the rounding of the Ness, or the entry between the Sutors, was prevented. The 'Tarbat' or portage was an important feature of early medieval seafaring. Tarbat names are most common on the west coast of Scotland, where there are eight examples, many of which hosted pivotal moments in history.[61] In 1263 Haakon IV, campaigning down the western seaboard, had his ships dragged across the isthmus between Loch Long and Loch Lomond and fought an inconclusive battle at Largs.[62] Tarbert on Sunart, which connects Ardnamurchan to Fort William (via Glen Tarbert), was the route taken by Donald Balloch and Clan Donald to rout Alexander Stewart Earl of Mar at Inverlochy in 1431.[63] By contrast, on the east coast, Watson can point to only two, one rather minor: 'On the east there are Tarbat on Ross and Tarbert in Fidra Isle in the Firth of Forth, the latter being probably the tiniest extant.'[64]

Other places, not now named as Tarbats, may have attracted portage, notably those that connect the waterways in the Great Glen. An early navigator, like Columba, would require portage at Fort William between Inverlochy–Gairlochy and the River Lochy, at Laggan between Loch Lochy and Loch Oich, and at Fort Augustus between Loch Oich and Loch Ness (the river Oich). From Loch Ness via the river Ness the waterway is clear into the Moray Firth. Clearly this ancient route had seen many changes before the Caledonian Canal was dug. In 1595 Gerhard Mercator shows the

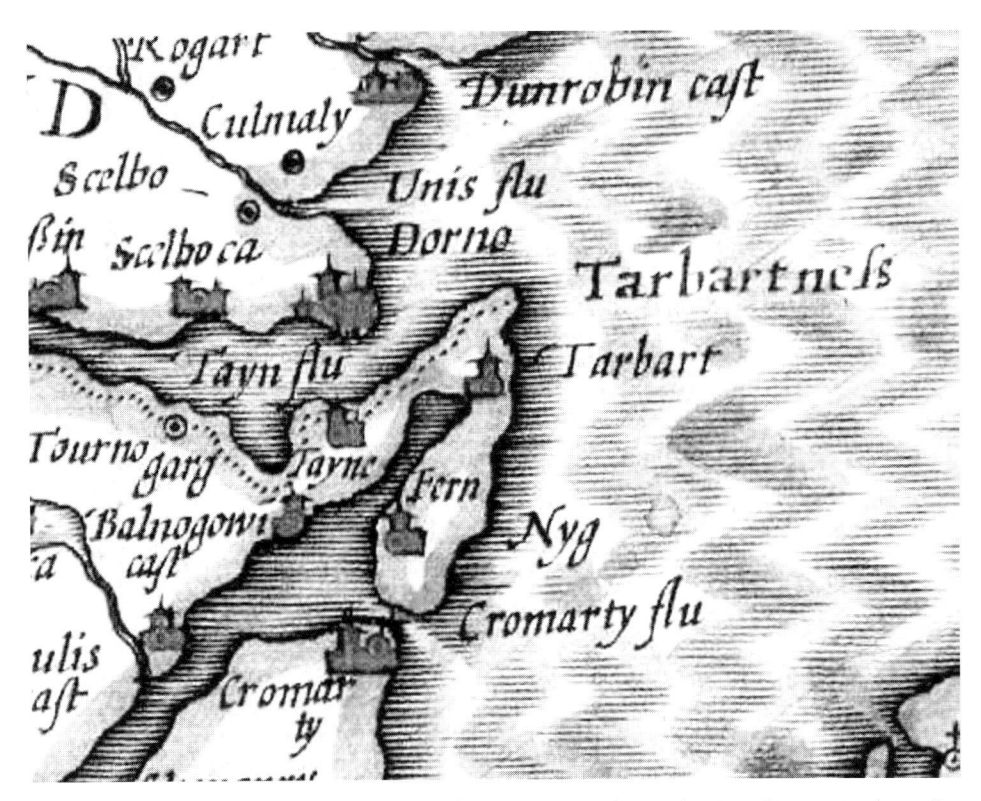

Fig. 9.4 The form of the Tarbat peninsula as represented on John Speed's map in the early seventeenth century.

Loch Ness–Loch Oich link as open water. Andrew Rutherford's map of 1745 shows only one portage on the Loch Ness route (between Loch Lochy and Loch Oich). Perhaps this is the only point that would have obliged travellers on the hypothetical route that connects Iona to Portmahomack to take their skin boats out of the water.[65]

The overbringing of boats across the Tarbat peninsula is thus not improbable, and there is indication of its route from early maps. Pont's map dated 1583–96 shows a river channel running from Loch Flynn (or Slin, now replaced by Loch Eye) southward to the Cromarty Firth. The river has two mills near Fearn, and a bridge near the Cromarty Firth, so has already been canalised. John Speed in 1610 shows an indent running in from Cromarty Firth west of Fearn and ending at Tarbart (*sic*) (Fig. 9.4). Speed also shows land routes running from Tarbat to Ben Nevis along the south side of Loch Ness, from Tarbat to Ilen Handa (Laxford) and from Elgin to Loch Ness along the Spey. Greenville Collins in 1693 shows very sandy shoals on the south edge of the Dornoch Firth, where Inver is. Clement Lemprière in 1731 shows a narrow channel connecting Loch Eye to the Cromarty Firth. Later travellers noticed the results of receding waters, with treacherous sand banks opposite Cromarty and Tain. In 1769 Thomas Pennant describes riding between New Tarbat (at the south end) and Tain as 'a tedious black moor'.[66] There is no doubt that we are dealing with a world that was once much more watery.

Even now it can be seen that the land north of the Bay of Nigg has been reclaimed and that Inver Bay can bring a light craft up to within a kilometre of Loch Eye. The present Loch Eye is only 8ft (2.4m) deep and replaces earlier lochs and lochans, perhaps broadened by medieval peat-digging. Around 1800 Loch Eye was said to be over 2 miles long and about ½ mile broad (3.2 × 0.8km). 'From this Loch proceeds the water to the mills of Fearn, and in its course forms two lesser lochs.'[67] The route from the Bay of Nigg to Fearn and thence to Loch Eye rises only 10m in 4km. That from Loch Eye to Inver is steeper but shorter. If the Bay of Nigg was flooded up to Fearn, the portage is only between 2.4 and 3km and much of it is by water. It can be noted, however, that it would function less successfully, or not at all, once the Abbey of Fearn had dried out the lands fringing the Bay of Nigg, and canalised the stream from Loch Eye to drive its mill.

We know nothing of the use of this hypothetical portage by the Picts, and precious little of Pictish use of the sea. In a famous passage, H. M. Chadwick wrote:

> The Picts must have possessed a fleet, at times if not always. Otherwise they could not have attacked the Orkneys, or kept them in subjection. In 729 AT [the *Annals of Tigernach*] record the wrecking of 150 Pictish ships at a headland called Ross Cuissini. It would seem that Pictish sea power was pretty well developed. Was it from Pictish (or Frisian) mariners that Bede, in his commentary on IV Kings xx, 9, derived his knowledge of the midnight sun? Perhaps the most remarkable feature of the seventh and eighth centuries was the long immunity from attack enjoyed by insular and coastal sanctuaries. I know of no instance between 617 and 793. This immunity can hardly be explained, unless the seas were then policed by power or powers possessing considerable naval forces; it was doubtless the collapse of these forces which brought about the Viking Age.[68]

It is not clear which 'insular and coastal sanctuaries' Chadwick had in mind, but we are not talking about a west coast archipelago here. The east coast has hardly any islands, and very few absolute necessities to get into a boat. On Pictish stones, boats are very rare and the one well-known example looks rather Norse.[69]

On the other hand, the stones are covered with images of horses, of which Picts would appear to be connoisseurs, and which would take them fast along the beaches and over the passes.[70] James Barrett's analyses suggest that the first deep sea fish were exploited in the Viking age.[71] There is thus a hint that the Picts were shy of sea travel. But, with so much left to discover, we are probably wise to leave the matter 'floating'. It would be no problem for Picts, as for Scots, to build hide boats and take them across a portage. The clinker-built boat, which dominates the east coast, was known to the Anglo-Saxons and to the Vikings and could have been built in the early historic Firthlands too. And, in the past, the Picts have always succeeded in surprising us with their advanced level of skills in all departments.

CONCLUSION

This very preliminary historical, archaeological and topographical excursion into the Tarbat peninsula allows us to call up a picture of its early days. The land took the form of a long hilly ridge separated from the mainland by a ribbon of lochs and marsh, and was thus very like an island. It provided a natural portage route between the Dornoch and Cromarty Firths. From the Bronze Age, if not before, it was fringed with burials – an isle of the dead. Some kind of Iron Age or early Pictish occupation is probable, with a fortification on the slopes of the Hill of Nigg and cultivation of some land with an ard. The natural landmark of the Tarbat Ness was known to the Romans and has remained at the centre of the Firthland stage so long as sea travel mattered.

The members of the monastic community at Portmahomack set themselves up in the sixth century at a previous burial site overlooking the beach. They developed a portage between Inver in the north to the Bay of Nigg in the south, passing by lochs and streams no doubt excavated for better ease of passage. The inshore waters of the Dornoch, Cromarty, Beauly and Moray Firths constituted their early Christian Pictish world. They recognised related communities at Iona, at Rosemarkie on the Black Isle, at Kinneddar in Moray and at many other places yet to be rediscovered. They were in touch with Ireland and Northumbria as leaders of a great monastic enterprise.

Towards the end of the monastery's life, monumental cross-slabs emblazoned with Pictish symbols stood at Nigg, Shandwick and Hilton of Cadboll, as well as at Portmahomack. Did they perhaps celebrate some lordship or secular establishment[72] or were they markers in a ritual landscape?[73] At Portmahomack four stone monuments stood around the church, marking out its inner precinct (see Chapter 5). Perhaps the four coastal sites together represented an expanded version of the monastic precinct, signifying a time, in the later eighth century, when the whole peninsula had become the monastic estate. Such protected, or rather proclaimed, spaces are features of early medieval monasticism – for example, in Ireland, where the *termon* was 'explicitly associated with refuge and with the limits of the holy in the seventh and eighth centuries'. Armagh, Clonmacnoise, Kildare and Scattery Island had locatable *termon* lands by the ninth century. Such reserved areas could be 3 miles or more (4.8km) across.[74] Given the elevated positions of the monuments at Portmahomack, Shandwick and Nigg above landing places, it is likely that each of these also functioned as a seamark, and all could have guided boats to beaches.[75]

However, these explanations do not entirely satisfy, since the existence of the places, certainly Portmahomack and probably Hilton of Cadboll, pre-date the erection of their crosses. By the Middle Ages we also have a proliferation of chapels to explain. Hugh Miller junior noticed that all the sculptured stone on Tarbat could be associated with churches and burial grounds and deduced: 'It is probable that all these are the sites of Culdee chapels.'[76] But what if some of those chapels had existed previously, as hermitages, or marking caves occupied by a holy man? This would imply that the monumental cross-slabs were added to a place already made famous by a saint. If so, perhaps it is the name of the saint, man or woman, that is spelt out on the cross-slabs in Pictish symbols. Perhaps the ornament and iconography of its faces, so complex and so multi-referential, actually compose an expression of the saint's life, a hagiography in stone.

Ascribing the figures and activities depicted on Pictish cross-slabs to a saint's life does allow an escape from the difficulties of their apparent eclecticism, and the need for four famous contemporaries to die at much the same time at four places on the peninsula. In saints' lives, animals talk, angels visit, mysterious strangers advise, miracles happen. 'St Nigg' was perhaps a famous leader who took the tonsure, retiring to a hermitage at Nigg. 'St Shandwick', a former warrior with a close relationship to animals. 'St Cadboll' an aristocratic woman who saw the heavenly light while out hunting. If the Pictish symbols name such people, the names could, of course, be those of saints already belonging to the broader Christian pantheon, St Paul at Nigg or the Blessed Virgin at Hilton. But I prefer to fill these missing centuries, between 550 and 800, with home-grown holiness. The cross-slabs would then remember legendary holy persons of the peninsula, depicting events in their lives. The context for such an investment would be the celebration of the rising fame of the monastery and its large estate by giving the peninsula a holy history set in stone. This might help explain why the monuments, so massive and so similar in style and fabric, are so different in every other way. By this argument, the construction of the sacred landscape on Tarbat was therefore already layered and retrospective in the late eighth century, referring to individuals who had contemplated alone, cultivated learning, taught and laboured early in the Christian project. Not inconceivably, the new landscape spun its web over places already made holy in pre-Christian, prehistoric times: the wells, caves and dwellings of the wise.

Notes

1. Graham and Gordon (1987: 266–8).
2. *FSA* 641.
3. Mowat (1981: 48).
4. *NSA* 462–3.
5. *FSA* 639; Historian Monica Clough considered that oats were hardly produced before 1800; the stable fare was more likely to have been the bannock, flat barley bread baked on an open hearth, rather than porridge.
6. The other component is not given, perhaps because it just consisted of small stones – i.e. plough pebbles; see Chapter 4.
7. *FSA* 597.
8. Mowat (1981: 8).
9. Miller ([1835] 1994: 37); *NSA* 30.
10. RCAHMS, Site 184.
11. Ibid., Site 189.
12. *NSA* 14, 460, 15^v.
13. *TSA*.
14. Now in Tain Museum; NMR, no. NH98SW0043. NGR 23 914 840: 'dug up near the church gates of Old Tarbat, Portmahomack, apparently from near the find spot of a Viking hoard' (Robertson 1983).
15. Jones *et al.* (1993: 70); Gregory and Jones (2001).
16. J. Fraser, in *Philosophical Transactions*, 21 (1699).
17. Dunwell *et al.* (1995b); Graham-Campbell and Batey (1998); Graham-Campbell (2006).
18. Graham-Campbell and Batey (1998: 69).
19. Dunwell *et al.* (1995b: 731–3); Proudfoot (1996); Driscoll (1998); Rees (2002); Alexander (2005).

20. Swift (1991: 31).
21. In Carver (1998b).
22. Watson ([1904] 1996: 57).
23. Davidson (1946: 26).
24. Watson ([1904] 1996: 56).
25. Ibid. p. 57.
26. The cross-slab at Nigg was seen by Petley in 1811–12, by Hugh Miller in the 1830s, by Stuart before 1856 and by Allen and Anderson before 1903: Petley (1831: 352); Miller ([1835] 1994: 41); Stuart (1856: 11); *ECMS* II. 75–83. *FSA* 594 gives the date it blew down as 1725.
27. Presumably south-west is meant.
28. Presumably north-east is meant.
29. *ECMS* II. 75, fig. 72.
30. *FSA* 592.
31. Henderson and Henderson (2004: *passim*).
32. Ó'Carragáin (1989).
33. *FSA* 594; *SSA* 28.
34. Cordiner (1780: 66).
35. The stone was subsequently seen by Petley between 1811 and 1812, by Hugh Miller in the 1830s, by Stuart before 1856 and by Allen and Anderson before 1903: Petley (1831: 346, plates XVIII, XIX); Miller ([1835] 1994: 41); Stuart (1856: 10); *ECMS* II. 68–73.
36. *ECMS* II. 68.
37. Robbins in Carver (1998b).
38. Henderson and Henderson (2004: 152).
39. Thanks to Kellie Meyer for discussion on Shandwick.
40. Sally Foster, pers.comm., citing Macfarlane (1906–8), vol. 3, pp. 17–19.
41. *ECMS* II. 61, citing Petley.
42. Isabel Henderson in the introduction to the *ECMS* reprint of 1993 gives Cordiner's dates as 1746?–1794.
43. Stuart (1856), vol. 1, p. 10.
44. *ECMS* II. 61.
45. Carver (1998b); *FSA* 383.
46. Sally Foster and Heather James, pers. comm.; my thanks to them for allowing me to see their conclusions from their interventions in advance of publication.
47. James *et al.* (forthcoming: ch. 9).
48. Henderson and Henderson (2004: 179–80).
49. *HE*, I.11.
50. Henderson and Henderson (2004: 128–9, 179–80).
51. *FSA* (389, 647) reports that 'the common people speak Gaelic'. But in 1845 (*NSA* 31), 'the Gaelic language is that generally spoken, but the English has made rapid progress of late'. In another century, English dominated.
52. Fraser (1986: 26–7, fig. 2.4).
53. Watson ([1904] 1996: 275, 277).
54. *FSA* 635.
55. Macfarlane (1906–8: vol. 1, p. 54).
56. Lady's Well; OS 1881 Sheet L, surveyed 1872.
57. *FSA* 648.
58. Stell, in *Bulletin* (1994), 40.
59. *FSA* 379–92; 651; Watson ([1904] 1996: 40); Mowat (1981); Calendar of Fearn Abbey; and see Chapter 8.
60. Tarbat, gael. *Taimbeart*, 'an overbringing' and specifically one that is always above water even at high tide (Watson [1926] 1993: 505).

61. Tairbeart on Lewis connecting the Atlantic to the Minch; Tarbert on Gigha connecting the Sound of Jura to the Sound of Gigha; Tarbat on Jura connecting Firth of Lorne (Colonsay, Iona) to the Sound of Jura (Kintyre); Tarbert on Kintyre connecting Sound of Jura (Jura) to Loch Fynne (Bute); Tarbet at Laxford connecting Handa Island to Loch Laxford; and Tarbet at Mallaig connecting Loch Nevis and Loch Morar; Tarbert on Sunart, which connects Ardnamurchan to Fort William (via Glen Tarbert).
62. Barrell (2000: 85).
63. Roberts (1997: 201).
64. Watson ([1926] (1993): 505).
65. Early craft in the Irish Sea were traditionally of hide on a wooden frame. See McGrail (1998); Cunliffe (2001: 66–8); for recent studies on portages in Scotland, see McCullough (2000); Phillips (2006).
66. Pennant (1790).
67. *FSA* 379–92.
68. Chadwick (1949: 47); Anderson ([1922] 1990: vol. 1, p. 226) remarks that possibly the place is Troup Head.
69. Cossins, see *ECMS* II. 217.
70. Lamb (1998: 268).
71. Barrett (1999).
72. James *et al.* (forthcoming).
73. Carver (2004).
74. Davies (1996: 5); Ó'Carragáin (2003b).
75. Carver (2004).
76. Miller (1889: 443).

CHAPTER 10

A holy place in history

We return from this archaeological expedition equipped with several new stories and a number of revised opinions – if not, we cannot claim that it has taught us anything much. In this chapter I retell the tales and reflect on them in the spirit of a long night at the Castle Inn, Portmahomack, a spirit of curiosity, pleasure, speculation and conjecture (Fig. 10.1). There is a new Pictish settlement in northern Scotland – Pictish because it belongs, scientifically, to the period of the sixth–ninth centuries, when the Britons living in that part of Britain were known as Picts, by them and by us. They were still Celts, however, and this no doubt affected their policies and attitudes. Their land was good land, some of the best in Britain.

We can reasonably suppose that these Britons had deep roots in their landscape, which was marked by many monuments, and the Moray Firth is an area where many different types of monuments meet.[1] In Neolithic Easter Ross and the Black Isle, Orkney-Cromarty and long cairn tombs predominate, while in Moray it is the Clava passage grave that provides the burial signature. There are four long cairns and seven

Fig. 10.1 Sunset over Portmahomack

great circular Orkney–Cromarty cairns that still ring the hills above Tain.[2] The long cairns are 30–65m long and up to 14m wide, and the circular cairns (four in Edderton, three in Scotsburn) are 20m across. The chambers use large slabs and lintels a metre and more long, and some have kerbstones.

These great monuments may not be especially prominent now, but they were certainly visible to the Picts and their medieval successors, who designated them as royal burial places and battle sites and used them to site gallows.[3] Richard Bradley remarks that 'the past provided a source of authority no matter how far practices had changed' and he notes that early medieval people seem to have invested Neolithic and Bronze Age sites with a new significance, citing the incorporation of barrows and stone circles at the seventh-century palaces at Yeavering and Millfield.[4] Moreover, prehistoric sites were often chosen in opposition to Roman. In East Anglia, the Angles resurrected Bronze Age practices for their burials, but on Christianisation chose Roman sites for their early monasteries. The early Picts emulated the Bronze Age standing stones, and sometimes marked existing examples with their symbols. The symbols themselves are owed at the least to the later Iron Age.

There are some interesting analogies here on the subject of standing stones and Christianisation. In Brittany, fellow Britons (Bretons) inherited a landscape of megaliths that already had its own repertoire of symbols: the 'axe-plough', the crook, the axe, horns, bull and snake, as well as numerous chevrons and concentric hoops. The single standing stone (menhir) was an early form, later combined into avenues (Carnac) or circles. Some menhirs in Côtes d'Armor were later 'converted' to Christian monuments. The menhir of Saint-Uzec was recarved at the top to show a cross and, in low relief, the Virgin Mary, the moon and the sun. The chapel of the Seven Saints at Vieux-Marché keeps in its crypt the assemblage from a chambered tomb.[5]

The sequence in Gotland (Baltic) offers another parallel vision of what Pictish sculpture might have been like if Christianity had not arrived, or arrived only in the eleventh century. Over 400 decorated stones are known from this island.[6] The earliest of them (AD 400–600) carry mainly geometric symbols, notably spirals with some images of animals and ships. The second group (600–700) are slabs with the famous 'phallus profile', and show an image of a bird or animal or a symbolic ship. In the eighth century, the monuments flower into elaborate picture stones, featuring horses, ships, fights, hunts and quotations from mythology. There then seems to be a hiatus before the appearance of runestones in *c.* 1000, where the cross is featured centrally at the top, surrounded by a garland of runes. The reading of the runestones leaves no doubt that they were intended as memorials: stones were raised by sons in memory of their father, by wives in memory of their husbands, by mothers in memory of their daughters. In east Sweden, the memorial was sometimes combined with the building and dedication of a bridge, mentioned in the inscription, the maintenance of which served to win prayers from the church.[7] Anne-Sofie Gräslund's study also demonstrates the broader role of women in matters of spirituality, acting as specialists in the pre-Christian period, controlling the process of Christianisation and losing their traditional authority in this sphere only when Christianity was institutionalised in the twelfth or thirteenth century. While no direct contact need be implied, and while the changes in Scandinavia took place in different circumstances, and in different centuries, we have much to learn from these sequences, on matters that have barely touched early historic Scotland – not just the rediscovery of women but their re-empowerment in prehistory.

The north Britons of Pictish times can be supposed to have read the vocabulary of their prehistoric landscape; it was the inherited text of their past, their origin myth, their permanent point of reference, their Bible before the Bible came. Did they also see the landscape as a number of territories, to be maintained? Bradley emphasises ritual regionality in Scotland for the prehistoric period, and finds, for example, that passage graves reused in the Beaker/Early Bronze Age are distributed north of the Beauly Firth.[8] Beside the chambered tombs mentioned above, there are many prehistoric discontinuities that appear to coincide with this same frontier, such as the southern limits of brochs or the northern limits of vitrified forts. Bradley wants us to see the Clava cairns as their own multi-referenced invention, linked to Kilmartin via the Great Glen and to the Aberdeen area in the early Bronze Age with its recumbent stone circles. 'Rather than describing the inner Moray Firth as a border zone – in any case an anachronistic conception – it might be better to think of it as a region in which at least three quite different cultural traditions came into contact',[9] which is, of course, exactly what a border zone is. Border people make references first one way, then another. That is what makes their regions special.

The regions can linger long. Alex Woolf has proposed that the Moray Firth area was the Picts' Fortriu, deriving the word from the tribal grouping *Verturiones* named by the Romans (see Chapter 7). Alexander Grant proposes that the Earldom of Easter Ross inherited the identity of the *Decantae*, and credits the reluctance of Ross to join Alba to a long and fairly independent gestation. A Pictish recognition of this province is therefore likely, and he sees it as signalled in the distribution of symbol stones. He also sees it in the establishment of the diocese, and before that in the eighth-century dedications to St Curadán.[10] Which brings us to the question of the Christianisation of the region, and the beginnings of a Christian establishment at Portmahomack.

Looking back from the twenty-first century, we find it hard to imagine a time without Christianity, a time without a central hierarchy, attempting to control thought and behaviour though a common world view. Perhaps there never was such a time: the Beaker culture offers a remarkable example of cultural orthodoxy in the early Bronze Age, so intensely felt that it was proselytised from Spain to Shetland in small boats. I fear that the herd instinct (and its concomitant, conviction politics) is something to be expected, if not accepted, as part of the human condition. An ideology from the Middle East was not a novelty in the Roman Empire, when soldiers and officials brought Mithraism, Judaism and Aristotelian philosophy to its frontiers, in our case as near as the Antonine Wall and perhaps to the Beauly Firth. Christianity was to have the advantage of adoption by the state after AD 313, so that those who received it in the fourth century and later received a strong dose of imperial aspiration, as well as the moral teaching of a prophet. If the teaching was intended to have a universal message, in Scotland its stage props were nevertheless almost entirely exotic: the hot sands of the desert, the hart panting for water, the asperges to lay the dust on the mosaic floors of the villas, the robes of Bedouin or late Roman senators adapted for monks and priests, writing in Latin and Greek, the books themselves, and so forth.

Theoretically, none of this was familiar to sixth-century Scotland, either as reality or as metaphor. At least this is the common perception: the Picts and the Scots knew the Roman Empire only at second hand, knew nothing about the Middle East or Greek philosophy or the Hebrew tracts. They knew precious little, it seems, other than that fish swam in the seas and spears wounded. They were blank slates on which missionaries could write. And yet within a few decades they had become fully functioning and inflexible exponents of the creed. A small proportion of scholars, mainly Christian themselves, are perfectly comfortable with this: it was possible because of the exceptional character of Christ's teaching. For the first time people were offered immortality. The crosses raised all over the land promised redemption, in this life and the next.

But redemption from what, and why for the first time? These are, of course, hard questions to answer, since we must oppose the inscrutable corpus of prehistoric monumentality to the voluble propaganda of the Christians. But it is simply impossible to believe today that the pre-Christian millennia had brought no wisdom, hope, learning, kindness or reason to the pre-Christian soul. It is also my thesis that a miraculous fully fledged conversion of entire peoples is not what we see in the monumentality of sixth–eighth-century Europe.[11] The Baltic, the North Sea, the Irish Sea and the Channel, all navigable in the sixth and seventh centuries, are notable for the variety of contemporary monuments that fringe their shores: ship burials in Uppland and East Anglia, symbol stones on Gotland and in Pictland, the first churches in Kent and Kerry. We no longer regard these phenomena as evidence for migration or diffusion, nor the arrival of the cross as the trajectory of creeping missions. People were arguing about their future, choosing with whom to align, and expressing their agenda in carved stone or earth mounds.

The argument for creative (not syncretic) thinking in the north of the sixth–eighth centuries takes three forms: first, that there were religious intellectual infrastructures on the ground already; secondly, that these included practices and attitudes that were compatible with Christianity, and, thirdly, that a great deal was known about Christian, Roman and Greek ideas, in Scotland as in Ireland, some decades before the appearance of the first missionary. Far from writing on a blank slate, there was an important discourse to be had, with Picts, as with Angles, as with Thessalonians. This enormous subject can scarcely be dealt with here, or indeed anywhere as yet, since archaeological inadequacy and intellectual timidity have left it in deep fog. Four poorly documented examples will have to suffice.

Many years ago, A. R. Burn wrote a paper in the *Glasgow Archaeological Journal* called 'Holy Men on Islands in pre-Christian Britain`, an example of learned, brilliant, inspiring and highly speculative scholarship.[12] The holy men were druids, and Burn showed that there were reasons for believing that they already practised monasticism. There were hermits, there were colleges, there were places where people talked and thought, in the late British Iron Age. The implication is that the introduction of Christian monasticism did not depend on the contrivance of the desert fathers with their pillar saints and stretched allegories about lions and ravens; this was merely news from abroad – not innovation but exemplars of similar practice.

A second example. A few years ago Natalia Venclova showed that the Celtic form of tonsure – a tonsure that shaved the front of the head and left the hair long at the back – was also owed to druids.[13] This would help to explain, of course, the deep intellectual confrontation that lay behind the well-known discussions reported by Bede. An apparently fatuous disagreement about the right way for monks to cut their hair conceals a more pertinent discourse about the learning that went with the haircut. Are we to abandon the wisdom and poetry of the centuries in favour of an exotic code? It is a question entirely relevant today, and it was answered by Oswy in the same manner that an Anglo-American politician might answer the puzzled thinkers of the modern Middle East: only our democracy will do.

With this tonsure in mind, it might be possible to throw light on that even more controversial matter of the date of Easter, computed in different ways, and therefore celebrated on different days in the Northumbrian and no doubt the Pictish court.[14] It may be that the western churches had received an earlier Mediterranean version and were thus at odds with the eastern. But that would be a trivial, scholastic, matter, solved within the college. But, as Bede's account of the Synod of Whitby makes clear, this was a political issue, to be resolved by the king. It implies that behind the confronted parties were deep matters of belief as well as alignment. Clearly the prehistoric British, the Irish and the Saxons already had an Easter, a spring equinox. But for the British and the Irish at least this was not a theoretical matter; it was embedded in many centuries of prehistoric stone circles that supplied not only the correct date, but much of the thinking that went with it. It is possible that the Angles had no great loyalty to the prehistoric landscape of Britain, but this can hardly be true for the Celts. The stone circles still marked the seasons and the movement of the spheres.

All these ideas rely largely on work that has yet to be done. But no fair-minded reader will disallow that the intellectual context in which Columba, Ninian, Nechtan and Bede laboured to promote their ideologies was interwoven with convictions and theories from a local deep past. And, while it may not have had a book of its own from which to debate the scriptures, its texts lay all round in the hills and coastlands, and all but the incomers found them perfectly intelligible. Most importantly, there was a tradition here, as in the world over, of holy men (and previously women) bringing healing and hope. And here we emerge once more into historical daylight, guided by Peter Brown and Alfred Smyth.

The role of the holy man (and woman) in restructuring the post-Roman world is now widely acknowledged, in Scotland[15] as in the Mediterranean.[16] The basic post-imperial model is that holy men provided a nucleus around which identities could form. They were in dynamic equilibrium with the warlords, one enforcing control with words, the other with swords. It would be no great surprise if the dialogue of north-east Scotland in the sixth–seventh centuries took that form, the obstinacy of the one gradually mollifying the rage of the other. In Chapter 9 I paint of picture of holy men and women occupying caves on the Tarbat peninsula, building reputations that are remembered in chapels, and eventually, long after the real details had been forgotten and displaced by the myths, as biographies in stone, the cross-slabs of saints. Such people are, of course, total fiction, and the hagiographical purpose of the cross-slabs is total conjecture. But my objective is to return to the distribution maps and broken carvings some of the intellectual passion that generated them.

Was Columba the holy man who brought Christianity to Easter Ross? At first the coincidences seem irresistible: his documented journey in *c*. 565, Adomnán's comment that he founded monasteries on the far side of the Druim Alban, the sixth-century start date for burials at Portmahomack, the possible derivation of Portmahomack from the same root *Colm* as Columcille, the similarity of the grave markers on Tarbat and on Iona. But doubts now creep in. There were even earlier burials than the sixth century on the peninsula. There may even have been earlier holy men. The monastery had a very slow start. Where is the imported pottery, from the Mediterranean, from Aquitaine, that was reaching the Irish Sea and Iona? Why is the church dedicated to St Colman, whose relics were thought to have been housed in the crypt in the Middle Ages? How much amnesia must we allow for, in order to maintain the idea of a Columban foundation?

It was never a popular option – 'evidence for Pictish Columban foundations in the kingdom [of the Picts] is very sparse indeed,' remarked Isabel Henderson[17] – although no one is likely to deny their existence or to diminish the influence of Iona. There are rivals for the palm of the local missionary: first, Ninian. Why else would the later monastery of Fearn be founded from Whithorn? Then, Egbert, the monk of Jarrow, who may have brought a Northumbrian version of Christian regulation to Easter Ross and Orkney in the eighth century.[18] And there was Curadán, whose church dedications have been mentioned.[19] The activities of Curadán could even be seen as of sufficient significance to propose an eighth-century diocese of Ross, with a seat at Rosemarkie, although the idea that 'Curadán presumably must be regarded as Bishop of the whole of northern Pictland' might be going a bit far.[20] Simon Taylor also maps an expansion of *kil* names that might find an equation with Curadán's project.[21] One possibility, therefore, is that at Portmahomack there was no Columba, there was only a Curadán.[22] His task was to modernise and Romanise the church, and we might surmise that among the chapels of the peninsula he chose the one by the best beach and galvanised it into international action. His eighth-century enterprise can offer a context to Portmahomack's productive Period 2, when vellum and metalwork were being produced in quantity and the monastic network was in a state of expansion. The location of some of the contemporary foundations can be guessed, inspired by sculpture and Isabel Henderson's reading of it: Kinnedar, Rosemarkie, Brodie, Burghead, Glenfernes, Elgin, Wester Delnies, Edderton, Nigg, Shandwick and Hilton of Cadboll. These places have been claimed as having a range of functions (pastoral care, administration of the Eucharist, monastic communities, pilgrimage) within an orthodox Christian infrastructure.[23] To those who like their conversions quick, comprehensive and inevitable, there are no difficulties here: it is a miracle of the usual kind. The region would acquire a bishop, a diocese, monasteries, parishes, congregations – the whole medieval package – within a few years. Archaeologically, this is currently incredible. The material culture of the eighth century looks nothing like that of the thirteenth – and so a reasonable person, recently descended from the Clapham omnibus, could be forgiven for concluding that it was indeed different.

Although an Anglian blast horn reached Burghead in the ninth or tenth century,[24] and the east coast route must have been active before the twelfth, leaving a trail of hogbacks,[25] eighth-century Portmahomack is connected to the south only by one tiny silver coin, a Frisian *sceat*, dated around 715. Our direct links to Northumbria are no better than those to Iona. The sculpture and the metal-working leave us in no doubt that the artists and artisans at Portmahomack were participants in the great adventure of insular culture. But it is not possible to point west or south (or north or east) as the only source of instruction. These were people whose output was determined by selectivity in sources and ideas, not by subjugation to superior dogma. What has come down to us is their first-hand view on life, death and the church.

By the eighth century at least, Portmahomack can be said to be a monastery, and its occupants were monks. The basis for this is the Latin inscription and the Apostles carved on stone, the making of vellum, the making of sacred vessels and a cemetery full of middle-aged and elderly men. The extraordinary architecture of the Smiths' Hall has also been advanced as evidence of learning (see Chapter 6). The argument depends on the convergence of a number of properties with the establishments described in texts. Adomnán's description of Iona and Bede's references to the monastic life lead us to expect a church, a precinct, a burial ground, rooms for study and prayer, roads, a mill, a farm, a smithy, a bakery, a garden and a membership that is continually on the move over a wide network.[26] Bede makes it clear that there are two styles of monasticism: the ascetic, Celtic kind, in which contemplation and self-torture are virtues, and the robust, productive, Northumbrian kind, in which new peoples are continually won over for Christ and the secular power of the church increases. He admires the former, but sees the latter as the necessary future. However crude this distinction in reality, or in my reading of it, it offers a possible explanation for the invisibility of Portmahomack in its first, sixth–seventh-century phase: a very small community, of both men and women, dedicated to prayer and devotion, to holiness, their slight archaeological imprint the result of a minimum dependence on material things. The only serious material investments that seemed necessary to them were the provision of fresh water and the encasing of the dead in large, naturally sheared, slabs of stone.

By the eighth century the general monastic echoes are strong, but we do not have to find in them any direct emulation of Iona or Jarrow. This was the age of originality, in which we can say with Rosemary Cramp: 'in the 7th and 8th centuries the diversity of the Rules of Life is reflected in the diversity of the plans. There may have been an ideal model for the churches . . . but these sites can in no way be seen as "type sites", and nor should this be expected on monastic sites of this period elsewhere.'[27] The geography that is argued for the Portmahomack site is, therefore, not claimed as typical of all, except in general aspects; but these aspects are not without interest. The church on the hill, with a churchyard, had by the eighth century superseded the straggling strings of graves along the ridge, and instituted an oval burial ground bounded by a bank. Four large cross-slabs marked three entrances, north, east and west, with one more cross at the east end of the church. The earliest of these (Cross A) was made in the later eighth century, while the latest addition (Cross D) was probably erected in the first half of the ninth century. A road, a neo-Roman road, led from the ridge down the hill towards the valley bottom, with working areas on either side. The east side of the road was associated with large quantities of cattle bones; perhaps this is where they were slaughtered, as they must have been, and the many assets separated from each other, the bones, the meat, the blood, conserved by smoking or salting. The hides went over the road to the workshop, where there stood a large bow-ended building, our Parchment-Makers' Hall. It had a pebbled or flagged surface to the north of it, incorporating a tawing tank; and to the south, a yard. Seeing this as an area for vellum production, as we do, associates this end of book production with quite an industry. The washing of bloody hides, trimming, soaking in an astringent synthesised from shells, de-hairing, de-fleshing, thinning (especially the hides of the elder cattle), preserving, stretching on frames, pouncing and smoothing. Maybe none of these craftsmen could read, maybe none of them could even chant, but they were nevertheless key servants in the monastic project. On the other side of the valley were their colleagues, the metal-workers, based inside and outside their Smiths' Hall. They too were involved in the more noisome and more dangerous end of the business: smelting, casting, finishing, shaping, inlaying bronze, glass, silver and gold (in order of decreasing certainty). So far as we can tell, and it is not very far, they were making the parts of chalices, patens and reliquaries, the arms and armament of the soldiers of Christ. Their building, it was argued, was made with as much attention to ritual symmetry as a metal escutcheon or the carpet page of a gospel book. These were not downtrodden artisans shacked up in the margins, slavishly following instructions of the lofty sponsors. They were servants of the servants of God, but they were also equal players, local movers, free spirits.

With no documents, we cannot say much about the rule at Portmahomack, but we should be content for it to be original, or – in the sense of later, institutionalised, Christianity – unorthodox. Nor would it be amazing if such a place subsisted outside any infrastructure or hierarchy of the type that would later become conventional. Christian historians long to find bishops and parishes as early as they can – but there is no need, and there is little evidence that monasteries of the seventh–ninth centuries had much of a pastoral role.[28] Those who have difficulty in believing in the viability of home-made or idiosyncratic versions of Christianity have only to visit the third floor of the National Museums in Edinburgh, where, laid out in a cascade diagram, are eighteen recognised and independent churches formed between 1700 and 1950. Where people think, and if no one stops them thinking, a variety of ideas is inevitable.

Another well-known attribute of the early medieval monastery is its attraction for Vikings. The argument that a Viking attack happened at Portmahomack is based on an extensive fire that swept through the workshop, which was followed by a dumping of sculpture, mainly belonging to Cross D. This was judged to have been both recently made, and freshly smashed, which puts the event close to its estimated date of manufacture in the late eighth or early ninth century. All the slabs were probably felled at that time, since larger weathered pieces belonging to Crosses A and C were lying in the grass of the churchyard before 1776, or had been incorporated into the foundations of a twelfth-century parish church, and buried. Fresher parts of Crosses B and C were to come to light from grave-digging or from excavations in the Glebe Field respectively. Given the likely date for Cross D, the raid should, therefore, date to the early ninth century. Radiocarbon dating brackets it between 780 and 830.

It was something of a surprise that the working part of the monastery was back in business so quickly, but there was clearly a major restructuring of the workforce. The vellum-workers had been laid off, and the metal-workers were removed to a roadside site beyond the pond. Their old hall was recommissioned as a barn for drying, malting and, possibly, brewing too. The metal-workers were soon augmented with a team of blacksmiths. It is hard to know the products of these craftsmen, and the best we can do is to table a general impression that the repertoire had become more secular. It is suggested that this later industrial phase ran from the ninth to the eleventh century and that the people of Portmahomack would have found themselves now of the Norse party, and now of the Scots, in the long struggle between the rival powers of Orkney and Moray. Given the mobility of those powers and their vacillating frontier, political control need not have been culturally branded by artefacts or buildings.

The Portmahomack experience may not have been unusual. After a prolonged onslaught, Iona too kept going from 807 to 825, dedicatees offering themselves as sacrifices to the furies. At Whithorn a fire of *c.* 845 was followed by a redevelopment supposed by its excavator to have begun with the rebuilding of one 'church' and then the building of another, together with an incongruous 'densely packed band of simple buildings'. The assemblage, however, is one of craft and domestic activity : iron-working debris, antler combs, glass finger-rings, a needle case, a steatite bowl, ornamental weight, fishing weight, silver ring money, copper alloy strip with Ringerrike ornament, a tenth-century buckle, a Tafl board and an antler handle. Peter Hill comments: 'The finds include a handful of tenth century objects of Norse type but these are too few to justify claims of Viking dominion.'[29] On the basis of these objects, Graham-Campbell and Batey say coyly: 'It appears most likely that the excavated settlement [in Period III] at Whithorn dates to the late Viking/late Norse period.'[30] Whithorn, it may be observed, became culturally Viking, in a way that Portmahomack did not.

For Monkwearmouth and Jarrow, Rosemary Cramp astutely notes that the key factor in the demise of a monastery is not fire (and the sword) but loss of endowment: 'Viking raids had so destabilised the economic system that by 800 even Christian kings were ready to take over and redistribute monastic land.'[31] There were signs of fire all the same: Building A at Jarrow was found still covered in charcoal. But Building D at the same site, the craftsmen's hall, continued to make combs and glass into the tenth century. There were no coins or pottery between the ninth and the eleventh centuries, so that the reduced circumstances in which these craftsmen continued to work were probably dominated by local needs and local powers. This provides an acceptable model for the end of Britain's first monastic experiment. While no one will to dare suggest that their Christianity was only skin deep, the workers and thinkers of the Tarbat peninsula would have found it easy to switch allegiance if their religion was positioned within a broader, less dogmatic, intellectual context than that demanded by Christian writers.

Conclusion

The archaeological journey undertaken by the Tarbat Discovery Programme is now at an end. Taking one small part of Scotland to speak for the whole, it has traversed much of the Christian experience. We have visited its beginnings in the sixth century and the building of the Visitor Centre arguably marks its ending in the late twentieth. Personally, I have no regrets about such an ending. Christianity is only one of many religions that humans have proclaimed and monumentalised in the landscape, and from a prehistoric perspective 2,000 or even 1,500 years is not a bad innings. We need not doubt that humans have had the same hunger for the understanding of dreams, life and death as long as they have occupied the earth. By deconstructing something as familiar as Christianity in an out-of-the-way place, we may gain an idea of how prehistoric worship worked, as contemplation, as discipline and as communal expression. As I know from my own upbringing as a Roman Catholic, Christianity generated art and ceremony of extraordinary beauty, and the age of experiment between the sixth century and the twelfth must have been particularly exciting to live through. But human values are those that map across all religions, including the lost majority that we now call prehistoric. Only archaeology offers access to the full range of this, the echo of the indomitable human spirit calling on its gods.

Notes

1. Henshall and Ritchie (2001: 31).
2. Long cairns 57, 45, 40, 27; Orkney–Cromarty cairns 2, 29, 30, 36, 46, 47, 48. There were no finds in these, but a barbed and tanged arrowhead, Beaker pottery, leaf-shaped arrow head, coarse pottery and saddle quern were found together in Ros 12, an OC tomb on the Black Isle.
3. Henshall and Ritchie (2001: 75).
4. Bradley (1993: 115, 117).
5. Briand 1997. Examples from Ireland include the cross carved on the Findermore stone, Co. Tyrone, a prehistoric monument located next to three ring-barrows (Herity 1995: 297) and the crosses carved on the kerbstones of the Neolithic passage grave at Lough Crew (Hughes and Hamlin 1973: 84).
6. Nylén and Lamm (1988).
7. Gräslund (2003: 491).
8. Bradley (2000: 3; illus. 177, p. 222).
9. Ibid. p. 229; see illus. 182.
10. Grant (2005, 88, 92); cf. Henderson (1958).
11. Carver (2003a: *passim*).
12. Burn (1969).
13. Venclova (2002).
14. Veitch (1997) notes that the tonsure was less important than the date of Easter, debate about which dragged on through the seventh and eighth centuries.
15. Smyth (1984).

16. Brown (1997).
17. Henderson (1975).
18. Lamb (1998: 260–1).
19. Macdonald (1992); Veitch (1997).
20. Grant (2005: 95); see also Macdonald (1992).
21. Taylor (1996).
22. cf. Veitch (1997: 637).
23. James *et al.* (forthcoming).
24. Graham-Campbell (1973).
25. Jesch (1993: 228–9).
26. See also Cramp (2005: 360).
27. Ibid. p. 362.
28. cf. ibid. p. 361.
29. Hill (1997: 48).
30. Graham-Campbell and Batey (1998: 205).
31. Cramp (2005: 360).

Digest of evidence

The following summaries are intended to provide a point of departure for future studies of the Portmahomack site and the Tarbat peninsula.

Details of the interim excavation results, of the objects found, of analytical work in progress, and contact addresses for researchers, will be found in the *Bulletins* and *Data Structure Reports* on line at www.http//:york.ac.uk/depts/arch/staff/sites/tarbat.html

The records and preliminary interpretation of the excavations are contained in seven volumes of *Field Reports*, which provide the data for the full *Research Report* being prepared for publication by the Society of Antiquaries of Scotland and the National Museums of Scotland and expected to be completed in about 2018.

All the objects found at Portmahomack are the property of the National Museums of Scotland, but a selection of the finest can always be seen on display at the Tarbat Discovery Centre in St Colman's Church, Portmahomack.

A1	Archaeological interventions at Portmahomack	204
A2	Excavated structures, other than churches	206
A3	Radiocarbon dates from the excavation campaign	207
A4	St Colman's church and its predecessors (Sector 4)	210
A5	Handlist of Pictish sculpture	214
A6	The monastic workshops, northern quarter (Sector 2)	218
A7	The monastic workshops, southern quarter (Sector 1)	221
A8	The Tarbat peninsula	224

A1 Archaeological interventions at Portmahomack

Int. No.	LOCATION	ACTIVITY	RECORDER	DATE
1	ZONE E	Trial excavation across enclosure ditch	Harden	Jun. 1991
2	ZONES D, E	Magnetometer survey	Garner-Lahire	Mar. 1994
3	ZONES D, E	Resistivity	Garner-Lahire	Mar. 1994
4	ZONES B–F	Contour survey	Copp	Mar. 1994
5	ZONE A	Contour survey	Copp	Mar. 1994
6	ZONE B	Churchyard map	Copp	Mar. 1994
7	ZONE E	Trial excavation in south field	Roe	Sept. 1994
8	ZONE D	Trial excavation in Glebe Field	Garner-Lahire	Sept. 1994
9	ZONES B–E	Radar survey	Sympkins	Sept. 1994
10	ZONE E	Trial excavation in west field	Garner-Lahire	Sept. 1994
11	ZONE E	Horizon 2 mapping in south field	Garner-Lahire	Aug. 1995
12	ZONE E	Horizon 0 mapping	Garner-Lahire	Aug. 1995
13	ZONE A	Crypt clearance	Harden	1992–5
14	ZONE D	Excavation in Glebe Field (N)	Garner-Lahire	1996–2007
15	ZONE J	Horizon 2 mapping and excavation	Garner-Lahire	1996
16	ZONE B	Excavation of service trench (N)	Garner-Lahire	1996
17	ZONE A	Excavation in church, east end	Roe	1996
18	ZONE B	Test pits around church exterior	Geddes	1996–7
19	ZONE A	Excavation in crypt	Roe	1997
20	ZONE A	Excavation in church, west end	Roe	1997
21	ZONE B	Watching brief on churchyard wall	Robins	1997
22	ZONE B	Excavation of service trench (S)	Roe	1997

Int. No.	LOCATION	ACTIVITY	RECORDER	DATE
23	ZONE A	Recording of church building	Jones	1997
24	ZONE D	Excavation in Glebe Field (S)	Garner-Lahire	1997–2007
25	ZONE E	Excavation in south field	Garner-Lahire	1997–2001
26	ZONE D	Pit dug for oil storage tank in Glebe Field	Garner-Lahire	1998
27	ZONE D	Pit dug for foundation of a bronze statue	Garner-Lahire	1999
28	ZONE B	Recording of memorials in churchyard	Carver	1998–2002
29	ZONE B	Recording in advance of a flag pole	Garner-Lahire	2005

A2 Excavated structures, other than churches

S1 Smiths' Hall/Barn in Sector 1
S2 Rectangular enclosure south of S1
S3 Bag-shaped building north of S1
S4 Tawing tank in Sector 2
S5 Oval building in Sector 1 (east)
S6 Rectilinear enclosure west of S1
S7 Dam and culvert: water management features in Sector 2
S8 Well adjacent to S1 in Sector 1
S9 Vellum-makers' hall in Sector 2

A3 Radiocarbon dates from the excavation campaign

Calibrated to 2sigma (95.4%) with OxCal3, unless otherwise stated.

Church and Cemetery

Burials at Balnabruach

Burial A GU-14998 410–200 BC (410–340 BC@58.1%)
Burial B GU-14999 AD 250–420 (AD 320–400@51.6%)
Burial C GU-15000 AD 250–540 (AD 320–470@79.7%)

Burials north of workshop

Cist burial 186 (Int14/F515) GU-14997 AD 430–610

In church

Carbonised grain from ditch F129/1345 GU-15001 AD 540–650

Phase 1 Burials (all human bone)

Cist burial 162 (Int20/F159/1373) GU-14996 AD 410–570
Cist burial 172 (Int20/F152/1373) OxA-9699 AD 430–650

Head support burial 128 (Int20/F103/1244) OxA-13487 AD 610–760
Burial 163 (Int20/F160/1374) OxA-13484 AD 610–770
Burial 165 (Int20/F158/1371) OxA-13509 AD 650–780
Burial 144 (Int20/F98/1232) OxA-13488 AD 650–780
Burial 160 (Int20/F148/1346) OxA-13486 AD 660–780
Head support burial 116 (Int20/F96/1228) OxA-13489 AD 660–820
Burial 147 (Int20/F125/1294) OxA-13485 AD 690–890
Burial 158 (Int 20/F138/1238) (blade injury) GU-9296 AD 680–900
Head support burial 152 (Int 20/F132/1307) (blade injury) GU-9297 AD 810–1020

Phase 2

Bell-casting pit (Int20/F107/1220) OxA-10536 AD 1040–1260 (68.2% 1050–1080 or 1150–1230)

Burial 117 (Int 20/F93/1222) (blade injury) GU-9298 AD 1150–1280
Burial 113 (Int20/F84/1206) OxA-13491 AD 1270–1400
Burial 99 (Int20/F76/1183) OxA-13490 AD 1280–1400
Burial 97 (Int20/F48/1107) OxA-13762 AD 1410–1455
Burial 90 (Int20/F45/1106) OxA-13521 AD 1410–1610

Burial began in the Iron Age (Phase 0). Burial in the church area with stone settings began before 570. Burial with stone settings (Phase 1) ended before 1020. Phase 2 burial began after 1159. Church 2 began between 1040 and 1260.

From the marsh and pool

Seeds from marsh, earliest deposits (Int24/2310/4910(27)) GU-15588 550–370 BC (89.6%)

Weed seeds from marsh, latest deposits (Int24/2310/4874(26)) GU-15587 AD 590–720 (90.1%)

Birch twigs from pool, earliest use (Int24/2296/4873(28)) GU-15589 AD 590–720 (91.5%)

Elder seeds from pool, end of use (Int24/2296/4863(29)) GU-15590 AD 640–810 (95.4%)

Stakes in stream (Int24/F404/2295) GU-15013 AD 650–780
Stakes in pool (Int24/F436/2224) GU-15014 AD 630–780

Workshops

Earliest cattle bones, east (Int14/2335) GU-15004 AD 650–780
Earliest cattle bones, west (Int14/F480/3122) GU-15005 AD 630–780

Use of hearth in yard (F445/2468) GU-15008 AD 610–770
Use of hearth in S9 (F495/2786) GU-15173 AD 650–780

Cattle metapodials aligned in workshop (Int14/F393/1957) GU-15006 AD 640–780
Dump of cattle metapodials in workshop (Int14/2000) GU-15007 AD 650–820

The dam and pool were constructed between 590 and 720. Leather-working activity began after 610, flourished between 650 and 780 and ended before 820. The pool was disused before 810.

Destruction

Burnt wattle from destruction layer (Int26/1030) OxA-9664 AD 330–560
Burnt stake from terrace wall (F490/2697) GU-15010 AD 410–570
Burnt wattle from terrace wall (F483/2584) GU-15011 AD 600–770
Wattle fragments from primary burning (Int14/2704) GU-15012 AD 650–830

Buildings constructed from timber cut after 330 and before 770 were burnt down after 650 and before 830.

After the raid

Metal-working hearth (Int14/F148/1412) GU-15015 AD 670–870
Cow burial (Int14/F304/1734) GU-15016 AD 820–1020

Raid had happened before 870. Given the terminal date for burials and vellum-working activities of 780, the latest date of burnt wattle of 830, and the last use of the pool of 810, the most likely date for the raid is after 780 and before 830.

Farm

Peat from outer enclosure ditch (Harden 1995: 226) GU-3265–3267 AD 140–410; 250–531; 350–590 (98%)
Wooden stake *in situ* in outer enclosure ditch (Int11/F158/1490) OxA-9663 AD 540–690 *superseded by* OxA-10159: AD 660–860.
Twigs from disuse of enclosure ditch (Int25/F132/1401) GU-15020 AD 680–900
Charcoal from ultimate backfilling of tributary ditch (Int11/F18/1143) OxA-9662 AD 780–1020.

Calcined animal bone from hearth in the Smiths' Hall (S1) (Int11/F65/1141) GU-11756 AD 760–900 (80.9%)
Grain from flue of S1 (Int 25/F79/1527) GU-15019 AD 1020–1180

Grain from central pit of oval structure S5 (Int 25/F13/1027) GU-15017 AD 680–900
Grain from ditch of S5 (Int25/F3/1153) GU-15018 AD 890–1030

The outer enclosure ditch was lined after 660 and disused before 900. Building S1 was last used by metal-workers between 690 and 900; and last used for crop-processing between 1020 and 1180. Building S5 was used for crop-processing between 680 and 900 and disused before 1030.

A4 St Colman's church and its predecessors (Sector 4)

Interventions: 13 (crypt), 17 (north aisle), 18 (architects' pits), 19 (crypt), 23 (fabric)

Components of the nine churches at Portmahomack

Church 1	Eighth century	Lower half of east wall of crypt, which may have formed a wall for an early stone church (Int19, F3 (19/3))
Church 2	Twelfth century	Rectangular building with south door (east wall 17/85; north wall 17/2 = 20/124, 127; construction trench 17/72, south wall 17/63; west wall construction cut 17/73, wall 20/73)
Church 3	Twelfth century	East end chancel added (north stub wall 17/66, south stub wall 17/69; north–south unidentified wall 17/86)
Church 4	Thirteenth century	New version of Church 3 with extensions west and east; east end crypt fashioned from the ruin of Church 1 (south wall 17/62 (footings) = 20/23, 17/63 = 20/89; north wall 17/17; wall 17/9; blocked doorway 17/68, 20/108 = 23/54, 20/87; postholes for construction 17/92, 93)
Church 5	Seventeenth century	With flagstone floor; doorway; north aisle; burial vault; MacKenzie Tomb; new vault and lights in east crypt; relieving arch at west end (flagstone floor 20/1000, 1001, 1007; 17/6, 1010, 1012, 1061, 1065; doorway 20/87, 131; north aisle 1/124, 80– 105, 11, 73, 81– 104; burial vault 17/113, 114, 115, 116, 117, 74, 5; MacKenzie Tomb 17/111; 23/1296; new vault and lights in east crypt 17/110; relieving arch at west end 23/1123)
Church 6	1756	Rebuilt north wall of nave; blocked doorway in south wall; west gallery; north gallery; doors in south wall; windows; door to gallery (north wall of nave 17/65 = 20/126; south wall 17/64=20/88; blocked doorway in south wall 17/70; west gallery 23/65; north gallery 23/66; doors in south wall 23/2, 23/60, 23/9, 23/12; windows 23/4, 23/8; Door to gallery 23/1)

Digest of evidence

Church 7	Late eighteenth century	New north aisle with upper storey; rebuilt east wall; flue for stove; fireplace; blocked doorway reused as window in west wall; new first floor; remodelled trapdoor to vault; window; vestry; door; pulpit door; blocking under arch *(rebuilt east wall 17/16; flue for stove 17/3; fireplace; blocked doorway reused as window in west wall 17/121; new first floor 23/66; remodelled trapdoor to vault 23/51; window 23/5; vestry 23/61; door 23/11; pulpit door 23/61; raised wall plate 23/1167; blocking under arch 23/1121)*
Church 8	Early nineteenth century	Roof raised by 1.07m; external masonry staircases to north aisle, east and west galleries; memorial to William Forbes and children (1841) 23/63, 23/1155
Church 9	After 1843	Renovated church after 1843; wooden floor, graffiti on west wall of north aisle, first storey; new vestry window; Macleod enclosure; memorials to Donald Macleod and sons (1874) *(wooden floor 17/1; graffiti on west wall of north aisle, first storey 17/122; new vestry window 23/10)*

Principal stratigraphic horizons and their component contexts

Horizon A	context 20/1383
Horizon B	contexts 20/1064, 20/1215, 17/1203, 17/1231
Horizon C	contexts 20/1298, 1031, 1056, 1225, 1217, 1191; 17/1051, 1202, 1240, 1244
Horizon D	contexts 17/1201, 1052, 1157; 20/1077
Horizon E	contexts 20/1052, 1058, 1045, 1152; burning 1151; mortar floor F61
Horizon F	contexts 20/1000

Features

Ditch under church 20/F129; 17/F100; burnt grain is 1345
Bell-casting pit preparatory to Church 2: 20/F107.
Bell-casting pit probably preparatory to Church 5: 20/F4, F147

Cemetery

Burials in the workshop area outside the churchyard: F515, F516, F517
Viking blade injuries: burials F152, F158, F149

Church 1

East wall of the crypt 19/F3, west wall 19/F4; north wall 19/F119; south wall 19/F118; aumbry 19/F40

The length of the north wall of the crypt is 6.76m and the south wall 7.20m.

The height of the surface of the buried soil 1383 inside the church was computed as 17.40m AOD. The ditch 20/129 cuts buried soil 1384, from highest point 17.36m; cist grave at west end and the west wall of Church 2 are cut from about 17.40m.

The base of the stones of the east wall (F3) lie at 14.73–14.87m, and the west wall (F4) at 14.93m. The crypt floor is currently at 15.025m. Top of the aumbry is at 16.41m AOD. F3 was reported by the architect as cut 1.5m into subsoil externally, implying a current subsoil surface at 16.5m at the east end. The south and east walls of the crypt were thirteenth-century dressed stone to a depth of 1m below the chamfered plinth (which was at 17.7m AOD), i.e. to c. 16.7m AOD, which should therefore represent the lowest Old Ground surface in the thirteenth century. The floor for Church 1 must have lain somewhere between 15m and 16.7m AOD (i.e. not lower than now, not higher than the thirteenth-century old ground surface). If the aumbry is in use in Church 1, then the floor could not have been much higher than it is now (15m AOD). If not, then the floor could be higher, but more than half a metre higher (15.50m) would imply impractically deep foundations. This would mean a floor level about equivalent to the present Step 2. Step 2 is at 15.41m, Step 9 is 17.40m, Step 10 is at 17.50m.

Medieval pottery: 19/1208/318; 17/1147/164.

Documentary references to a church at Tarbat

(after Fraser and Munro 1988, with additions)

The Middle Ages

[AD 565]	According to *Origines Parochiales Scotiae*, St Columba built a church at Tarbat and this had survived as a vault 30ft long (i.e. the crypt of Tarbat Old Church). The church was dedicated to St Colman.
c. 1220	Abbey of Fearn founded probably at mid-Fearn near Edderton. By 1227 it had been moved to its present site on the hill of Fearn on the Tarbat isthmus.
1255	A church at Portmahomack served by a canon of Fearn.
1274	Vicarage revenues assigned to a canon of Fearn.
c. 1487	Members of a party of Mackays from Sutherland killed at Tarbat church. The church is also burnt and Angus Mackay died in the fire.
1529	Pope Clement VII confirmed to the canons of New Fearn all their possessions, including the vicarage of the church of St Colman.

Tarbat at the Reformation

c. 1560	The Reformation.
1623	James Cuthbert, Provost of Inverness and his wife Jeane Leslye commemorated in N aisle.
1626–8	Fearn parish, including the abbey, separated from the parish of Tarbat, to which it had originally belonged.
1634	Sir John Mackenzie is chief heritor and has the right to the north aisle.

1642	William Mackenzie, minister, provided with new tomb in the north aisle by Sir John Mackenzie.
1690	The Revolution Settlement. Tarbat until then nominally a *mensa* of the Bishop of Ross; now under the control of the minister, congregation and heritors.
Late 17th century	Tarbat becomes one of fourteen churches funded by George, Lord Tarbat, first Earl of Cromartie as heritor. Construction of the harbour at Portmahomack begun. The pier is constructed by Alexander Stronach, 1698.
1706	'St Colmshaven' and 'Malcolm's haven' are terms used to refer to Portmahomack. 'Castlehaven' of 1701 is probably Portmahomack (rather than Port a' Chaistell).
1709–28	A manse constructed, which included a stable ('consisting of three Highland couples under one roof on the west side of the close'), a barn, byre and kitchen.
1721	Church is in a ruinous condition.
1739	Church in a *very* ruinous condition.
1756–62	The whole church dismantled except for the west gable and bell tower and rebuilt on the old foundations and within existing dimensions.
1762	The manse rebuilt.
1764	The present bell refounded from the previous bell by John Milne of Edinburgh.
1776–80	The church harled inside and outside. Sir John Gordon's aisle refitted for the benefit of parishioners.
1780–5	Major repairs and alterations. The north aisle lengthened by 10ft (3m). The side walls and roof of the aisle raised to the same height as the nave. Joists were laid from the front of the aisle to its gable to create a top storey for Sir John Mackenzie. The lower storey was fitted with seats to accommodate parishioners generally.
1801	Manse totally rebuilt. The Glebe enlarged from 4 acres to 6 acres and 2 roods. The laird of Geanies made over a small part of his land that adjoined the north-east part of the Glebe.
1804–7	Churchyard dyke (i.e. the boundary wall) built. It enclosed 11 2/3 roods, or 14,121 sq yd (11805m^2; about 3 acres).
1843	The Disruption: formation of the Free Church. The minister and the bulk of the congregation deserted the parish church and set up the Free Church of Tarbat.
1851	A grass Glebe is provided for the minister.
1853	At this point the congregation of the Free Church is 1000; of the parish church 85.
1856	Inspection recommends extensive repairs to the church, manse and outbuildings. Church walls, the harling, the roof, stone stairs, windows and doors all needed repair.
1868	The churchyard enlarged again.
1874	The land held by Mr Campbell, the minister, amounted to 12 acres.
1893	Churchyard extended again.
1899	A Viking-period silver hoard discovered beneath the churchyard wall.
1908	Church bell recast.
1928	Church, manse and Glebe transferred from heritors to the Church of Scotland Trustees.
1946	Church declared redundant.

A5 Handlist of Pictish sculpture

PORTMAHOMACK

About 250 pieces have so far been unearthed, which are thought to derive from at least nine grave markers, four cross-slabs, a sarcophagus, a shrine and an architectural finial. Unlike those at Hilton, Shandwick and Nigg, all the Portmahomack cross-slabs were broken up before the eighteenth century, and one at least before the twelfth.

TR1–19 Represent chance discoveries, mostly made before 1994. Nos 20–225 were recovered during the University of York's research project, described in this book. All the Portmahomack stones belong to the National Museums of Scotland, although at any one time a large number of them will be on exhibition at the Tarbat Discovery Centre in Portmahomack. The remainder can be seen on exhibition at the National Museums, Chambers Street, Edinburgh, or by appointment in the NMS store.

Descriptions of TR1–10 will be found in *ECMS* III. 88–95. Other references are included below. The corpus as a whole is currently being studied for definitive publication in the research report.

Abbreviated Catalogue

Modern measurements are given in metric.

TR1	Base of a cross-slab, including the tenon. Face 1: border of vine-scroll ornament similar to that on Hilton of Cadboll, framing part of a figurative scene. Face 2 (side): crescent and V-rod; a sword or 'tuning fork' symbol; a serpent and Z-rod; an animal – perhaps the Pictish dolphin. Face 3 (side): interlace. Face 4 (now effaced; likely to have featured a cross). 630×1120×150mm. Probably the base of a cross-slab.
TR2	Four pieces from an upright cross-slab, with central interlace shaft and panels ornamented with serpents. Probably the 'Danish Cross' seen in the churchyard in the nineteenth century. Conjoined panel *c.* 2ft 8in × 1ft 7in × 2ft. (810 × 230 × 50mm).
TR3	Fragment of relief sculpture, with interlace. 6in × 3.5in × 2in thick (150×90×50mm).
TR4	Fragment of upright cross-slab, bearing raised fillets and interlace. 12in × 9in × 2in thick (300 × 230 × 50mm).

TR5	Central boss from a cross-slab comprising seven small bosses in a wreath of interlace. 1ft 1in diameter × 2.5in thick (330mm in diameter and 60mm thick).
TR6	Central boss of a cross-slab, with wreath ornamented in key pattern. 360 × 345mm.
TR7	Fragment with spirals in relief and hooked peltae. 260 × 170 × 25mm.
TR8	Triangular fragment of an upright cross-slab, bearing key pattern in relief. 270 × 100 × 65mm.
TR9	Triangular fragment of an upright cross-slab. Face 1: middle of a panel of spiral-work with small triangular dots. Face 2: portion next to the edge of a panel of interlaced-work. 9in × 7in × 8in thick (230 × 180 × 200mm).
TR10	Inscribed stone. Face 1: the apex of a square panel containing spiral ornament in relief. Matches TR20, the 'Apostle Stone'. Face 2: on a narrow side, an inscription in relief insular majuscules. 480 × 310 × 200mm.
TR11	A 'small boss richly fretted like a knot of young adders interlaced' in olive green sandstone (now lost).
TR12	Fragment of relief sculpture with a cockerel and a fox carved in shallow relief. 7in × 8in × 2in thick (180 × 200 × 50mm). (NMS, IB209.)
TR13	Fragment with recessed crosses and key pattern. Face 1: strip of key pattern. Face 2: 3 crosses. 35 × 425 × 75mm. (*PSAS* 73 (1939), 333.)
TR14	Fragment with interlace. Incorporated into the relieving arch at the west end of the church.
TR15	Cross-slab with maltese cross formed from five circles. 3ft 4in long by 2ft broad by 7in thick (1000 × 610 × 180mm) (now lost) (Ritchie 1915).
TR16	Fragment with letter 'A' in insular majuscule. Included in the blocking of the south door at the east end of the nave of St Colman's church. Dimensions 250 × 220mm.

Found between 1991 and 1994

TR17	Three conjoining fragments with interlace. 215 × 190 × 25mm thick.
TR18	Fragment with spiral decoration. 82 × 111 × 72mm thick.
TR19	Roughly shaped rectangular stone bearing a simple cross in relief. 340 × 126 × 80mm.

Found during the University of York's Research Campaign (began 1994)

TR20	The 'Monk Stone' 'Dragon Stone' or 'Apostle Stone' ; fragment from a large cross-slab. Face 1: panels of spirals forming part of a cross, inset by a composite beast ('dragon'). Border 40mm; ribs 20mm; volute 60 × 25mm. Face 2: two lions disputing a deer carcass, a bear and a row of four clerics. Border (top) 40mm wide. Complete face 50mm across and 60mm down. 710 × 410 × 178mm thick (thickness varies 160–180mm). Probably belongs to the same monument as TR10.
TR21	Small cross-slab bearing a hollow-armed cross one side and a chisel-ended cross the other. 510 × 195 × 45mm.
TR22	The 'Boar Stone'. Possible sarcophagus lid. Face 1 (side, horizontal): lion and boar in relief in panels. Panels 300 × 160mm (lion);

	330 × 160mm (boar); rebate 25 × 25mm (1ft × 1ft) in profile. Panels separated by ribs 55mm wide. Face 2 (end): cross in relief. 1065 × 460 × 230mm.
TR23	Tiny fragment with spiral in relief. 55 × 30mm.
TR24	Roughly shaped stone with simple cross scratched upon it. 470 × 245 × 130mm.
TR25	Roughly shaped stone with simple cross incised on it. 231 × 195 × 47mm.
TR26	Cross-shaft reused as lintel in north light of crypt *in situ*.
TR27	A stone post with side-grooves, possibly a 'shrine-post' or part of a *cancellum*. Removed from an unknown location in the graveyard. 560 × 150 × 140mm; groove is 35mm wide internally.
TR28	Trial piece or partially worked slab with rendering of bull, cow (or two cows) one licking a calf, in low relief; also part of horseman/woman. Possibly intended as a screen and maybe unfinished. 775 × 480 × 100mm (max. thickness 80mm) (with TR35). Joins with TR35.
TR29	Piece with part of stepped cross in low relief. 325 × 325 × 72mm.
TR30	Part of cross-slab with incised hollow-angled cross. At least 560 × 620mm. Incorporated into the church south wall, but no longer visible.
TR31	Part of cross-slab with incised hollow-angled cross. At least 190 × 180 × 70mm. Incorporated into the south wall of the church but no longer visible.
TR32	Small fragment with plain border against an incised decoration of tendrils similar to those on TR18. On the edge is part of a key pattern. 135 × 85 × 50mm (140 × 90 × 60mm). Ribs 35mm wide.
TR33	Cross-slab with cross in low relief which has parallels at Iona. 524 × 212 × 56mm.
TR34	Fragment of cross-slab with hollow-angled cross in low relief.
TR35	Fragment with rendering of a lion, the forelegs of which conjoin with the feet on TR28. Above this a cloven footed 'manticora' is depicted possibly menacing a lamb. The top of the fragment displays a finished edge marked by four incised lines. 380 × 330 × 80mm.
TR36	Small fragment of spiral carved in relief. 85 × 50 × 30mm.
TR37	Small fragment of double strand interlace. 89 × 45 × 20mm.
TR38	Fragment of median strand interlace probably from the same piece of carving as TR37. Comprises two conjoining pieces. 114 × 88 × 35mm.
TR39	Fragment of yellow micaceous sandstone with a prominent interlace boss. 100 × 100 × 50mm. Found by Richard Blosse in 1999 among stones bought by Ann Perry, for whom he was building a garden wall. The stones originated from the manse steading, which had recently been demolished.
TR40	Sandstone fragment bearing geometric ornament carved in relief on the front and back faces. 370 × 270 × 190 mm (measured as 360 × 290 × 200mm). Found by Richard Blosse in1999 among stones bought by Ann Perry, for whom he was building a garden wall. The stones originated from the manse steading which had recently been demolished.
TR41	Fragment of a hollow-armed cross. 185 × 116 × 33mm.
TR42–113	Fragments of moulded border belonging to a cross-slab or cross-shaft.

TR114–47	Fragments of spiral ornament belonging to a cross-slab or cross-shaft.
TR115–199	Fragments of interlace ornament belonging to a cross- slab or cross-shaft.
TR201	Fragment bearing the face of a holy man.
TR204–9, 216, 218, 221–2	Fragments bearing animal ornament.

NIGG

NH 856747	Cross-slab. Erected in the Church at Nigg. One loose fragment from near the top was found in 1998 and may be seen in the Museum at Tain. Described in Chapter 9 (Nigg Trust).

SHANDWICK

NH 856 747	Cross-slab. *In situ* on the hill above Shandwick village. The cross is protected by being placed in a glass cabin. Entry to the cabin is allowed by obtaining the key from the custodian (see the notice on the site). Described in Chapter 9 (Shandwick Trust).

HILTON OF CADBOLL

Originally located at NH 883 791; RCAHMS 1979, no 210	The upper and larger part of the cross-slab is in the National Museums of Scotland in Chambers Street, Edinburgh where it is displayed in the prehistory section. The lower and smaller part is in the care of the Hilton Trust, which displays it in the Leisure Centre at neighbouring Balintore. Several thousand small fragments, which were generated when the cross was trimmed in 1676, are now in the care of the National Museums of Scotland. A reconstruction of the Hilton cross-slab by Barry Grove stands near the Chapel of St Mary at Hilton of Cadboll. One side replicates the upper part of the Hilton stone in the NMS. The other side carries a reconstruction of an ornamental cross which is largely imaginative. Described in Chapter 9 (Hilton Trust).

A6 The monastic workshops, northern quarter (Sector 2)

(Interventions 14, 24)

Principal buried soil in Int. 14, Sector 2: context 1384.

Early hearth F535; Fe blade 4311, worked bone 4401. Hearth F535 contained a pellet of copper alloy. Slag and a fragment of mould were also found in buried soil, 2480.

Early water management: cistern F530 fed by ditch F534. There were three other stone-lined pits, less than a metre in diameter F470, 473, 399. F470 had a slab base. Wicker-lined well F527; charcoal pit F573.

Later water management: dam F440; culverts F431, 432; covers F430. Capstones 3572; kerb wall across the valley F394. These were the last features to be excavated and their interpretation should be refined by further analysis.

Road 1 F469; east ditches F471A, 472A; west ditches F468/475.

Road 2: F18; recommissioned ditches F471C (highest fill 1891/2538) and F472C (alias F180; highest fill 2672, 2556).

Parchment-makers

S4 Tawing tank. Trough F72; pebbling F50, 82; culvert F376; drains F378, 380, 385.

S9 Workshop: north wall F514; south wall F434; Postholes: F498, F499, F508 squared post ghost, F511, F513, F22, F29, F230, F231, F233, F234, F275, F276, F277, F279, F280, F283, F288, F370, F133, F506, F372; hearth F495. Stone and clay lump F512.

Yard: Hearth F474; terrace wall F480. The working floor is 2109. Bone rows: 1959, 2511, F373. Pits F558, 575; Piles of ash 1886, 1917.

Hot air ducts: F467, F379 (= Int26/F22), F395.

Viking Raid

Primary burning: white, yellow, pink and orange: 1662, 2701, 2704 (heather, rope, wattles, poles), 1916, 2602 (against yard wall F480), 1949 (plank), 1868 (bird), F490 and F483 burnt wattle, 1364 (within tawing tank); inside drainage gully for S9, F31 (2958); last layer of hearth in S9 (2745); charred thatch in S9 (2889).

Dumping of sculpture 1588, 1506, 1510, 1721; 2645, 2537 in F180; trample 2587.

9th–11th-century metal-workers

Hearths: F353, 474, 478, 479, 484; F148, with a Cu droplet, slag, crucible frags, mould was constructed over hearth F493.

Crucibles: 2547, 2567, 2571, 2567: moulds: 2548, 2678; whetstones: 2539, 2609.

Carnelian gem from 14/2701 = 2687; touchstone from 14/2687. 2687 was the sandy floor of the workshop lying directly over the burning layer 2701.

Sceat from context 1510, or from 1505, the fill of a small pit F185, or more probably from 1510, the charcoal sculpture bearing layer that it cut (24/1505/2283).

Reticella vessel fragment 24/2885; cylindrical blue glass bead with zig-zag inlay from mill pond; spacer bead 24 module B4; mould from F180/2620.

Residual Cu alloy objects: plaque 14/1002/1286; strap-end 14/1002/1285; fretwork handle 14/1501/2277; dress pin 24/1002/504; dress pin 24/1292/527; ornate disc with spirals 14/1225.

Snaffle bit: 14/2609.

Painted pebble from context 2578.

Debris (earliest is 2631, latest is 2649); dumps (earliest is 2731, latest is 2570).

Post-holes in metal workshops: F215–223; squared posts F491 and F486.

Posts in pool: F348, 436, 438 (square post).

Metal-working west of road: Pit F482 with conical crucible and iron pieces.

At north end: earliest hearth F299; stake buildings F93, F100; paved areas F121; 17+ postholes; figure of eight hearth F35; 8 metal-working pits (F11, 25, etc.); 6 hearths (F57, 167, etc.);.

Book plaques and comb: 14/1002/1296, 1295, 271.

11th–13th century residential

Domestic pits (F139 with residual bone pins from vellum-workers); 19 post-holes (F29, F360, etc.); 4 gullies (F127, F263, etc.); culvert lined with Calf Stone (F166). Period 4C; rubble layer 1074, 1153, 1843; huge domestic rubbish pit F2; 3 other domestic pits F345, 366, 369; 7 gullies or windbreaks (F23, F145); 8 post-holes (F163, F224, etc.).

Collapse of terrace wall F147; stagnant water 2204; rubble over boggy pond 1326.

Rubble layers 1074, 1153, 1843; huge domestic rubbish pit F13; other domestic pits F345, 366, 369; 7 gullies or windbreaks (F23, F145); 8 post-holes (F163, F224, etc.).

Later use

Ploughsoils 1284; shell middens F156.

Field boundary 24/F97.

A7 The monastic workshops, southern quarter (Sector 1)

(Interventions 11, 25)

Plough soils

Plough soil test: module C1, C2 and half of B4.

Ancient plough soil 1371, 1381; ploughmarks 1385; Module G6 marked by ard scratches, cut by outer enclosure ditch. Ard marks in E7, E8, F5, F6. Plough pebbles were first recognised in Sector 2 workshops, where they had probably been brought within cut turf for building.

Early metal-workers on backfilled inner enclosure ditch

Int 25/F179 = Int 11/F176, investigated in two contiguous stretches 1250 of F176 and 1377 of F179.

Defined features: Int25/F3, F176, F179, F216, F203; 5 post-holes F202, etc.; l hearth F208 and hollows F214, 216.

Finds: glass rod, glass droplets, lumps of raw blue glass, fragment of shallow clay vessel with coating of yellow glass; opaque white glass stud; blue glass stud with inlaid metal wire: Int25/686; Int25/687, Int11/3469, 4131, 4132, 4152.

Leat, with metal-working debris F18; scoops and root pits F220.

Outer enclosure ditch

Ditch F132. Section through F132 in P3/P7. Twigs and tree trunks from 1404. Top of the boulder clay in the side of the ditch at 14.40m AOD. Boulder clay upcast F154. Track F101.

Smith's Hall and Barn (S1)

Components of structure

	Original (Phase 1)	Refurbishment (Phase 2)	Dismantling (Phase 3)
East end			
E1	F150 (Cr 40cm, Ps)	F148 (double; Ps).	Removed (F149)
E2	F464 (Ps)	F426 (Ps) F427 (buttress)	Removed
E3	(F429) (Ps)	F442 (Cr 40cms) F448 (buttress; Cr 40cms)	Replaced by F439, F441 (buttress)
E4	F472 (Ps)	(F472) and F471 (buttress)	(F470, 467 – unrelated)
E5	F47 (Ps)	F47 (replacement) and F402	
E6	(F409) (Ps)	F49 and F52 (buttress?)	
E7	F455/473 (Cr 40cm, (Ps)	F466/462 (Ps) and F463 (buttress)	
E8	(F402) No Ps	F129 (Cr 30cm) and F128 (buttress)	
West End			
W1	F118/9 (Cr, Ps)	F117 (Sq)	
W2	F443 (Ps)	F453	Removed
W3	F132 (Cr 30cm, Ps)		
W4	F134 (Cr 25cm, Ps)		
W5		F435 (buttress to W8); Angle of buttress 60 deg. F115 (Cr replacement)	Removed
W6		F131 (Cr 30cm)	
W7		F135 (Cr 25cm) F438 (replacement)	
W8		F136 (buttress to W9) Angle of buttress 56 deg.	
W9		F133 (Cr 40cm)	
W10		F114 (Sq, Ps; buttress) Angle of buttress 60deg	
W11		F138 (N) (Cr 25cm) F138 (S) Buttress (Cr 40cm) Angle of buttress 70deg.	
Doorway			
P1	(F432)	F110; F445 (buttress) F454 (Sq); F450/459	F126 Removed
P2	(F451)	(buttress); F113 /1783 (Sq)	
P3	(1767)	F130	
P4	F461 (Cr; Ps)		
Perimeter wall	F40 (1056)		
Heating	Hearth F65	Flue F67/79	
Marker pit	F430		

Note: Key to post structure: Ps – padstone; Cr – circular scantling; Sq – square or rectangular scantling.

Top of subsoil at 15.10–15.52m AOD.

Hearth: Int11/F65/1141; fragment of bronze 3391, iron rod 575, flint scraper 592, cereal grain 3390.
Whetstone: F462/find 455.

Crop-processing structure to the east of Int. 25 (S5)

Ditch is F3. Post-holes are F11, 14,15,16, 22, 69. Stone-lined hearth F13 (1027) lined with pitched stones 1037.

Hut circle under S5: F31.

Post-holes near S5: 25/F172, 174, 175, 176. Preserved timber post, find no. 578 in 1327 in F174.

Well S8

Well F36; channel 11/F18. The well was 2.3m in diameter. At 14.40 m AOD; bottom of shaft 14.08m.

A8. The Tarbat peninsula

Sources for Fig. 9.1

Pictish names (from Watson 1904 unless otherwise indicated)

Pitkerrie: G. *Baile-chéiridh*. ?Dark place.

Four pit names (Fraser 1986: 26–7, fig. 2.4): Pitculzean in Nigg (pit of little wood); Pitcalnie in Nigg; Pitkerrie in Fearn; Pitmaduthy (pit of Macduff) in Logie Easter.

Also Pithogarty (pit of the priest) and Pitnellies both in Tain.

Pitfaed: G. *Baile Phàididh*. Watson says it is 'of doubtful meaning' but has the same form as the other Pit names. It is near the *Tobar ma Chalmag*. Watson sees Allan in Allansallach, near the port of Wilkhaven as Pictish meaning 'a swampy place' (Watson 1904: 275, at note to p. 43, Clay of Allan).

Portage

TARBAT (*Arterbert* in 1227) is probably from G. *Tairbeart* meaning an isthmus or peninsula, but may be from an older P-Celtic (British) word meaning headland.

Dallachie: G. *loch an dàilich* ? loch of the meetings.

Lochslin: G from *slinn* a weaver's sley. 'Lochslin, as a loch, has disappeared, and survives only in the names Lochslin Farm and the ancient ruin of Lochslin Castle' (Watson 1904: 42).

Locheye: G. *loch na h-iudhe*. Uidh from Norse *eith*, isthmus. Might refer to slow running water between lochs.

Mounteagle: G. *cnoc na h-iolaire*. Also *an eith*. So this name also perhaps refers to slow running water.

Ports and havens

PORTMAHOMACK is from the G. meaning the Port of Colman or Cholmag.

Port a' chait: Cat's port; cf. Cadboll.

Wilkhaven translates Port nam faochag [=wilk; =?whelk]. It was Allan-sallach [ford] and had a chapel dedicated to St Bride.

Balintore was G. Bail' *an todhair* (village of bleaching – i.e. flax). It was also Abbot's Port, Abbot's haven.

Port a' Chaisteil: Castle-haven.

Port na baintighearna: Lady's haven (Hilton beach).

Port an Druidh is west of Shandwick.

Shandwick had a Ballnamorich Fisher town in 1786.

Wells G. Tobar

Tobar ma Chalmag: Colman's well is 'behind the library' at Portmahomack.

Tobar na baintighearna: 'Lady's haven well' at Hilton beach.

Tobar na slainte (well of health): at Shandwick.

Nigg had twenty wells, including a Tobar a' bhaistidh baptismal well (just above the old UP church).

Sixteen chapels recorded on the Tarbat peninsula

1. Portmahomack, St Colman's church (extant).
2. Portmahomack, Chapel Hill (place name extant).
3. Portmahomack, Dunbar chapel, still visible in 1791 (*FSA* 648).
4. Portmahomack, Teampul Eraich, near the old castle of Tarbat. 'Near it is a plentiful spring of water which continues to bear the name of Tobair Mhuir or Mary's Well. A small cave or grotto is shown as the abode of the priest' (*FSA* 648). Teampall-Earach, 'Easter Temple', is RCAHMS, Site 245.
5. Portmahomack, St Brigit's chapel; site recorded at *Allansallach*, 'a short mile' east of Portmahomack church, by Macfarlane (1906–8: vol. 1, p. 215). Presumably near Wilkhaven (Watson 1904: 45).
6. Portmahomack, St John's chapel, stood a 'large mile' from Tarbat parish church (Macfarlane 1906–8: vol. 1, p. 215; RCAHMS, Site 244).
7. Portmahomack, Bindal Hermitage. The site of an old hermitage situated on the shore of the Moray Firth *c.* 1.5 miles (2.4km) north-east of Bindal. A wall *c.* 7ft high and 4ft broad (2.1 × 1.2m) is supposed to have provided the east, north and south sides, while the west side was the cliff (*ONB* 1872). RCAHMS describes the boundary wall as drystone built and averaging 1.3m wide and 1.7m high with an entrance gap *c.* 2.0m wide towards the south end of the east wall (visited 14 September 1972). Appears to have been an early rectangular building, with an enclosure and clearance heaps (heaps of stones removed from the surface before the land was ploughed for the first time) (RCAHMS, Site 280; NH 9387 8502). Bindal is Norse meaning 'sheaf-steading'. Nearby is *Stiana Bleadar* (Norse = Stone spot).
8. Balnabruach, a chapel recorded by Davidson (1946: 27).
9. Wester Arboll, John Baptist's chapel (Macfarlane 1906–8: vol. 1, p. 215).
10. Hilton St Mary's by Cadbollmount was still visible in the nineteenth century; see *OPS*, vol. 2, p. 434; *ONB* bk 11, Fearn Parish 28 (*OPS*, vol. 2, pp. 441–3).
11. Hilton St Mary's chapel on the seashore, recorded in 1529 and still visible in 1855 (RCAHMS, Site 210).
12. Shandwick chapel, 'the walls of which stood pretty entire till within a few years' (*FSA* 592).
13. Old Shandwick chapel (fifteenth century). Exposed at the edge of a quarry (NH 8582 7453).
14. Castlecraig in Nigg parish formerly contained *an Annaid*, 'The Annat', which refers to a chapel with relics of the founder (Watson 1904: 52–3). Castle built by William the Lion at Dunskeath in 1179 (at Castlecraig) (*NSA*, 25).

15 Nigg: in addition to Nigg parish church (extant), the traditional site of a chapel dedicated to St Barr (RCAHMS, Site 227). Alston (1999: 181) says this chapel was at Geanies.
16 Another old chapel at Culiss (Nigg), where there is a small enclosure that goes by the name of Chapel Park. 'Scarce a vestige of the building remains' (*FSA* 592).

Bibliography

Maps

Gerhard Mercator (1595), *Scotiae Regnum*, N Sheet.
Gerhard Mercator (1595), *Scotiae Regnum*, S Sheet.
Timothy Pont (1560?–1614?), Tarbet [*sic*] Ness, Easter Ross *c.* 1583–96. Adv. MS 70.2.10 (Gordon 20).
W. Hole (1607), *Scotiae Regnum*, Marischal 8.
John Speed (1610).
John Adair (1650–1722), Bart 26; MS 1651Z 69/01.
Greenville Collins (1693).
Clement Lemprière (1731), *A Description of the Highlands of Scotland*.
Andrew Rutherford (1745) [EMS.5.90b], *An Exact Plan of His Majesty's Great Roads through the Highlands of Scotland*.

References

Adam, R. J. (1991) (ed.), *The Calendar of Fearn: Text and Additions 1471–1667* (Edinburgh: Scottish Historical Society).
Adomnán of Iona (1995), *Life of St Columba*, ed. and trans. with an introduction by R. Sharpe (London: Penguin).
Aitchison, Nick (1999), *Macbeth: Man and Myth* (Stroud: Sutton Publishing).
Akerström-Hougen, G. (1981), 'Falconry as a motif in early Swedish art: Its historical and art historical significance', in Rudolf Zeitler (ed.), *Les Pays du Nord et Byzance* (Uppsala: Almqvist and Wiksell), pp. 263–93.
Alcock, Leslie (2003), *Kings and Warriors, Craftsmen and Priests in Northern Britain AD 550–850* (Edinburgh: Society of Antiquaries of Scotland).
Alexander, Derek (2005), 'Redcastle, Lunan Bay, Angus: The excavation of an Iron Age timber-lined souterrain and a Pictish barrow cemetery', *PSAS* 135: 41–118.
Allen, J. Romilly and J. Anderson [1903] (1993), *The Early Christian Monuments of Scotland* (Balgavies: Pinkfoot Press).
Alston, D. (1999), *Ross and Cromarty. A Historical Guide* (Edinburgh: Birlinn).
Anderson, A. O. [1922] (1990), *Early Sources of Scottish History AD 500–1286* (Stanford, CA: Stanford University Press).
Ashmore, Patrick J. (1980), 'Low cairns, long cists and symbol stones', *PSAS* 110: 346–55.
Ashmore, Patrick J. (2003), 'Orkney burials in the first millennium AD', in Downes and Ritchie (eds) 2003: 35–50.
Bailey, Richard (1996), *England's Earliest Sculptors* (Publications of the Dictionary of Old English, 5; Toronto: Pontifical Institute of Medieval Studies).
Baldwin, J. R. (1986) (ed.), *Firthlands of Ross and Sutherland* (Edinburgh: Scottish Society for Northern Studies).

Barber, J. W. (1981), 'Excavations on Iona 1979', *PSAS* 111: 282–380.
Barker, P. (1977), *Techniques of Archaeological Excavation* (London: Batsford).
Barrell, A. D. M. (2000), *Medieval Scotland* (Cambridge: Cambridge University Press).
Barrett, James H. (1999), 'Archaeo-icthyological evidence for long-term socioeconomic trends in Northern Scotland: 3500 BC to AD 1500', *Journal Archaeological Science*, 26: 353–88.
Barrow, G. W. S. (1981), *Kingship and Unity: Scotland 1000–1306* (Edinburgh: Edinburgh University Press).
Batey, C., J. Jesch and C. D. Morris (1993) (eds), *The Viking Age in Caithness, Orkney and the North Atlantic* (Edinburgh: Edinburgh University Press).
Bieler, L. (1979) (ed.), *The Patrician Texts in the Book of Armagh* (Scriptores Latini Hiberniae, 10; Dublin: Dublin Institute of Advance Studies).
Blackburn, M. (1998), 'An eighth century coin from the Glebe Field', *Bulletin*, 4: 15–17.
Blair, J. and C. Pyrah (1996) (eds), *Church Archaeology: Research Directions for the Future* (York: Council for British Archaeology, Research Report 104).
Bourke, Cormac (1995) (ed.), *From the Isles of the North: Early Medieval Art in Ireland and Britain* (Belfast: HMSO).
Bradley, R. (1993), *Altering the Earth: The Origins of Monuments in Britain and Continental Europe* (The Rhind Lectures 1991–2; Edinburgh: Society of Antiquaries of Scotland).
Bradley, R. (2000), *The Good Stones: A New Investigation of the Clava Cairns* (Edinburgh: Society of Antiquaries of Scotland).
Briard, J. (1997), *The Megaliths of Brittany* (Luçon: Éditions Gisserot).
Broun, Dauvit (2005), 'The Seven Kingdoms in *De Situ Albaniae*: A record of Pictish political geography or imaginary map of ancient Alba?', in Cowan and McDonald (eds) 2005: 24–42.
Broun, Dauvit and T. O. Clancy (1999) (eds), *Spes Scotorum – Hope of the Scots: St Columba, Iona and Scotland* (Edinburgh: T. and T. Clark).
Brown, T. Julian (1972), 'Northumbria and the Book of Kells', *Anglo-Saxon England*, 1: 219–46.
Brown, Michelle P. (2003), *The Lindisfarne Gospels. Society, Spirituality and the Scribe* (London: British Library).
Brown, P. R. L. (1997), *The Rise of Western Christendom: Triumph and Diversity* AD 200–1000 (Oxford: Blackwell).
Burn, A. R. (1969), 'Holy men on islands in pre-Christian Britain', *Glasgow Archaeological Journal*, 1: 2–6.
Cameron, N. (1994), 'St Rule's Church, St Andrews, and early stone-built churches in Scotland', *PSAS* 124: 367–78.
Cameron, N. (1996), 'The church in Scotland in the later 11th and 12th centuries', in Blair and Pyrah (eds) 1996: 42–6.
Campbell, E. (2001), 'Were the Scots Irish?', *Antiquity*, 75: 285–92.
Cant, R. G. (1986), 'The Medieval church in the north: Contrasting influences in the Dioceses of Ross and Caithness', in Baldwin (ed.) 1986: 47–58.
Card, Nick and Jane Downes (2003), 'Mine Howe: The significance of space and place in the Iron Age', in Downes and Ritchie (eds) 2003: 11–19.
Carver, M. O. H. (1987), 'S Maria foris portas at Castel Seprio: A famous church in a new context', *World Archaeology*, 18.3: 312–29.
Carver, M. O. H. (1998a), 'Conversion and politics on the eastern seaboard of Britain: Some archaeological indicators', in Crawford (ed.) 1998: 11–40.
Carver, M. O. H. (1998b), 'Hilton of Cadboll: An Archaeological Assessment and Project Design' (unpublished paper, University of York).
Carver, M. O. H. (1998c), *Sutton Hoo:. Burial Ground of Kings?* (London: British Museum Press).
Carver, M. O. H. (2001), 'Why that? Why there? Why then? The politics of early medieval monumentality', in A. Macgregor and H. Hamerow (eds), *Image and Power in Early*

Medieval British Archaeology: Essays in Honour of Rosemary Cramp: 1–22 (Oxford: Oxbow).

Carver, M. O. H. (2003a), 'Northern Europeans negotiate their future', in Carver (ed.) 2003b: 3–14.

Carver, M. O. H. (2003b) (ed.), *The Cross Goes North: Processes of Conversion in Northern Europe, AD 300–1300* (York: York Medieval Press).

Carver, M. O. H. (2004), 'An Iona of the East: The early medieval monastery at Portmahomack, Easter Ross', *Medieval Archaeology*, 48: 1–30.

Carver, M. O. H. (2005a), *Sutton Hoo: A Seventh Century Princely Burial Ground and its Context* (London: British Museum Press).

Carver, M. O. H. (2005b), 'Sculpture in action: contexts for stone carving on the Tarbat peninsula, Easter Ross', in Foster and Cross (eds) 2005: 13–36.

Carver, M. O. H. and C. A. Spall (2004), 'Excavating a *parchmenerie*: Archaeological correlates of making parchment at the Pictish monastery at Portmahomack, Easter Ross', *PSAS* 134: 183–200.

Chadwick, H. M. (1949), *Early Scotland* (Cambridge: Cambridge University Press).

Clancy, Thomas O. and Gilbert Márkus (1995), *Iona: The Earliest Poetry of a Celtic Monastery* (Edinburgh: Edinburgh University Press).

Close-Brooks, J. (1984), 'Pictish and other burials', in Friell and Watson (eds) 1984: 87–114.

Colardelle, R. (1986), *Grenoble aux premiers temps chrétiens* (Paris: Guides archéologiques de la France 9).

Colardelle, R. (1996), 'Saint-Laurent et les cimetières de Grenoble du IVe au XVIIIe siècle', in Henri Galienié and Elisabeth Zadora-Rio (eds), *Archéologie du cimetière chrétien* (Tours: Féracf and La Simarre) 111–24.

Cordiner, Charles (1780), *Antiquities and Scenery of the North of Scotland, in a Series of letters to Thomas Pennant* (London and Edinburgh: s.n.).

Cowan, E. J. (1993), 'The Historical Macbeth', in Sellar (ed.) 1993: 117–41.

Cowan, E. J. and R. Andrew McDonald (2005) (eds), *Alba: Celtic Scotland in the Medieval Era* (Edinburgh: John Donald).

Cramp, Rosemary (2005), *Wearmouth and Jarrow Monastic Sites* (2 vols; London: English Heritage).

Crawford, Barbara (1987), *Scandinavian Scotland* (Leicester: Leicester University Press).

Crawford, Barbara (1995), *Earl and Mormaer: Norse–Pictish Relationships in Northern Scotland* (Rosemarkie: Groam House Lecture).

Crawford, Barbara (1996) (ed.), *Scotland in Dark Age Britain* (Aberdeen: Scottish Cultural Press).

Crawford, Barbara (1998) (ed.), *Conversion and Christianity in the North Sea World* (St Andrews: Committee for Dark Age Studies, University of St Andrews).

Cunliffe, Barry (2001), *Facing the Ocean: The Atlantic and its Peoples 8000 BC to AD 1500* (Oxford: Oxford University Press).

Dalland, M. (1992), 'Long cist burials at Four Winds, Longniddry, East Lothian', *PSAS* 122: 197–206, fiche 2.

Dalland, M. (1993), 'The excavation of a group of long cists at Avonmill Road, Linlithgow, West Lothian', *PSAS* 123: 337–44.

Davidson, J. M. (1946), 'A miscellany of antiquities in Easter Ross and Sutherland', *PSAS* 80: 2–33.

Davies, W. (1996), ' "Protected space" in Britain and Ireland in the Middle Ages', in Crawford (ed.) 1996: 1–19.

Downes, Jane and Anna Ritchie (2003) (eds), *Sea Change. Orkney and Northern Europe in the Later Iron Age AD 300–800* (Balgavies: Pinkfoot Press).

Driscoll, S. (1998), 'Picts and Prehistory: Cultural resource management in early medieval Scotland', *World Archaeology*, 30: 142–58.

Dunbar, John (1981), 'The Medieval architecture of the Scottish Highlands', in Maclean of Dochgarroch (ed.) 1981: 28–70.
Dunbar, John (1996), 'The emergence of the reformed church in Scotland c. 1560–c. 1700', in Blair and Pyrah (eds) 1996: 127–34.
Dunwell, A. J., T. Neighbour and T. G. Cowie (1995a), 'A cist burial adjacent to the Bronze Age cairn at Cnip, Uig, Isle of Lewis', *PSAS* 125: 279–88.
Dunwell, A. J., T. G. Cowie, M. F. Bruce, T. Neighbour and A. R. Rees (1995b), 'A Viking Age cemetery at Cnip, Uig, Isle of Lewis', *PSAS* 125: 719–52, fiche 4.
Edmonds, Mark (1992), 'Their use is wholly unknown', in Niall Sharples and Alison Sheridan (eds), *Vessels for the Ancestors: Essays on the Neolithic of Britain and Ireland in Honour of Audrey Henshall*: 179–93 (Edinburgh: Edinburgh University Press).
Fairhurst H. (1971), 'The wheelhouse site A'Cheardach Bheag on Drimore machair, South Uist', *Glasgow Archaeological Journal*, 2: 72–106.
Fanning, T. (1981), 'Excavation of an Early Christian cemetery and settlement at Reask, Co. Kerry', *Proceedings of the Royal Irish Academy*, 81C: 67–172.
Fenton, A. [1976] (1999), *Scottish Country Life* (East Linton: Tuckwell Press).
Fenton, A. and B. Walker (1981), *The Rural Architecture of Scotland* (Edinburgh: John Donald).
Fernie, E. (1986), 'Early Church architecture in Scotland', *PSAS* 116: 393–411.
Fisher, I. (2001), *Early Medieval Sculpture in the West Highlands and Islands* (Edinburgh: Society of Antiquaries of Scotland).
Foster, Sally (1998) (ed.), *The St Andrews Sarcophagus: A Pictish Masterpiece and its International Connections* (Dublin: Four Courts Press).
Foster, Sally M. and Morag Cross (2005) (eds), *Able Minds and Practised Hands: Scotland's Early Medieval Sculpture in the 21st Century* (Leeds: Society for Medieval Archaeology and Historic Scotland).
Fraser, A. and F. Munro (1988), *Tarbat: Easter Ross. A Historical Sketch* (Evanton: Ross and Cromarty Heritage Society).
Fraser, I. A. (1986), 'Norse and Celtic placenames around the Dornoch Firth', in Baldwin (ed.) 1986: 23–32.
Friell, J. G. P. and W. G. Watson (1984) (eds), *Pictish Studies* (Oxford: British Archaeological Reports 125).
Graham, Angus and Joanna Gordon (1987), 'Old harbours in northern and western Scotland', *PSAS* 117: 265–352.
Graham-Campbell, J. (1973), 'The 9th century Anglo-Saxon horn mount from Burghead, Morayshire, Scotland', *Medieval Archaeology*, 17: 43–51.
Graham-Campbell, J. (1995), *The Viking-Age Gold and Silver of Scotland (AD 850–1100)* (Edinburgh: National Museums of Scotland).
Graham-Campbell, J. (2006), 'Some reflections on the distribution and significance of Norse place-names in northern Scotland', in Peter Gammeltoft and Bent Jørgensen (eds), *Names through the Looking-Glass: Festschrift in Honour of Gillian Fellows-Jensen*: 94–118 (Copenhagen: C. A. Reitzels Forlag A/S).
Graham-Campbell, J. and C. Batey (1998), *Vikings in Scotland: An Archaeological Survey* (Edinburgh: Edinburgh University Press).
Grant, Alexander (2005), 'The Province of Ross and the Kingdom of Alba', in Cowan and McDonald (eds) 2005: 88–126.
Gräslund, Anne-Sofie (2003), 'The role of Scandinavian women in Christianisation: The neglected evidence', in Carver (ed.) 2003b: 483–96.
Gregory, Richard A. and the late G. D. B. Jones (2001), 'Survey and excavation at Tarradale, Highland', *PSAS* 131: 241–66.
Greig, Colvin, Moira Greig and Patrick Ashmore (2000),'Excavation of a cairn cemetery at Lundin Links, Fife, in 1965–6', *PSAS* 130: 585–636.

Guttmann, E. B. A., S. J. Dockrill and I. A. Simpson (2004), 'Arable agriculture in prehistory: New evidence from soils in the Northern Isles', *PSAS* 134: 53–64.

Hamilton, J. R. C. (1956), *Excavations at Jarlshof, Shetland* (London: HMSO).

Harbison, P. (1970), 'How old is the Gallarus oratory?', *Medieval Archaeology*, 14: 34–59.

Harden J. (1995), 'A potential archaeological context for the early Christian sculptured stones from Tarbat, Easter Ross', in C. Bourke (ed.), *From the Isles of the North: Early Medieval Art in Ireland and Britain*: 221–6 (Belfast: HMSO).

Harding, D. W. and I. Armit (1990), 'Survey and excavation in West Lewis', in Ian Armit (ed.), *Beyond the Brochs*: 71–107 (Edinburgh: Edinburgh University Press).

Hare, M. and A. Hamlin (1986), 'The study of early church architecture in Ireland: An Anglo-Saxon viewpoint with an appendix on documentary evidence for round towers', in L. A. S. Butler and R. K. Morris (eds) *The Anglo-Saxon Church*: 130–45 (York: Council for British Archaeology, Research Report 60).

Heald, Andrew (2003), 'Non-ferrous metal-working in Iron Age Scotland (c. 700 BC to AD 800)' (unpublished Ph.D. thesis, University of Edinburgh).

Henderson, I. H. (1958), 'The origin centre of the Pictish symbol stones', *PSAS* 91: 44–60.

Henderson, I. H. (1975), 'Inverness, a Pictish capital', in *The Hub of the Highlands: The Book of Inverness and District*: 91–108 (Edinburgh: Inverness Field Club and James Thin).

Henderson, Isabel (1993), 'The shape and decoration of the Cross on Pictish cross-slabs carved in relief', in M. Spearman and John Higgit (eds), *The Age of Migrating Ideas* 209–18 (Edinburgh: National Museums of Scotland and Alan Sutton Publishing).

Henderson, I. H. and G. Henderson (2004), *The Art of the Picts: Sculpture and Metalwork in Early Medieval Scotland* (London and New York: Thames and Hudson).

Henshall, A. S. and J. N. G. Ritchie (2001), *The Chambered Cairns of the Central Highlands: An Inventory of their Structures and their Context* (Edinburgh: Edinburgh University Press).

Herity, M. (1995), *Studies in the Layout, Buildings and Art in Stone of Early Irish Monasteries* (London: Pindar Press).

Higgitt, J. (1982), 'The Pictish Latin inscription at Tarbat in Ross-shire', *PSAS* 112: 300–21.

Hill, P. (1997), *Whithorn and St Ninian: Excavation of a Monastic Town 1984–1991* (Stroud: Whithorn Trust and Alan Sutton Publishing).

Holbrook, Neil and Alan Thomas (2005), 'An early-medieval monastic cemetery at Llandough, Glamorgan: Excavations in 1994', *Medieval Archaeology*, 49: 1–92.

Howard, Deborah (1995), *Scottish Architecture: Reformation to Restoration 1560–1660* (Edinburgh: Edinburgh University Press).

Hughes, K. and A. Hamlin (1973), *The Modern Traveller to the Early Irish Church* (London: Society for the Promotion of Christian Knowledge).

Hunter, J. (1986), *Rescue Excavations on the Brough of Birsay 1974–82* (Edinburgh: Society of Antiquaries of Scotland).

Hunter, F. (2007), *Beyond the Edge of the Empire: Caledonians, Picts and Romans* (Rosemarkie: Groam House Lectures).

James, Heather (2005), 'Pictish cross-slabs: An examination of the original archaeological context', in Foster and Cross (eds) 2005: 95–112.

James, Heather, Isabel Henderson, Sally M. Foster and Siân Jones (forthcoming), *A Fragmented Masterpiece: Recovering the Biography of the Hilton of Cadboll Pictish Cross-Slab* (Glasgow: University of Glasgow).

Jesch, Judith (1993), 'England and Orkneyinga Saga', in Batey, Jesch and Morris (eds) 1993: 222–39.

Jones, B., I. Keillar and K. Maude (1993), 'The Moray aerial survey: Discovering the prehistoric and protohistoric landscape', in Sellar (ed.) 1993: 64–70.

Laing, Lloyd (2000), 'How Late were Pictish Symbols employed?' *PSAS* 130: 637–50.

Lamb, Raymond (1998), 'Pictland, Northumbria and the Carolingian Empire', in Crawford (ed.) 1998: 41–56.

Lane, A. and E. Campbell (2000), *Dunadd: An Early Dalriadic Capital* (Oxford: Oxbow).
Lang, J. (1999), 'The apostles in Anglo-Saxon sculpture', *Early Medieval Europe*, 8.2: 271–82.
Lowe, C. (2006), *Excavations at Hoddom, Dumfriesshire: An Early Ecclesiastical Site in South-West Scotland* (Edinburgh: Society of Antiquaries of Scotland).
McCormick, Finbar (1997), Iona: The archaeology of the early monastery', in Cormac Bourke (ed.), *Studies in the Cult of Saint Columba*: 45–68 (Dublin: Four Courts Press).
McCullough, David A. (2000), 'Investigating portages in the Norse maritime landscape of Scotland and the Isles' (unpublished Ph.D. thesis, Glasgow).
Macdonald, A. (1992), *Curadán, Boniface and the Early Church at Rosemarkie* (Rosemarkie: Groam House Lectures).
Macdonald, A. D. S. and L. R. Laing (1970), 'Early ecclesiastical sites in Scotland: A field survey: Part II', *PSAS* 102: 129–45.
McErlean, T. and Crothers, N. (2007), *Harnessing the Tides. The Early Medieval Tide Mills at Nendrum Monastery, Strangford Lough* (Belfast: Environment and Heritage Service).
MacFarlane, W. (1906–8), *Geographical Collections Relating to Scotland*, ed. G. Mitchell and J. T. Clark (3 vols; Edinburgh: Scottish History Society).
MacGibbon, David and Thomas Ross (1896), *The Ecclesiastical Architecture of Scotland: From the Earliest Christian Times to the Seventeenth Century* (Edinburgh: David Douglas).
McGrail, S. (1998), *Ancient Boats in North-West Europe* (London: Longman).
Mackenzie, Alexander (1977), *The Prophecies of the Brahan Seer*, ed. Elizabeth Sutherland (London: Constable).
Maclean of Dochgarroch, Loraine (1981) (ed.), *The Middle Ages in the Highlands* (Inverness: Inverness Field Club).
Macleod of Cadboll, Lt Col. R. B. (1956), 'Donations to the Museum: Ten fragments of sculpted stone from Tarbat', *PSAS* 87: 239.
Marshall, Dorothy (1977), 'Carved stone balls', *PSAS* 108: 40–72.
Marshall, Dorothy (1983), 'Further notes on carved stone balls', *PSAS* 113: 628–30.
Miller, Hugh, Sr [1835] (1994), *Scenes and Legends of the North of Scotland* (Edinburgh: B&W Publishing).
Miller, Hugh, Jr (1889), 'Note on fragments of two sculptured stones of Celtic workmanship found in the churchyard of Tarbat, Easter Ross', *PSAS* 23 [11 NS]: 435–44.
Miller, Hugh, Jr and the Revd Donald Macleod (1889), 'Notice of the discovery of a hoard of silver penannular armlets and coins at Tarbat, Ross-shire', *PSAS* 23: 314–17.
Morris, C. D. (1993), 'The Birsay Bay project', in Batey, Jesch and Morris (eds) 1993: 285–307.
Mowat, I. R. M. (1981), *Easter Ross 1750–1850: The Double Frontier* (Edinburgh: John Donald).
Mulville, Jacqui, Mike Parker Pearson, Niall Sharples, Helen Smith and Andrew Chamberlain (2003), 'Quarters, arcs and squares: Human and animal remains in the Hebridean Late Iron Age', in Downes and Ritchie (eds) 2003: 20–34.
Murray, Diana and Ian Ralston (1997), 'The excavation of a square-ditched barrow and other cropmarks at Boysack Mills, Inverkeilor, Angus', *PSAS* 127: 359–86.
Murray, Gordon (1986), 'The declining Pictish symbol – a reappraisal', *PSAS* 116: 223–53.
Nylén, Erik and Jan Peder Lamm (1988), *Stones, Ships and Symbols: The Picture Stones of Gotland from the Viking Age and before* (Stockholm: Gidlunds Bokförlag).
Ó Carragáin, E. (1989), 'The Meeting of Saint Paul and Saint Anthony: Visual and Literary Uses of a Eucharistic Motif', in P. Wallace and G. Niocaill (eds), *Keimeila*: pp. 1–58 (Galway: Galway University Press).
Ó Carragáin, T. (2003a), 'Pre-Romanesque churches in Ireland: Interpreting archaeological regionalisms' (unpublished Ph.D. dissertation, University College, Cork).
Ó Carragáin T. (2003b), 'A landscape converted: Archaeology and early church organisation on Iveragh and Dingle, Ireland', in Carver (ed.) 2003b: 127–52.

Omand, D. (1984) (ed.), *The Ross and Cromarty Book* (Golspie: Northern Times).
Oram, Richard (2004), *David I: The King who Made Scotland* (Stroud: Tempus Publishing).
O'Sullivan, J. (1994a), 'Excavation of an early church and a women's cemetery at St Ronan's medieval parish church, Iona', *PSAS* 124: 327–65, fiche A5–D11.
O'Sullivan J. (1999), 'Iona: Archaeological investigations 1875–1996', in Dauvit Braun and Thomas Clancy (eds), *Spes Scottorum: Hope of Scots. Saint Columba, Iona and Scotland*: 215–43 (Edinburgh: T. and T. Clark).
Pernnant, T. (1790), *A Tour in Scotland 1769* (5th edn; London: no publisher recorded).
Petley, Charles (1831), 'A short account of some carved stones in Ross-shire, accompanied by a series of outline engravings', *Archaeologia Scotica*, 4: 345–52.
Phillips, Christine (2006), 'Portages in early medieval Scotland: The Great Glen route and the Forth–Clyde isthmus', in Christer Westerdahl (ed.), *The Significance of Portages*: 191–8 (Oxford: British Archaeological Reports, International Series 1499).
Proudfoot, Edwina V. W. (1996), 'Excavations at the long cist cemetery on the Hallow Hill, St Andrews, Fife', *PSAS* 126: 387–454.
Ralston, I. (1996), 'Four short cists from north-east Scotland and Easter Ross', *PSAS* 126: 121–55.
Ralston, I. (1997), 'Pictish Homes', in D. Henry (ed.), *The Worm, the Germ and the Thorn: Pictish and Related Studies Presented to Isabel Henderson*: 19–34 (Balgavies: Pinkfoot Press).
Reed, David (1995), 'The excavation of a cemetery and putative chapel site at Newhall Point, Balbair, Ross and Cromarty, 1985', *PSAS* 125: 779–91.
Rees, Alastair R. (2002), 'A first millennium cemetery, rectangular Bronze Age structure and late prehistoric settlement at Thornybank, Midlothian', *PSAS* 132: 313–55.
Rees, A. R. and W. L. Finlayson (1997), 'A Long Burial at Innerwick, near Dunbar, East Lothian', *PSAS* 127: 601–7.
Ritchie, Anna (1997), *Iona* (Edinburgh: Historic Scotland).
Ritchie Anna (2003), 'Paganism among the Picts and the conversion of Orkney', in Downes and Ritchie (eds) 2003: 3–10.
Ritchie, Anna and Graham Ritchie (1991), *Scotland. Archaeology and Early History* (Edinburgh: Edinburgh University Press).
Ritchie, J. (1915), 'Description of a simple Inscribed Cross observed in the Churchyard of Tarbat and now destroyed', *PSAS* 49: 304–6.
Roberts, John L. (1997), *Lost Kingdoms: Celtic Scotland and the Middle Ages* (Edinburgh: Edinburgh University Press).
Robertson, A. S. (1983), 'Roman coins found in Scotland, 1971–82', *PSAS* 113: 405–48.
Ruckley, Nigel and Martin Carver (1998), 'Stone for carving: The Tarbat geological research project', *Bulletin*, 4: 12–15.
Samson, R. (1992), 'The reinterpretation of the Pictish Symbols', *Journal of British Archaeological Association*, 145: 29–65.
Sellar, W. D. H. (1993) (ed.), *Moray: Province and People* (Edinburgh: School of Scottish Studies).
Sharpe, Richard (1995) (ed. and trans.), Adomnán of Iona *Life of St Columba* (Harmondsworth: Penguin).
Sharples, Niall (1999), *The Iron Age and Norse Settlement at Bornish, South Uist: An Interim Report on the 1999 Excavations* (Cardiff: University of Cardiff, Studies in Archaeology, Report No. 16).
Sharples, Niall (2005), *A Norse Farmstead in the Outer Hebrides: Excavations at Mound 3, Bornais, South Uist* (Oxford: Oxbow Books).
Smyth, Alfred (1984), *Warlords and Holy Men* (Edinburgh: Edinburgh University Press).
Stell, G. (1986), 'Architecture and Society in Easter Ross before 1707', in Baldwin (ed.) 1986: 99–132.

Stell, G. and E. Beaton (1984), 'Local building traditions', in Omand (ed.) 1984; 207–18.
Stuart, John (1856), *The Sculptured Stones of Scotland*, vol. 1 (Aberdeen: Spalding Club).
Swift, C. (1991), *Ogam Stones and the Earliest Irish Christians* (Maynooth: Department of Old and Middle Irish, St Patrick's College)
Taylor, S. (1996), 'Place names and the early church in eastern Scotland', in Crawford (ed.) 1996: 93–110.
Thomas, A. C. (1961), 'The animal art of the Scottish Iron Age and its origins', *Archaeological Journal*, 118: 14–64.
Thomas, A. C. (1963), 'The interpretation of the Pictish symbols', *Archaeological Journal*, 120: 31–97.
Thomas, A. C. (1981), *Christianity in Roman Britain to AD500* (London: Batsford).
Thomas, F. (1867), 'On the primitive dwellings of the Outer Hebrides', *PSAS* 7: 153–95.
Veitch, K. (1997), 'The Columban church in Northern Britain 664–717: A reassessment', *PSAS* 127: 627–47.
Venclova, N. (2002), 'The Venerable Bede, druidic tonsure and archaeology', *Antiquity* 76: 458–71.
Wainwright, F. T (1955) (ed.), *The Problem of the Picts* (London: Nelson).
Watson, W. J. [1904] (1996) *Place-Names of Ross and Cromarty* (Evanton: Highland Heritage Books).
Watson, W. J. [1926] (1993), *The History of the Celtic Place-Names of Scotland* (Edinburgh: Birlinn).
Woolf, Alex (2006), 'Dún Nechtain, Fortriu and the Geography of the Picts', *Scottish Historical Review*, 85.2: 182–201.
Youngs, Susan (1989) (ed.), *The Work of Angels: Masterpieces of Celtic Metalwork, 6th–9th Centuries AD* (London: British Museum).

Index

Adomnán of Iona, abbot and author, 23, 24, 25, 196–7
Adoratio crucis, 107
age at death
  of monks, 78
  of parishioners, 78, 159
Aitchison, Nick, historian, 146
alcohol, 37
Allen, J. Romilly, Pictish scholar 5, 9
Anderson, Joseph, Pictish scholar 5, 9
Anderson, Katie, excavator, 44, 59
Andrew, St, 110
Angles, 25
annat, place name, 184
Anthony, St, 178
'Apostle Stone' *see* sculpture, TR20
apostles, 108, 110; *see also* sculpture, TR20
aquamanile, 47, 158
'archaeology pit', 66
architects' test pits (Int.18), 42
astringent, for parchment, 124; *see also* vellum
Aud the Deep-minded, 144, 146
aumbry, 85

back-pains, 78–80
bag-shaped building *see* Structure 1
bait, for fishing, 56
Balnabruach, 81, 177
baptistery, 51, 183
Barrow, Geoffrey, historian, 151
battles
  in Fortriu, 144
  at Mons Graupius, 22, 176
  at Nechtansmere, 23, 25
  prehistoric, 192
  of Tarbat Ness, 147, 174
Beauly Firth, 176
Bede, the Venerable, 10, 22–5, 197
bell-making, 45, 152, 154, 156
big toe, 47, 161
Black House, Hebridean, 132
blast horn, Anglian, 197
'Boar Stone' *see* sculpture, TR22
bone, animal, 53, 133
  in rows, 123–5
  see also vellum, cattle bone
bone, human, 45, 47, 76–81, 159
  reburial, 47–8

Boniface *see* Curadán
book-plaque, 58
Bornais, 125, 132
Bradley, Richard, prehistorian, 192–3
Bridei son of Mailchon, king of Picts, 23, 24
Britons, 22, 25
Brittany, monuments, 192
Broichan, king's wizard, 24
bronze-working, evidence for *see* metal-working
Brothwell, Don, osteologist, 47
Broun, Dauvit, historian, 142, 144
Brown, Julian, scholar, 11
Brown, Peter, historian, 195
Burghead, sculpture at, 144
buildings archaeology, 34, 48–9
burials
  barrows, 19, 96
  Beaker, 175–6, 193
  Bronze Age, 81, 175–6
  cist burials, 8, 45, 46, 76–82, 176
  head-support, 45, 79
  Iron Age, 81, 94
  Medieval, 47
  pillow *see* head-support
  in the workshops, 62, 76–7
  Viking, 176
Burn, A. R., scholar, 194
Burns, Robert, poet, 38

Cadboll Castle, 180
Cadboll Fisher, 180
Caledonians, 75
'Calf Stone' *see* sculpture, TR28/35
Cameron, Neil, 90
camp site, 37–8
Campbell, Revd D., minister and historian, 6, 80
cancellum, 97
carnelian gem, 58
carved stone balls, 19–20, 48, 73–4
Castel Seprio, Italy, 81
Castle Inn, Portmahomack, 38, 191
cattle
  bones, 53, 60, 76, 92, 123–5, 133; *see also* vellum
  depicted, 59; *see also* sculpture TR28/35
  drinking place, 52
  hide, 120–6

Celtic church, 24, 197
　buildings, 87–90
　reform of, 151
cereals *see* grain
Chadwick H. M., early Medieval scholar, 186
chafing dish, 47, 158
chamfered plinth, 45, 157; *see also* Church 4
Chapel Hill, 80
chapels, on the Tarbat peninsula, 80, 184
charcoal filtration, 75
Christianity
　conversion to, 18, 23, 24, 25, 82, 96, 104, 192–200
　reformed in 8th century, 24
　reformed in 12th century, 151
　reformed in 16th century, 163
　reformed in 1843, 169
　varieties of, 198
　see also Roman Catholic
churchyard, 8, 31, 32, 34, 84, 87, 168, 171
Clach a' Charaidh *see* Shandwick
Clarke, David, museum curator, 53
clay and bool, 132
clay-silts, 57–8, 60, 126, 140
Close-Brooks, Joanna, archaeologist, 44
coffins, 47, 160–1
Colman, St, 10–11, 159; *see also* St Colman's church
Columba, St, 10, 23, 75, 196
Columcille *see* Columba
comb, 58
community, descendant and local, 31–2, 65
conservation, of the site, 67
Constantine, Roman emperor, 104
Constantine, king of Picts, 144
Cordiner, Charles, antiquary, 5
Craig Phadraig, 36, 92
Cramp, Rosemary, archaeologist and art historian, 17n, 197
Crawford, Barbara, historian, 145
Crawstane, The, 95
cropmark, 13, 27, 49
cross, as symbol of Christianity, 96, 104, 107, 194
cross-slabs and high crosses, 96–7; *see also* sculpture, Gotland
crucibles *see* metal-working
culdees, 146, 151, 187
cultural resource management, 31
culvert *see* drains, ancient
Curadán, missionary, 25, 193, 196

dam, 55, 58, 59, 118; *see also* water management
'Danish Cross' *see* sculpture, TR2
Danish princes, 177
Dark Ages, 25, 33
David, King, 105, 108
deposit model, archaeological, 26–30, 55–6, 59

diseases, of monks, 77–8; of parishioners, 160
display to public, 65–7
'Dragon Stone' *see* sculpture, TR20
drains, ancient, 45, 59
　timber-lined, 45, 77
drains, modern, 51, 56
druids, 194
Druim Alban, 22
Duff, Alexander, 180
Duffus, St, 183
Duncan, king in Moray, 146, 151
Dunoon, George, schoolmaster, 5
Dunrobin Castle, museum at, 6–7
Dunskeath, 152
Dupplin Cross, 111, 114, 144

Easter controversy, 10, 24, 195
Easter Rarichie, 176
Easter Ross, 193
Einar the Turfer, 145–6
enclosure ditch, inner, 51, 92, 119, 134
enclosure ditch, outer, 27, 49, 51, 52, 119, 152, 221
Eucharist, 91, 107, 158, 163, 196
Europe, early kingdoms of, 18
　evaluation, archaeological, 27, 29, 41, 58
　see also strip-and-map
excavation, archaeological, 33, 34, 37, 57
　in the church (Sector 4), 37, 39, 41–9
　in Glebe Field (Sector 2), 30, 39, 55–65
　in the Gordons' field (Sector 1), 35, 39, 49–55
　at Hilton, 180, 182
　interpretation on site, 64
　interventions, 34–5, 204–5
　mistakes, 61
　sectors, 34–5, 39
　at Shandwick, 179
　by Tarbatness Road (Sector 3), 30, 39

faces
　of monks, 77–8
　of parishioners, 160
Fearn Abbey, 91, 151, 158, 163, 173, 180, 184–6
Fernie, Eric, 90
Fibonacci series, 130–1
Field School, 37
Finian *see* Ninian
Finlay (Finlaech), father of Macbeth, 144–5
fire, devastation by, 58–9, 135–9, 219
　in the 15th-century church, 159
fishing, 175, 186; *see also* bait
Forbes, William, minister, 166–7
Fortriu, province of, 25, 144, 193
Free Church, 169–71
Frisia, 139

gaming board, 47
Garner-Lahire, Justin, excavator, 39, 55

Geanies, 103, 168, 180
Geddes, Fred, architect, 34, 39, 40, 48–9
geophysical survey, 27
glass-making, evidence for, 53, 54, 128–9, 133–4, 139
Glebe, 55, 168, 171
Glebe Field excavations *see* excavations in Sector 2
gold-working evidence for, 58, 139
Golden Number, 130
Golden Section, 130–1
Gordon, James and Douglas, of Portmahomack, landowners, 27, 31, 49
Gordon, John, laird, 166
Gotland, monuments in, 192
graffiti, 170
grain, 76, 175
  grain-drying, 141
Grant, Alexander, historian, 151, 193
Gräslund, Anne-Sofie, archaeologist, 192–3
grave-markers, 97–100
Great Glen *see* Loch Ness
Grove, Barry, sculptor, 103
Gruoch (Lady MacBeth), 146

hair, human, 47
Hallow Hill, The, 81
hammerscale slag, 133
Harden, Jill, archaeologist, 13, 41, 43
heating ducts, 53, 58, 125, 141
Henderson, George, art historian, 104, 182
Henderson, Isabel, art historian, 11, 96, 104, 182, 196
henges, prehistoric, 19–20, 195
Heritage Lottery Fund, 33, 37
heritors, 163, 169, 171
hermits *see* holy men
Higgins Gardner, designers, 66
Higgitt, John, art historian, 8, 11
Highland Clearances, 169
Highland Council, 31, 32, 33
Hilton of Cadboll
  site, 34, 177, 180–2
  cross-slab, 6, 107–8, 182, 217
  replica, 181
Historic Scotland, 61, 180
hoard of coins and ring silver, 7, 143, 147
Hoddom, monastery at, 34
holy men, 184, 187–8, 194–6
holy wells *see* wells
Hooper, Elizabeth, artist, 110
horizon mapping *see* strip-and-map
horizons in church, 45, 76–7
Hummler, Madeleine, excavator, 39, 53, 126
Hundason, Karl, 145–6

ice houses, 175
Inscription, from Portmahomack *see* sculpture at Portmahomack, TR10
interventions *see* excavation

Invergordon Castle, lapidarium at, 6, 11
Inverness, 23
Inverness Scientific Society, 9
Iona, monastery at, 10, 12, 26, 89, 100, 106, 132–3, 147, 158, 199
Ireland *see* Celtic
Iron Age activity, 54, 59, 75, 94, 176; *see also* burials, pre-monastic features
iron-working, evidence for, 58, 152

Jarrow and Monkwearmouth, monastery at, 24, 197, 199
Jerromes, Roy and Faith, 38
Joass, Revd J. M., antiquary, 8, 44
Johnson, Duncan, farmer, 27
Jones, Barri, aerial archaeologist, 12–13, 176
Jones, Martin, buildings archaeologist, 48–9

Keillar, Ian, aerial archaeologist, 12–13, 176
Kells, Book of, 8, 106–7
Kiln-Barn *see* Structure 1
King, Sarah, osteologist, 77–8
kingdoms, of the North Sea, 18
Kinnedar, monastery at, 144
Kirsty Beg, 183

Laing, Lloyd, 96
lairs (burial places in churchyards), 31, 168
languages
  British, 21, 22, 183
  English, 21, 22
  Gaelic, 21, 22, 183
  Latin, 22, 158
  Norse 21, 183
  Pictish, 21, 22, 183
leather shoe, 47
levelling, of the land, 57, 119
Lindisfarne Gospels, 8
Lindisfarne, monastery at, 10, 147
Llandough, Wales, 81
Loch Ness
  monster, 23
  thoroughfare, 10, 75, 147, 184–5
Low, Revd Stewart, minister, 47
lume, 121, 132
Lundin Links, 82
lunnellarium, 125

Macbeth, king in Moray, 94, 144–7, 151
McCally, Donna, excavator, 47–8
Mackay, William, grave-digger, 7
Mackays of Strathnaver, 159
Mackenzie, George *see* Tarbat, Lord George
Mackenzie, Sir John, laird, 163
Mackenzie, William, minister, 164–5
Macleod, Revd Donald, minster, 7
Macleod family of Invergordon, 6, 11
Macleod, John, Free Church minister, 32
MacTaggart, Farquhar, Earl of Ross, 151, 158
Mael Brigte, Moray warrior, 144

Magna domus, at Iona, 132
malt, 141
manse, 8
manuscripts *see* vellum
marsh, 76, 118
mason's mark, 161
matriarchy, among the Picts, 22
memorials
  in the church, 164–7
  in the churchyard, 167–9
metal-working, evidence for
  in 6th–7th centuries (Period 1), 76
  in 7th–8th centuries (Period 2), 53, 54, 119, 129, 133–4, 221
  in 9th–11th centuries (Period 3), 58, 59, 137–40, 152, 219
  see also gold, iron, silver
metrics, of churches, 90, 156
  on manuscripts, 106
  of sculpture, 105
  in Sector 2, 134
  of Structure 1, 128–32
Meyer, Kellie, art historian, 107–8, 117n, 180, 182
mill (horizontal water-mill), 62, 118
  at Fearn, 184–6
  see also water management
Miller, Hugh, senior, geologist, 5
Miller, Hugh, junior, 5, 7, 103, 187
Mine Howe, 75, 141
monasteries, Dark Age (or early Medieval), 196–7; *see also* Hoddom, Iona, Jarrow, Kinnedar, Rosemarkie, Whithorn
monasteries, expansion of, 135, 178
monastery, at Portmahomack, 14, 197
  in 6th–7th centuries (Period 1), 76–93
  in 7th–8th centuries (Period 2), 94–135
monastic estate, 187
monastic rule, 197–8
monks, at Portmahomack, 75–80, 197
monuments, early Medieval, 18, 25; *see also* sculpture
Mormaers, lords of Moray, 144
moulds *see* metal-working
Munro, Finlay, historian, 32
Munro, George, resident, 51
Munro family, 160

'natural' *see* subsoil
Nechtan, king of Picts, 24
Nechtan's path, 177
Nechtansmere *see* battle
Nigg
  site, 34, 177, 178
  cross slab, 9, 34, 108, 178, 217
Ninian, St, 23, 196
Norsemen, 25, 147, 176, 186; *see also* Vikings
Northumbria, 88, 197
nuts, 53

Ó'Carragáin, Tomás, archaeologist, 88
ogam, inscriptions in, 18–19
opposition, to the project, 31–2
Orkney
  buildings in, 132
  churches in, 89
  see also Mine Howe
Oswy, King of Northumbria, 10, 24
Oykell estuary, 145

paradise, 180
parchment *see* vellum
parchmenterie, 126
parish church *see* St Colman's Church, Church 2–9
Paul, St, 178
pebbles
  Pictish, 140
  for ploughs *see* plough pebbles
  for vellum working, 124
Petley, Charles, antiquary, 5
Picti, 3, 22
Pictish, archaeological sites, 3, 26, 132
  buildings 134; upper floor, 140–1; *see also* Structure 1 and Structure 9
  cross-slabs, as hagiography, 187–8, 195; *see also* sculpture
  historical events, 23
  horses, 182, 186
  monasteries, 26
  nation, 17, 26, 191
  sculpture *see* sculpture
  ships, 186
  symbol stones, 19, 94–6, 107–8; *see also* sculpture
  women, 22, 23, 77, 80, 82, 92, 182, 192–3
place names, 21, 147, 183, 196
plague, at Portmahomack 5
plough pebbles, 51, 73
ploughing, ancient, 51, 54, 73, 75, 221
ploughing, modern, 50, 175
Poitiers, hypogeum, 88
pool, 59; *see also* water management
portage, 35, 173, 184–6
Portmahomack village, 3; *see also* St Colman's church, churchyard, manse, monastery
pottery, post-Roman, absence of, 92
pottery, Medieval, 50, 56, 58, 60, 152
prehistoric religion, 191–200
prehistoric territories, 191–3
pre-monastic features, 52, 59, 62, 73–5, 188
primary burning *see* fire
Prince Charles, Duke of Rothesay, 66–7
project design, archaeological, 16, 26, 33, 34, 37, 38, 197; *see also* conservation, display
pubic hair, 47

radiocarbon dates, 207–9
rampart, 52
Reformation, The, 47, 161–3

Regulus, St, 183
relics, 10, 87
research programme, 34
rig and furrow, 50, 51
ring-silver, 8, 142–3, 147
Ritchie, Anna, Pictish scholar, 34, 45
'Road 1' (paved), 60, 118
'Road 2' (pebbled), 56, 60, 136, 138–9
Robbins, Graham, archaeologist, 177
Robertson, Niall, excavator, 44
Roe, Annette, excavator, 39, 40–9
Roman Catholic church, 158, 163–4, 200
Romans, 176
Rosemarkie, monastery and bishopric at, 144, 196
Ross, churches in, 89
Ross, D. J., merchant, 11
Rosses of Balnagowan, 159
rubbish pits, Medieval, 58, 121
Ruckley, Nigel, geologist, 103
runestones, 192

Saints see Andrew, Anthony, Boniface, Colman, Columba, Curadán, Duffus, Ninian, Paul, Regulus; see also holy men
St Colman's church, 5, 12, 26, 40, 67, 153–4, 210–13
  belfry, 164
  Church 1 (8th century), 49, 82–91
  Church 2/3 (12th century), 42, 43, 49, 152–6
  Church 4 (13th century), 42, 49, 156–160
  Church 5 (17th century), 49, 160–1, 163–4
  Church 6 (18th century), 49, 164, 166
  Church 7 (18th–19th century), 49, 166
  Church 8 (early 19th century), 49, 166
  Church 9 (after 1843), 49, 170
  Church 10 (after 1997), 171
  churches of, 49
  crypt, 10, 13, 43, 82–7, 159
  poor loft, 164
  restoration of, 32, 41
St Serf's Island, 146
sandbags, 30, 45
sceat, 139, 197
Scots, 25
sculpture, Pictish, 21
  at Portmahomack, 5–13, 42–4, 59, 82, 153, 168–9; see also Chapter 5, 94–117, and Digest A5, 214–17
  destruction, 138; see also fire
  Early modern, 168
  geology see stones for building and carving
  iconography, 104
  Medieval, 42, 160, 162
  ornament, 105–10
  paint on, 102
  on the Tarbat peninsula see Hilton of Cadboll, Nigg and Shandwick
  TR1 (Cross A), 6, 66, 104, 110–12, 115

TR2 (Danish Cross, Cross B), 5, 106, 110–12, 115
TR5, 6
TR6, 7
TR7, 7
TR8, 6
TR10, 8–9, 107
TR12, 11
TR13, 11
TR14, 11
TR17–18, 13
TR20 (Dragon Stone, Apostle Stone, Cross C), 44, 106–12, 115
TR21, 42, 102–3, 116
TR22 (Boar Stone), 42, 97, 101
TR24, 97–8, 115
TR28/35 (Calf Stone), 59, 97, 101, 107–8, 139
TR201 (Apostle fragment), 101
TR42–223 (Cross D), 102, 111–15, 138–9
seafaring, 173–4, 184, 186
seamarks, 178, 187
seaweed, 124–5; see also vellum
sectors see excavation
sex
  of monastic community, 78
  of parishioners, 78, 159
Shandwick
  cross-slab, 34, 107–8, 217
  site, 34, 177–9
Sharples, Niall, archaeologist, 125, 132
shells, 56, 124
Shepherd-Barron, Caroline, 14, 16, 31
shoe, 15th-century, 47, 159, 161
shroud-pins, 47
Sigurd's Mound, 145
Sigurd the Mighty, 144
Sigurd the Stout, 145
silver-working, evidence for, 58, 139
Smith's Hall see Structure 1
Smyth, Alfred, historian, 147, 195
snaffle bit, 140
social context, of the project, 31–4, 47
souterrains, 19, 54
spade, 126
Spall, Cecily, excavator, 39, 60, 124
Speed, John, map by, 185
spirals, 106
spirorbis, 124
standing stones, prehistoric, 19, 94
  Pictish see sculpture
Stell, Geoffrey, scholar, 11, 183
stone, for building and carving, 78–80, 85, 91, 102–4, 131, 154, 156
stone circles see henges
stool of repentance, 163
strip-and-map, 29, 30, 37, 50
Structures, excavated, 206
Structure 1 (Smith's Hall and Kiln-Barn), 28–30, 50–5, 126–33, 140–2, 222–3

Structure 4 (Tawing tank), 28, 55–6, 60, 120–1, 218
Structure 5 (Grain-processing hut), 52–5, 142, 223
Structure 9 (Vellum-makers' Hall), 60, 121–2, 139, 218
Stuart, John, antiquary, 5
subsoil, 28, 30, 45, 50, 57, 62
superstition, 164
Sutton Hoo, Anglo-Saxon burial ground, 17, 50
sword-cuts *see* wounds
synthesis, 67–70

Tarbat Ness, 176; *see also* Tarbat peninsula, Torfness
Tarbatness Road, excavation at *see* excavations
Tarbat Discovery Centre, 33, 65–67, 200
Tarbat Discovery Programme *see* project design
'Tarbat foot', 129–34
Tarbat Historic Trust, 12, 14, 30, 32, 37, 41, 171
Tarbat, Lord George, Earl of Cromartie, 163–4
Tarbat Old Church, 5, 170; *see also* St Colman's church
Tarbat peninsula, 3, 73, 145, 147, 173–90, 195, 224–6; *see also* chapels, place names, wells, Hilton of Cadboll, Nigg, Shandwick.
Tarbat portage, 35, 173, 184–6
Tarradale, 176
tattoos, 23
tawing *see* Structure 4
teeth, 77
termon, 112, 187
terrace walls, 59, 118
Thomas, Charles, archaeologist, 94
Thorfinn the Mighty, Earl of Orkney, 90, 145

Thorfinn, Skullsplitter, 144–5
timber churches, 91
tonsure controversy, 10, 24, 195
Toop, Nicola, excavator, 57
Torfness, 145
turf, 121, 132, 136, 145, 175

United Tarbat East Church of Scotland, 5

vallum see enclosure ditch
Vass, Billy, farmer 31
vellum, preparation of, 60, 119–25, 218
Venclova, Natalia, archaeologist, 195
Verturiones, 75, 193
Vikings, 8, 80, 176, 198; *see also* burials, fire, Norsemen, language, wounds
Vitamin D deficiency, 160
vitrified forts, 19

water collectors and wells
  in Sector 1 (S8), 54, 141–2, 223
  in Sector 2, 75
  see also water management
water management, 55, 62, 76, 118–20, 183
Watson, W. J., place-name scholar, 183
weather, 37, 39
wells, on the Tarbat peninsula, 183–4
whalebone, 131
whelks, 124
whetstones, 124, 133
Whitby, Synod at, 10
'White Church', the, 5; *see also* St Colman's church
Whithorn, monastery at, 23, 24, 158, 199
William the Lion, 152, 184
Woolf, Alex, historian, 25, 144, 193
wounds, 80

York, University of, 32